D0283045

Journalism Ethics

Journalism Ethics

Philip Seib
Kathy Fitzpatrick

HARCOURT BRACE COLLEGE PUBLISHERS

Fort Worth   Philadelphia   San Diego   New York   Orlando   Austin   San Antonio
Toronto   Montreal   London   Sydney   Tokyo

Vice President, Publisher	Christopher P. Klein
Acquisitions Editor	Carol Wada
Developmental Editor	Helen Stimus
Project Editor	Karen R. Masters
Production Manager	Carlyn Hauser
Art Director	Brian Salisbury
Electronic Publishing	Laurie E. McIlroy

ISBN: 0-15-502962-2

Library of Congress Catalog Card Number: 96-75852

Address for Editorial Correspondence: Harcourt Brace College Publishers, 301 Commerce Street, Suite 3700, Fort Worth, TX 76102.

Address for Orders: Harcourt Brace & Company, 6277 Sea Harbor Drive, Orlando, Florida 32887-6777. 1-800-782-4479 or 1-800-433-0001 (in Florida)

Printed in the United States of America

6 7 8 9 0 1 2 3 4 5 066 9 8 7 6 5 4 3 2 1

Preface

Almost everyone has something to say about journalism ethics.

Those people who are the subjects of news stories often complain that journalists work in an ethical void, trampling on privacy, sensationalizing, playing fast and loose with the truth. News professionals themselves proclaim their allegiance to fairness and accuracy, but most news organizations operate with few, if any, formal ethical guidelines. News consumers—the public—rely on journalists for information but are skeptical about the profession's commitment to behaving ethically.

This mix of opinions also affects journalism education. Students hoping to get into the news business are told that ethical standards are important, but then they learn that precise, definitive rules are in short supply. Answers to most questions about ethics begin with, "It depends."

This book is not meant to address every aspect of journalism ethics. Rather, we wrote it to provide a sampler of topics that can be discussed in the classroom to stimulate thinking about why ethics matters. These issues and cases should elicit a variety of comments and suggestions about the duties of the journalist and the course of action he or she should follow. This is not a matter of finding the "right" answer. In most instances, the real test is to explain why a particular decision was made.

With no shortage of ethics textbooks on the market, we designed this volume for use in a variety of courses in mass communication and journalism, including (but not limited to) survey, media ethics, and reporting. Some of the topics we address are only lightly covered in other texts: the evolving ethical challenges of new technology, such as "real-time" news and computerized alteration of visual images; the case for compassion in news gathering; the importance of diversity in the gender, ethnicity, and sexual orientation of those who cover the news and of those who are covered; the significance of the "civic journalism" movement; and the expanding tabloidism in print and electronic news.

Chapter 1 explores the theoretical bases of journalism ethics, looking at various approaches to ethical reasoning. As pragmatic as much of news ethics must be, the field also should have a well constructed philosophical foundation. Industrywide organizations (such as the Society of Professional Journalists) and some news organizations have created codes of ethics, but most important is how journalists themselves apply these codes or put their own standards to work as they do their jobs. A profession's ethics are only as good as those of its individual practitioners.

In Chapter 2, conflicts of interest are examined. The news business as business is addressed, with particular attention to the conflicts between doing journalism and making money. The influence of corporate parents on the news is considered, most notably in terms of the blurring of lines between news and entertainment and in friction between interests owned by the same conglomerate.

Personal interests can also create conflicts. Suppose that an organization that is the subject of a reporter's coverage invites that reporter to give a speech for a hefty fee. Is that just the journalist's personal business, or should his or her news organization impose some rules about outside income?

Chapter 3 inspects the sometimes wobbly bridges between the news business and two other mass media professions: advertising and public relations. Ad dollars provide most of the revenue for print and broadcast companies, so the voices of advertisers cannot be ignored.

But when advertisers' demands infringe on the integrity of the news product, matters of commerce become issues of ethics. What happens, for example, when newspaper reporters find shoddy practices in local automobile dealerships and those dealers threaten to stop advertising in the paper if the story runs?

Public relations practitioners are principal sources of much information that reaches the public as news. Public relations professionals, however, are in the business of making their clients look good. As gatekeepers determining what is news and how it is to be presented to the public, journalists must be more than mere pass-through mechanisms for public relations messages.

Chapter 4 looks at sensationalism. Some stories are blown out of proportion, with reporters ignoring a lack of newsworthiness and making their highest priority the satisfaction of the public's curiosity, no matter how morbid. News gathering becomes a feeding frenzy; self-restraint vanishes. Even though journalists are by nature invaders of privacy, some limits on intrusiveness should be observed.

When stories are sensational and newsworthy, the task for journalists is to have a sense of proportion and to not lapse into reporting that is more frantic than logical. For example, much of the coverage of the 1994–95 O. J. Simpson case was a prolonged example of press excess.

When considering sensationalism, particular attention should be paid to pictures—still photographs or the moving images on the TV screen. Their graphic intensity has enormous power to enhance the impact of important news or to distort the essence of the story.

The tactics of news gathering are examined in Chapter 5. Does the end justify the means? Does getting a newsworthy story justify using hidden cameras, undercover reporting, ambush interviews, and maybe even breaking the law? Also at issue are relationships between journalists and their sources: when to grant confidentiality, whether to pay for information, how close a relationship to establish with a source. And after a story has appeared, suppose the journalist finds out it contained mistakes. What ethical (not legal) reasons make correcting the errors important?

In Chapter 6, the duties of journalist as citizen and as watchdog are scrutinized. When covering war, crime, and the courts, do duties of citizenship transcend those of news gathering? Are they compatible? In political coverage, what is the journalist's responsibility to the integrity of the electoral process and the workings of government? This chapter looks at just a few aspects of these kinds of coverage as a way to establish context for considering the journalist's multifaceted role in helping make democracy work.

Chapter 7 considers compassion—a characteristic some journalists think is essential and others think is superfluous. Journalists are human beings, as are the people they write about. How these individuals look at each other will affect news coverage. Perhaps a theoretical case can be made for reporters stripping themselves of feelings, but it is hard to imagine a reporter being unmoved by the slaughter of innocents in Oklahoma City, Sarajevo, Rwanda, and elsewhere. And it also is difficult to imagine people's lives not being affected when the news media hold them up for public inspection.

The rapidly changing technology of journalism is examined in Chapter 8. In the global village today, the time between an event happening and its being reported often shrinks to zero. That profoundly alters the role of the journalist, sharply reducing the time needed to make editorial judgments about newsworthiness and accuracy.

Also, the machinery of journalism has changed to make reality more susceptible to tampering through techniques such as hard-to-detect electronic manipulation of photographic composition. This revolution shows no signs of slowing. With electronic newspapers and interactive newscasts on the way, will journalists' ethics keep pace?

Chapter 9 offers a look at some additional changes in the news business, particularly the growing emphasis on diversity in the news product and in the newsroom. The news business has long been dominated by Anglo men. That is changing. Decisions about coverage and hiring increasingly recognize race, gender, sexual orientation, ideology, and other factors.

Another change is the renewed nurturing of ties between news organizations and the communities they serve. "Civic journalism" and "public journalism" are the principal labels used by news organizations that gear their coverage toward meeting the needs and helping to solve the problems of their news consumers.

In Chapter 10, issues from earlier chapters are reviewed to get a sense of where journalism is heading and the importance of ethics in getting there.

One of the most fascinating aspects of the news business is its constant change. Every day brings new stories for journalists to tackle. The technology of journalism changes almost as rapidly, providing new ways to get more information and to deliver it faster. And journalism schools are producing a generation of news professionals who will look far different from their predecessors. Their diversity will enrich news coverage.

All these changes have ethical components. In some instances, solid ethical standards are improving the quality of journalism and making it even more significant to the people who rely on it. On the other hand, some proponents of "flash and trash" have been too nonchalant about ethics and have lowered the reputation of journalism to sordid depths.

Ethics does matter. This book, we hope, will explain some of the reasons why.

Acknowledgments

We would like to thank all those in academia and the news business whose thoughtful consideration of ethical issues has educated us as we have worked in this field and written this book.

We especially appreciate support from our colleagues at Southern Methodist University, among whom are John Gartley and Darwin Payne.

Special thanks go to those who provided us with clippings and other information, including David Dawson, Alan Otten, and Charles Seib. Emily Pourchot did a superb job as research assistant.

Brief Contents

Contents

CHAPTER ONE

Ethics and Journalism

It was late in the day when the fax came in to the newsroom on the eve of the election. The incumbent governor was running against a popular business leader who had won the hearts (and presumably the votes) of many supporters. Public opinion polls had the candidates neck-and-neck, with few commentators willing to predict the outcome. The fax stated that the newspaper should check out rumors that the "business" candidate had ties to individuals who recently had been accused of insider trading by the Securities and Exchange Commission (SEC). A few phone calls confirmed that the alleged criminals were, in fact, old fishing buddies of the candidate and that all of them had participated in a private "investment club" while in law school. More phone calls yielded no additional information before deadline. As a reporter for the local newspaper, will you write a story that will appear on the morning of election day? Why or why not?

The television reporter and camera crew arrived at the scene just as the victim was being carried out of the house on a stretcher. An elderly woman, living alone, had been brutally slain by an escaped convict who had entered the house through an unlocked bedroom window. After beating her to death with a baseball bat, the murderer ransacked the house, apparently in search of valuables. The camera crew captured the image of the woman's bruised and bloody, partially clad body being covered by paramedics. Should the tape be aired? Why or why not?

As a prominent news anchor of a network affiliate, you are invited to deliver the keynote address at the national convention of the National Rifle Association. You may choose the topic of your remarks. The "honorarium" to be provided for your time is $30,000. Will you accept? Why or why not?

Your new assignment as a court reporter for a prominent newspaper takes you to Galveston, Texas, to the trial of an alleged child molester. During a break in the preliminary hearing (before a jury has been selected), the prosecutor tells you that the defendant made a full confession when arrested, although he (the defendant) now claims that his admission was coerced and that he is not guilty. You are unable to confirm this report before your deadline. When you file a report about the day's activities, will you mention the alleged confession? Why or why not?

As the education reporter for the city's leading newspaper, you plan to cover the news conference at which the appointment of the new, and first female, president of the state's largest university will be announced. While researching background information, you discover that the new president is involved in a homosexual relationship. This information did not surface during the interview process and has not been reported. Will you include it in your story? Why or why not?

These are types of questions that journalists face every day. Unfortunately, there are no easy answers or magic formulas for reaching ethical decisions. That's why journalism ethics must be contemplated before deadlines arrive. In the news business, decisions must be made quickly with little time for reflection. Ensuring that those decisions are grounded in ethical values requires both an understanding of ethics and a commitment to journalistic integrity.

Understanding Ethics

Ethics involves defining individual, organizational, and societal values that are morally acceptable and using those values as the basis of human behavior.[1] Although ethics and morality are not the same, the two words are easily confused. While morality refers to behavior that is socially acceptable, ethics deals with the criteria by which decisions about right and wrong are made.

The primary approaches to ethics are based on teleological or deontological principles. Teleology (the study of "ends") is based on the premise that the usefulness of acts, measured by how much good is produced, is most important in analyzing ethical behavior. The ethical decision is the one that produces the greatest balance of good over evil.

Deontology (derived from *deontos* or "duty") relies on the premise that human beings are obligated to treat others with dignity simply because they are human. Based on this humanistic approach, people have a duty to respect other people's rights and to treat them accordingly. A good example of deontological thinking is the Declaration of Human Rights. This document guarantees certain human rights that should not be violated by others. Whether an act infringes on such rights is a primary factor for evaluating if it is ethical.

In journalism, a teleological approach is sometimes rejected because it requires the prediction of outcomes. Journalism professor Herbert Strentz suggests that news coverage decisions should be based on questions of accuracy and context rather than on imagined consequences:

> One of the most difficult lessons for a reporter to learn is that in deciding whether to cover an event or issue, the possible consequences of such coverage are among the least reliable criteria for decision making.
>
> Consequences of the story usually are beyond the control of the reporter. The accuracy and the relative interest and importance of the news item to readers and viewers are more within the bounds of judgment that reporters and editors are qualified to

make. Not reporting an event or issue because of imagined harm it might do is likely to lead to little reporting at all. On the other hand, reporting an event or issue because of the good it will do is likely to lead to disappointment. That is why the reporter is better advised to think in terms of accuracy and context and in terms of a story's immediacy, prominence, and proximity than in terms of good or bad news.[2]

According to journalism professor Ralph Barney:

[J]ournalists, to be moral, should not be so concerned with the casualties as with the war effort, the effort to collect and distribute information. The guiding generalization is that damage resulting from disclosure of information is seldom as great as damage resulting from suppression. . . . Certainly, once we accept a principle of the primacy of information distribution, we can turn our attention to the business of assuring the fewest casualties. In my view, we too often accept the shortsighted view that any casualties are unacceptable, allowing us to reduce information distribution merely on speculation of damage.[3]

The teleological approach is also criticized because it can be used to justify questionable practices if the end result is positive.

CASE: The Fire Escape Collapse

A newspaper photographer was covering a fire in Boston when a fire escape collapsed, sending a child and her godmother plunging to the ground. The scene captured on film showed the two in midair with arms and legs outstretched. Later that evening the godmother died as a result of injuries sustained in the fall. The photo originally ran in the *Boston Herald American* and was later distributed by the Associated Press and picked up by more than one hundred newspapers worldwide. Within twenty-four hours, efforts to improve fire escapes in Boston were underway.

In an ethics case study regarding the publication of the photo, journalism professors Philip Patterson and Lee Wilkins examine whether the end (repair of aging fire escapes) can be used to justify

Stanley Forman

the means (running the photo). "When the local news peg (the fire) is absent, what is the ethical reasoning for running the photo?" they ask.[4] Can societal good be used to justify publication of personal tragedy?

The news industry apparently thinks so. The photographer who took the picture, Stanley Forman of the *Boston Herald American*, was awarded the Pulitzer Prize for the photo. The

National Press Photographers Association also named the photo "Picture of the Year."[5]

A Philosophical Approach to Ethical Decision Making

In journalism ethics classrooms, the philosophies of John Stuart Mill, Immanuel Kant, John Rawls, Aristotle, and other philosophers are often introduced in an attempt to get beyond *what* one should do to *why* one should do it. The exploration of classical philosophical thought provides a backdrop for discussion of why ethics is important and how ethical concepts can be applied in the workaday world of journalists. Although some of the writings could use a little journalistic editing to make them easier to comprehend, the basic ideas provide thoughtful alternatives for resolving ethical dilemmas.

For example, John Stuart Mill would advise that ethical decisions in journalism be based on an evaluation of alternative acts to determine which would produce the greatest good for the greatest number of people. The route that offers the most benefit and the least harm should be followed.

Immanuel Kant would suggest that the best test for evaluating the ethics of a particular act is to determine whether the principle upon which the act is based could be applied universally. In other words, Kant would expand the logic of the Bible's "Golden Rule" to include a *categorical imperative,* which requires that actions be judged by whether they conform to a universal moral law that is unconditionally binding on everyone.

John Rawls's *veil of ignorance* approach to ethical decision making would require that decision makers mentally place themselves in the positions of every person affected by a particular decision and negotiate to reach agreement.

Aristotle's *golden mean* approach would seek to resolve ethical dilemmas by finding the "mean," or moral midpoint, which lies somewhere between the two extremes of "excess" and "deficiency."[6]

These philosophical frameworks illustrate that modern-day ethical dilemmas are not unique, says Carl Hausman in *Crisis of*

Conscience. "Thinkers have grappled with similar dilemmas for centuries," Hausman observes. "And while they don't have the answers for all the mind-bending questions that confront journalists, they can help apply a little method to our particular brand of madness."[7]

CASE: Televised Executions

Consider the question of whether state executions of convicted killers should be photographed and/or televised by applying the philosophies of Mill, Kant, Rawls, and Aristotle. Think about all the individual and institutional interests involved in the decision and how each might react to or be affected by news coverage of the event.

What good might result from televising executions? What harm?

Is there a universal "law" that could be applied to resolve this issue?

How can the public's need to know be balanced with the rights of those affected by news coverage? Does the public have a right to witness the death-chamber results of its laws? What, if any, rights of the convicted criminal and his or her family should be considered? How important are privacy concerns?

What competing ethical principles can be identified? Is there a middle ground that would accommodate all rights and interests?[8]

The "Potter Box" Approach to Ethical Decision Making

A popular contemporary model of ethical decision making was devised by Dr. Ralph Potter of the Harvard Divinity School. The "Potter Box" approach requires the decision maker to consider important values and principles and to prioritize loyalties to important constituents to reach an ethical outcome. Potter's four-step process involves (1) defining the situation, (2) identifying values, (3) selecting principles, and (4) choosing loyalties.[9] This model of moral reasoning incorporates the central issues involved in ethical dilemmas and provides an excellent guide to aid journalists in reaching ethical decisions.

The "Potter Box" Approach
to Ethical Decision Making

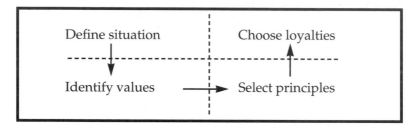

Although simple in design, the "Potter Box" forces the decision maker to make difficult choices. Competing values, competing principles, and competing loyalties confuse and complicate the process. Choices in one quadrant affect choices in the others. To reach resolution, the decision maker must determine which values, principles, and loyalties are *most* important and be prepared to defend those decisions.

Identifying Values

Identifying the values on which a system of ethics should be built is not an easy task, but it is a necessary one. Without an established set of common values, decision makers are forced to evaluate issues on a case-by-case basis, relying simply on situational ethics without any guiding principles.[10]

Values represent the enduring beliefs that people find important. Individuals have value systems that reflect their upbringing and experiences. Institutions have value systems that, generally, are defined by institutional executives. Industries and professions also have value systems. For example, a traditional journalistic value is the pursuit of truth. Regardless of intervening forces and factors, the ideal of discovering truth guides journalists in their work.

A value system provides the foundation of ethical behavior. In an organizational setting, policies and actions are based on institutional values. As an organization grows and changes to adapt to a changing environment, values stay the same—they endure and guide the organization through the process of change. The same is true for individuals. Decisions are made on the basis of whether they adhere to personal values.

Michael Josephson, founder of the Josephson Institute for the Advancement of Ethics, has identified ten "universal and time-less" values that he views as essential to the ethical life. Consider which of these values are important for journalists:

- Honesty
- Integrity
- Promise-keeping
- Fidelity
- Fairness
- Caring for others
- Respect for others
- Responsible citizenship
- Pursuit of excellence
- Accountability[11]

The process of identifying *journalistic* values ensures that journalistic decisions are not based on personal biases or prejudices, but rather that they reflect the ideals of journalism. Journalistic values should be based on the media's role within society and on the obligation to provide valid accounts of the events and issues that shape people's lives. Truth-telling, accuracy, independence, and fairness top the list of journalistic values.

Truth-telling is paramount. Distorted news distorts reality for those who rely on the news media to provide information that allows them to make informed decisions. Although some distortion is inherent in the news condensation process, information can be perverted in other ways as well. If individual reporters allow personal prejudices to slip in or if editors cut information that helps put the story in context, then news consumers receive a picture of reality that falls short of truth.

Accuracy is also critical to the ethical performance of a journalist. Stories free from mistakes should be the goal. Journalists tempted to cut ethical corners for the sake of scooping the competition or meeting a deadline might consider the advice offered to new employees in a United Press International manual: "The very reputation of the UPI will be riding on every word that leaves your typewriter. When you place the UPI logotype on a dispatch, you will be issuing both a personal and corporate guarantee to a UPI subscriber that it is accurate in every detail. That guarantee must not be given lightly . . . Do not confuse speed with excellence. The motto is, 'Get It First, But First Get It Right.' Make no mistake, the second half of that motto is the more important."[12]

Journalistic independence must be maintained. When special interests are allowed to influence media behavior, distortion of the news occurs. Conflicts of interest and perceptions of conflicts of interest arise in all areas of work—when news sources become a little too friendly, when trips or other items are offered in attempts to get journalists on-site at a special event, when reporters support political candidates in their free time—the list goes on and on. Journalists don't have to live their lives in caves, but they should strive to ensure that their work remains free from outside influences.

Fairness is especially important because of the powerful influence of the media on public reaction to events and issues. When the media present a skewed version of a story, then people's attitudes are skewed accordingly. Being fair means being just and impartial.

Other values should be considered in the process of gathering and delivering the news. According to professors Patterson and Wilkins, the following are particularly important in defining news:

- Dignity—leaving the subject as much self-respect as possible
- Reciprocity—treating others as you wish to be treated
- Sufficiency—allocating adequate resources to important issues
- Accuracy—getting the facts correct; using the right word and putting things in context

- Tenacity—knowing when a story is important enough to require additional effort, both personal and institutional
- Equity—seeking justice for all involved in controversial issues; treating all sources and subjects equally
- Community—valuing social cohesion equally with individual honor
- Diversity—covering all segments of the audience fairly and adequately[13]

Establishing Principles

Ethical principles derive from shared values and provide the "rules" by which journalists operate. Principles guide decision making and provide the justification for choosing between alternatives. As the authors of *Media Ethics* point out, "the purpose of sound ethical reasoning is to draw responsible conclusions that yield justifiable results."[14]

Principles take a variety of forms, ranging from legal statutes to detailed codes of conduct to simple guidelines like "Do unto others as you would have them do unto you."

Law and Ethics   Most people reject the idea that the law provides the best foundation for ethical decision making. Although the law provides a good starting point, it simply does not go far enough to establish the principles on which ethical issues should be resolved.

In essence, what the law represents is yesterday's ethics. Notwithstanding the argument that morally unacceptable legal systems are still legal systems, in a democracy the laws generally reflect what society views as acceptable behavior.[15] As societies develop and evolve, so do social values. And, eventually, the laws are changed to reflect those shifts in values.

In the meantime, the ethical standards by which organizations and individuals are judged are generally way ahead of the legal system. Consider the trend in corporations to develop and promote more socially responsible business practices. Companies are responding to public demands for improved ethical performance, recognizing that simply complying with legal requirements is not always enough to meet the special ethical demands of important constituents.[16]

Laws determine what *can* be done. Ethics dictates what *should* be done.

In comparing government-regulated British media to the U.S. media, British journalism professors Andrew Belsey and Ruth Chadwick observe that laws don't necessarily define ethical conduct:

> Clearly, even if (most) legal restrictions were lifted [in Britain], ethics in journalism would still be required, and it is notable that in the USA, where the law is less restrictive, ethical debate among both theoreticians and practitioners of journalism is lively, widespread and accepted as normal.
>
> Ethical discussion is essential because there are many ways in which the media can offend without straying beyond the law: inaccuracy, lies, distortions, bias, propaganda, favouritism, sensationalism, trivialisation, lapses of taste, vulgarity, sleaze, sexism, racism, homophobia, personal attacks, smears, character assassination, cheque-book journalism, deception, betrayal of confidences and invasions of privacy. And this is by no means a complete list.[17]

But it is a long one.

Industry Codes of Ethics   News industry associations have developed codes of ethics to which members are supposed to subscribe and to which they can be held accountable. Industry codes are important because they reflect the standards developed by and for journalists to guide their work. They also represent the standards by which media performance can be measured.

Sigma Delta Chi, the forerunner of the Society of Professional Journalists (SPJ), adopted its first code of ethics in 1926. The code, which was essentially an endorsement of the American Society of Newspaper Editors (ASNE) code of ethics written three years earlier, was viewed as a significant first step toward the increased professionalism of journalism.[18]

In a historical study that tracked the development of the SPJ's code of ethics, John Galey found that the evolution of the code is a good gauge of changing media attitudes toward professionalism. For example, major revisions to the code in 1973 reflected increasing concerns regarding a perceived lack of media accountability. The revised code stated, "Journalists should be accountable to the public. . . . Open dialogue with our readers, viewers and listeners should be fostered."[19] A "pledge" was also added: "Journalists should actively censure and try to prevent violations of these standards, and they should encourage their observance by all newspeople."[20] This focus on responsibility was viewed as offensive by some SPJ members, however, and in 1987 the pledge was replaced with a section called "Mutual Trust" that softened the earlier language.[21]

Organizational Codes of Conduct   In "Creating the Conditions for Ethical Journalism," Deni Elliott argues that a "journalist can only be as ethical as her news organization allows for her to be. The news organization creates the conditions for ethical journalism to occur."[22]

One way in which news organizations establish an ethical climate is through written policies and procedures of their own. Although most also subscribe to industry standards of conduct, customized codes of ethics have become commonplace in newsrooms throughout America. A recent national study of newspapers and television stations found that close to half of the newspapers (44 percent) and television stations (49 percent) surveyed had written codes. Almost all of the others said they relied on "unwritten" policies.[23] (See, as an example of a written code, the *Dallas Morning News* guidelines in the Appendix.)

Of course, more than a written document is required to truly institutionalize ethics. As journalism professor David Boeyink found in a study of the effectiveness of codes of ethics in fostering social responsibility in newsrooms, other factors are critical in shaping an ethical environment. First, management must be committed to the written institutional ethics standards, and, second, ethical discussion and debate must occur within the newsroom to bridge the gap between ethical standards and concrete cases.

"Without a culture in which ethics is seen to matter, few ethical standards can be expected to be effective," says Boeyink. "[T]he presence of a code is unlikely to be valuable in a setting in which no one has a reason to pay attention to its content— where it is not seen as an expression of important institutional values."[24]

Even in situations where institutional support exists, codes are often dismissed as having little practical value for journalists in the dynamic environment of the news business. In *Ethics in Human Communication*, Richard L. Johannesen outlines the frequent objections to codes of ethics:

1. They are filled with meaningless language, "semantically foggy clichés," and thus are too abstract, vague, and ambiguous to be usefully applied.
2. The existence of codes of ethics seems not to have promoted a significant improvement in the ethics of communication.
3. There exists a danger that a code will be viewed as static, as settling matters once and for all.
4. Standards in a code may appear to be universal when they are not.
5. A formal code would inappropriately restrict the journalist's constitutional rights of free speech and free press.
6. They lack effective enforcement procedures to punish violators; they have no "teeth."
7. Many codes are dismissed as mere public relations ploys aimed just at enhancing the group's image of responsibility with the public.[25]

These objections illustrate the difficulty in designing an effective code of ethics that will be both acceptable to and accepted by members of an industry or organization. To avoid many of these problems, codes should explain the ethical philosophy behind ethical behavior such that journalists are stimulated to think about not only what is right or wrong, but also why it is right or wrong.[26] Rather than simply providing a list of *do*s and *don't*s, codes should articulate the importance of adhering to ethical norms.

Professor Brian Richardson suggests that, rather than a rule-based, restrictive approach that focuses on what journalists should *not* do, an affirmative approach to teaching ethics is more effective. In fact, Richardson says, journalists often fear ethics because of the way it is presented to them:

"The way we teach ethics sends students and working journalists the message that ethics is about what they cannot do, that ethical behavior is more about keeping secrets from people rather than publishing information for people," says Richardson. "If ethics is about what they cannot do, then they know where to pigeonhole ethics—among other threats to First Amendment guarantees. Faced with being told what they cannot do, journalists will—with good cause— rely on their fundamental ethic: Publish, because knowledge is good and ignorance is bad."[27]

Richardson suggests that when ethics is presented as an affirmative process, journalists recognize the fundamental place for ethics in journalism. He recommends that ethics training be based on the following four standards:

1. It should be **affirmative,** telling journalists what they should do rather than what they should not do, "because journalism is about informing, not withholding."
2. It should be **systematic,** offering a workable, flexible, and defensible way to proceed to make ethical decisions, "because journalists facing daily deadlines do not have time to reinvent the wheel every time they have to make a decision."
3. It should be **integrative,** allowing for ethics to be inseparable from doing good journalism.
4. It should be **definitive,** showing primarily through case studies that there are right and wrong answers to ethical questions.[28]

Fresh ideas for integrating ethics into journalism are valuable because industry and institutional mandates can go only so far in improving journalistic practices. Simply making journalists more sensitive to the responsibilities and moral implications of journalism will have little impact unless individual journalists value ethical performance.

"So much of contemporary journalism involves immediate response that the ethical formation of the individual news person is crucial in deciding how he or she will cover a story," says Robert Schmuhl in *The Responsibilities of Journalism.* "Given the wondrous new communications technology, there is usually little time to consult codes or to consider the commentary generated by internal or external critics about similar situations. What the news person does at the moment will frequently develop out of the moral principles and standards that have been internalized over time."[29]

The key to ethical journalism is held by the individual reporters, editors, directors, and photographers who bring America the news every day. Ethical decision making ultimately comes down to a single individual who has to make the hard decision, drawing on the best information and advice available. As editor and publisher Clarence Pennington observes, "Newspapers and editors may compose masterful journalism ethics codes, but they will not succeed until individual journalists become enthusiastic participants. As always, we must earn readers' trust one journalist at a time."[30]

Choosing Loyalties

The media must balance public interest and private concerns. In the effort to create an informed public through unbiased and complete coverage of important issues, journalists are often required to juggle competing loyalties and to determine which should take precedence in a given situation. Those loyalties include the following:

Society Serving the public interest is a guiding principle of the news media. Although there is much agreement on *this* point, there is considerable debate on how public interest can best be served. As

Louis Day points out in *Ethics in Media Communications: Cases and Controversies*, "Considerations of societal duties are more complex than they appear. In the real world society is not some monolithic entity but consists of many different groups, among which choices sometimes have to be made: news sources, public figures, minorities, senior citizens, children, the handicapped. It is the balancing of these interests that presents a real challenge to media practitioners in the rough and tumble world of a diverse civilization."[31]

Industry/Profession   Unethical practices by professionals reflect negatively on every practitioner in their respective industries. Certainly, this is true for journalism. Reporters and editors are obligated to question how their acts will affect their professional colleagues individually and the industry generally. Maintaining the credibility of the news media as an institution should be high on every journalist's list of ethical duties.

Employer   Loyalty to the organization that puts food on the table is also important. Media professionals are obligated to support the organization's mission and to avoid causing harm to the company. Whether organizational policies should be violated for what is perceived to be a "greater good" is a difficult question sometimes faced by journalists. Another is whether journalists owe a special duty to those who make it possible for the employing organization to operate — advertisers, subscribers, and so forth.

Self   Finally, journalists have a duty to themselves. Personal integrity plays an important role in the ethical decision-making process. The popular "mirror test" is often used to help determine when, or if, personal values should be sacrificed for the benefit of a perceived higher value.

The Journalist as Professional

A question that often arises in considering these important duties is whether journalists must meet special "professional" obligations in gathering and reporting the news. In other words, are journalists professionals?

A *profession* is defined as "an occupation requiring advanced education and training, and involving intellectual skills, as medicine, theology, engineering, teaching, etc."[32] True professions are most often judged according to whether they meet five criteria: (1) specialized educational preparation, (2) dedication to the public's welfare, (3) a distinct body of knowledge, (4) an enforceable code of conduct, that is, a shared body of values and standards, and (5) individual accountability.

Consider how journalism stacks up against these criteria. Is there a specific course of study required before one can call him or herself a journalist? Are journalists committed to serving the public interest? Is there an established body of literature that defines the practice of journalism? Is there an agreed-upon code of ethics to which all journalists must adhere or else risk losing their right to practice journalism? Finally, are journalists individually responsible for their work?

Clearly, based on these criteria, journalism is *not* a profession. Although members of the news media collectively are committed to serving the public interest, and they have developed an expansive body of knowledge, and they are individually responsible for their actions, there are no special educational requirements that one must complete before becoming a journalist. There is no legally enforceable code of ethics that reflects industrywide agreement on how journalists should behave.

And that's just the way it should be, according to many in the industry. Jeffrey Olen argues in *Ethics in Journalism* that journalism should not be considered a profession for two important reasons:

> First, professionalism is not consistent with the spirit of the First Amendment. Freedom of the press, after all, is not a right that belongs to the institution of journalism. It belongs to every individual. Furthermore, it is not something that we need qualify for. Individual employers may decide whether we have the qualifications for a particular job, but no professional organization may decide whether we have the qualifications for the exercise of our First Amendment rights.

Second, journalists, unlike attorneys, do not characteristically have clients who must be protected against incompetence or quackery. A bad magazine, newspaper, or broadcast news show might bore, infuriate, or mislead me, but it will not harm me in the way that bad legal representation will. And all sorts of eccentric journalism ought to be tolerated. Certainly, nothing along the lines of a bar association ought to decide which ones should not be tolerated. We do not, in short, need to be protected from "unprofessional" journalism. If anything, we need to be exposed to the widest variety of journalism.[33]

Most arguments against state licensing of journalists are based on the need to safeguard press freedom. As the watchdog of the government and other centers of power, the media protect vital public interests. Under the protection of the First Amendment, journalists gather and distribute information that the public has a right and need to know.

Such a calling makes the media itself an immensely powerful institution. So powerful, in fact, that it also needs watching. But if the news media police everyone else, who will police the media? There is little news coverage of the news business.

The illogic of this is striking: No other American institution of comparable power escapes press scrutiny. But for the most part, news organizations exempt themselves from the oversight they impose as a matter of course on their fellow power holders.[34] Reporters remain ready to blow the whistle on misconduct by wielders of clout in politics, business, and other fields, but, with few exceptions, journalists back away from reporting the transgressions of their own industry.

The reluctance of the media to report on itself hurts the relationship between the press and public. Longtime newspaper industry leader Norman Isaacs wrote: "I'm among those who believe journalists have alienated millions of citizens who think the press needs curbing. Those journalists who have insisted on their right to examine and assess anyone and anything, while simultaneously rejecting any such evaluation of their own work and conduct, have fouled the press's nest."[35]

CASE: Pickup Crash Test

On November 17, 1992, NBC's "Dateline" aired a story about alleged safety problems with General Motors's pickup trucks. The concern was that pickups built in 1973–1987 had fuel tanks mounted on the sides, allegedly making them particularly vulnerable to leaks and explosions on side impact. In a "live" crash test, "Dateline" showed two pickups involved in a side collision that resulted in a fiery explosion.

Unfortunately, "Dateline" failed to mention that it had installed remote-controlled, incendiary devices under the two pickups tested. When initially accused of deceiving viewers, the network vehemently denied that it had rigged the explosion. When it became clear that the test was rigged, the network charged that General Motors was simply trying to divert attention from the safety issue. NBC later issued an embarrassing on-air apology to General Motors and viewers for the misleading tape.

The network's initial response to the criticism was far worse than the mistake, says *Detroit News* Washington bureau chief James P. Gannon:

> NBC displayed an arrogant defensiveness that characterizes the
> media's response to criticism. . . . Even while admitting NBC
> secretly used toy rockets to ensure a fiery crash for its cameras,
> [NBC News president Michael] Gartner defended the program as
> "fair and accurate" and attacked GM for trying to "divert atten-
> tion." The day after issuing this go-to-hell missive, NBC telecast a
> humiliating apology accepting every major point of GM's criti-
> cism. . . . The damage to NBC's reputation—and by extension to
> all the media—is incalculable. Our bedrock asset is public trust.
> Anything that shakes people's faith in that is a mortal sin.
> Confession helps, but does not heal the damage.[36]

That damage is reflected in recent public opinion polls that show that the press has experienced a steady erosion in public confidence over the past twenty years.[37] Studies conducted by the National Opinion Research Center found that in 1973, 23 percent of the respondents to a national survey said they had "a great deal" of confidence in the press. In 1983 that number had dropped to 14 percent, and by 1994 only 10 percent had "a great deal" of confidence in the press. The only institutions to receive either comparable or lower ratings were Congress and organized labor.[38]

A 1990 Gallup survey showed that public perception of press believability dropped significantly during the five-year period of 1985–1990, accompanied by a decline in the public's view of press performance. The survey showed a 10 percent increase (from 43 to 53 percent) in the belief that news reporting was often inaccurate, and a 15 percent increase (from 53 to 68 percent) in the belief that coverage was biased. The erosion in believability was true for all types of media, including the daily newspaper.[39]

Notwithstanding that public perceptions of the media are sometimes skewed by unflattering portrayals of journalists in movies, books, and television, the extent to which journalists themselves are responsible for their image problems should be addressed. Although some concerns regarding media credibility have nebulous bases, others can be attributed directly to ethical missteps on the part of journalists.

This book explores the ethical challenges routinely faced by journalists in an attempt to raise consciousness about ethical issues and to help journalists cultivate ethical competence. It was written not with the hope that agreement will be reached regarding what constitutes ethical behavior in every instance, but rather with the hope that increased attention to ethics will improve journalism.

For Discussion

1. Compare the Code of Ethics of the Society of Professional Journalists with the codes developed by the *Dallas Morning News,* the Radio-Television News Directors Association, The National Press Photographers Association, and the American Society of Newspaper Editors (see Appendix for texts of the codes). What common values are evident? Is there a need for diverse codes, or is one sufficient to guide all journalists in their work? Why or why not?

2. Are written codes appropriate in journalism, or does its nature ensure that such codes will be broad to the point of vagueness or narrow to the point at which they obstruct news gathering?

3. To whom does a journalist owe his or her greatest loyalty? What duty is owed to the subjects of stories?

4. Using the "Potter Box" approach to ethical decision making, analyze the following situation: A reporter for the local newspaper receives from an anonymous source a list of videotapes allegedly rented by a mayoral candidate at a local videotape rental store. Included on the list are selections such as *Debbie Does Dallas* and other racy titles. A part-time clerk at the store provides "off-the-record" confirmation that the candidate did, in fact, rent the tapes. Should the reporter write a story about the candidate's viewing habits? Should the paper run it? Walk through the steps of the "Potter Box" to reach a decision.[40]

5. Why is media credibility with the public important?

6. Should journalists be expected to openly censure colleagues and competitors guilty of ethical lapses?

CHAPTER TWO

Conflicting Interests

It's easy to forget that journalism is a profit-making enterprise—
if you're not working in the newsroom, that is. Journalists face
constant pressures from business managers to produce news that
not only keeps America informed of the day's events, but that also
sells. Operating in an environment where success is measured by
bottom-line results, journalists struggle to balance profitability
and social responsibility.

The Business of News

"Extra! Extra! Read all about it!"

The news media have experienced dramatic change since the
news was marketed on street corners by young boys shouting
these words. Today, sophisticated marketing strategies help
news organizations deal with the complexities of market forces
and the economic realities of the news business. Those realities
include increasing competition, monopoly ownership, and a
bottom-line focus.

This list says little about journalistic integrity, quality news, or
ethical reporting. It simply reflects the fact that most news organizations are profit-driven institutions that must make money to survive. What this means for journalists is that they are frequently

caught between the public service priorities of journalism and organizational concern for the bottom line. Often forced to focus more on what sells than on what's important, many journalists are increasingly concerned about the declining quality of journalism.

The seriousness of this issue was illustrated by the 1995 resignations of the top two editors of *The Des Moines Register.* Editor Geneva Overholser and managing editor David Westphal left *The Register* in the wake of an industrywide debate about whether journalistic quality is being sacrificed to corporate pressures for profits. "I understand newspapers are a business," said Overholser. "I wish newspapers made money to do a better job of serving the readers. In fact, newspapers, like other businesses, have to keep their shareholders happy. The result sometimes is that the business pressures are at odds with serving readers' needs."[1]

After leaving Des Moines, Overholser (who later noted that personal reasons also played a part in her decision to move on) said she heard from a lot of newspeople who share her concerns about business pressures on journalism. "I can't tell you how much mail I got from editors saying, 'Oh, the economic pressures are horrible. I can hardly stand it.' And then they'd say things at the end like, 'P.S. Don't quote me.'"[2]

Financial pressures affect the quality of news in numerous ways, most notably in the dwindling resources dedicated to gathering and reporting information. As the price of newsprint goes up, news budgets go down. As concerns about a news organization's stock go up, news budgets go down. For lots of other reasons, news budgets go down. The result in many cases is that journalists aren't able to do the kind of work they entered journalism to do.[3]

Operating without adequate resources, reporters, editors, and news directors sometimes fill the news hole with either what is available or what is most easily covered. Hastily scanned wire service reports, slightly edited news releases, and prepackaged video provided by public relations sources often make up the day's news. In some newsrooms, investigative reporting is a luxury that can no longer be afforded.

All this seems to paint a rather bleak picture for the future of journalism. Although profits may represent success to shareholders, financial gain may mean a departure from traditional journalistic values for those in the newsroom. Of course, that's not the case in all news organizations. Good journalism can be profitable.

Media Monopolies

The 1995 marriages of Westinghouse and CBS, Walt Disney Company and ABC, and Time Warner and Turner Broadcasting were celebrated with much fanfare and much concern about the impact of these unions on the news. The concentration of the news media in the hands of big corporations with diverse interests spurred questions about potential conflicts in covering stories involving corporate interests.

In *The Media Monopoly*, Ben Bagdikian observes that "many of the corporations claim to permit great freedom to the journalists, producers, and writers they employ. Some do grant great freedom. But when their most sensitive economic interests are at stake, the parent corporations seldom refrain from using their power over public information."[4]

That power can sometimes have a chilling effect on news coverage. For example, when Westinghouse acquired CBS, questions were raised about future coverage of the corporation's interests in electric-power generating equipment used in nuclear power plants. Veteran environmental affairs writer Karl Grossman suggested that CBS coverage of nuclear safety issues was unlikely to occur. "Censorship in the United States really functions as a sin of omission," Grossman said. "The reporters will know that this is a very, very sensitive issue in the eyes of management. The investigative reporting that is desperately needed, when it comes to nuclear technology, will just not happen."[5]

This conflict of interest issue has a flip side. When Disney merged with ABC, for example, the writers covering Disney productions had to worry about both negative and positive reviews of Disney interests. "Good Morning America" film critic Joel

Siegel explains that concerns about writers pandering to corporate interests create the biggest problem when the news is positive. "Because we're more conscious of the public perception, we're more careful," he said.[6] Siegel noted that although his bosses have advised him to mention the network in any positive reviews of Disney productions, in negative reviews, it is not required.[7]

Consider another example:

As the book review editor for the local newspaper, you must review a new book that chronicles the development of the city and its pioneering leaders. The book, written by a distinguished professor and well-respected local historian, is quickly becoming a best-seller. Part of its success is due to the fact that it includes stories about the corrupt affairs of some of the city's founding fathers. One of these fathers just happens to be the grandfather of the corporate executive who owns your newspaper. The grandfather reportedly was an active member of the Ku Klux Klan and a participant in some shady business dealings that sent his former business partners to prison. Will you include this information in your review?

News and Entertainment

Corporate control of the news business is also blamed for a news menu in which meat and potatoes have been replaced with lighter fare. The line between news and entertainment has become so blurred that even those in the industry struggle to separate the two.

Dan Rather says, for example: "They've got us putting more and more fuzz and wuzz on the air, copshop stuff so as to compete not with other news programs but with entertainment programs, including those posing as news programs, for dead bodies, mayhem and lurid tales. Action, Jackson, is the cry. Hire lookers, not writers. Do powder puff, not probing interviews."[8] In other words, do what sells.

Sometimes selling means distorting legitimate news to cash in on its entertainment value. The O. J. Simpson case was a prime example. For television news executives, the case was the summer of 1994's biggest hit, observes Jacqueline Sharkey in *American Journalism Review*. "In a climate in which ratings are of prime importance, entertainment values, traditionally reserved for sit-coms and dramas, now play a major role in news decisions. The Simpson coverage frames the time-honored debate in the starkest of terms: Is it the role of journalism to simply give people what they want, or should journalists remain gatekeepers in order to give people what they need to know?"[9]

That's a tough call when ratings zoom off the charts. ABC News's senior vice president Richard Wald justified his network's coverage, saying that covering topics in which people are interested is central to "the business of mass daily journalism. There is an elitist attitude that because it's interesting, it must be wrong."[10]

Because television news, particularly, must compete with entertainment programming for advertising dollars, news directors are pressured to make news interesting. A story like the Simpson case is tailor-made for capturing viewers' attention. When the celebrity aspects of a story become more important than the social issues, however, the public is ill-served.

Another troubling effect of entertaining news is that the role of the news media as the primary conveyors of important information is diminished. In this era of "new journalism," readers and viewers struggle to determine what's news and what's entertainment. Information sources ranging from supermarket tabloids to talk radio to the evening news seem to be equal in weight and authority. People are left to wonder: What is truth—and where can I find it?

Ratings Games

The quest for higher profits forces editors and news directors to think more like marketers than journalists, according to James Gannon, who heads *The Detroit News*'s Washington Bureau. "If readers aren't interested in government or foreign policy, then figure out what they are interested in."[11]

This marketing-oriented approach to the news is most evident during the sweeps periods when television viewership is measured.

Stations scramble to ensure that their offerings will attract the most "customers." Sometimes, ethical lapses occur.

CASE: Michael Jackson Interview

When "PrimeTime Live"'s Diane Sawyer interviewed Michael Jackson and his wife, Lisa Marie Presley, during the June 1995 sweeps period, Jackson was allowed to view the tape before it aired. When he objected to the way the lighting created lines in his face, ABC reportedly agreed to adjust the tape electronically. This departure from industry standards raised questions concerning the integrity of the report.

Although most stations have policies that prohibit the screening of stories by news sources, ABC justified the decision by saying it was "simply addressing a technical glitch."[12] This explanation met with considerable skepticism, particularly after earlier reports that the network had agreed to air Jackson's *Scream* video during the broadcast.[13]

Television reporter Karl Idsvoog points out the problems that can occur when market forces dictate both what and when important information reaches the public. "The decision on when a piece runs is no longer determined just by asking is the report concise, clear, and well-produced; is it fair, thorough and accurate? There are now more critical questions. What's the lead-in? Where do we place the promotion? Will it deliver better numbers on Monday or Wednesday?"[14]

Idsvoog notes that news managers are no longer rewarded for solid journalistic achievement. Rather, "[w]e reward those managers who are able to deliver the numbers. In the short term, that may work. In the long run, we're waiting for more ethical disasters which will hurt the entire profession."[15]

What happens, for example, if a station holds a story concerning questionable health practices at a local clinic, and someone dies because of those practices? Although it's unlikely that the station could be held legally liable for withholding the information, the potential damage to the station is still severe. "How would you like an attorney grilling your reporter about how long she/he had to sit on a story to make sure that it could be broadcast during ratings?" Idsvoog asks. "What would that do to the newsroom image that your promotion department spent so much time and money cultivating?"[16]

Balancing Social Responsibility and Profitability

When news decisions are controlled by media owners and managers rather than by journalists, the potential for conflict exists. Primary emphasis on marketing strategies contradicts journalism's enlightenment role. As competition increases, those conflicts may get worse. News organizations will be forced to consider how they can ethically respond to the marketplace.

Industry commentators offer conflicting views on what that response should be. Some promote strict adherence to traditional values. Others believe that the news media must become more audience-driven or lose their position as leaders in the information business. Still others find a middle ground that can accommodate both journalistic and financial interests. Consider these diverse perspectives:

Writing for *Editor & Publisher*, Bill Winter suggests that a market-driven approach to journalism is simply a needed response to changing times and a changing market. Winter argues that those who mourn the passing of traditional journalistic values overstate the case and fail to appreciate the need for new and different approaches to information gathering and dissemination.

> Given the realities of newspaper circulation trends and changing demographics, lifestyles, and reader interests, a strong case can be made that newsrooms damned well better be changing their approaches to readers and that any insistence on clinging to old forms and old newsroom decision-making processes is a prescription for death—maybe not even a slow death. . . . I have not yet figured out how our unique First Amendment values can be defended by newspapers that have expired because they could not make a buck to pay the salaries and buy the newsprint and the ink, presses, and delivery trucks. Let's face it: *The Arkansas Gazette, Dallas Times Herald*, and other recent and sorely missed

casualties of the economic wars are not helping us much these days in the fight to protect a free press.[17]

Veteran journalist Leonard Silk takes a different view:

> Those . . . who sense that there is something wrong when the press puts its own financial interests above the broad public interest are right; they recognize that the press does have responsibility to the public, and to truth, which must take precedence over its immediate quest for profit. . . . It is considered outrageous, and properly so, when a newspaper lets its own quest for profits dictate its editors' judgment of the news, how to play it, what to cover, what not to cover, and how to editorialize about it or stand silent. An honest, accurate, disinterested, and courageous press is what economists call a "public good"—something from which the entire community stands to benefit. However, the payments for the benefits resulting from that public good may not go to those who create it. In fact, a good newspaper may die, although it served its community well.[18]

In the *Journal of Mass Media Ethics,* John McManus suggests a type of Aristotelian middle ground: "News is necessarily a commodity when produced by commercial corporations, but to be ethical from a utilitarian perspective, it must be something more than a commodity as well. It must observe the public service norms of journalism, even though such observance almost inevitably reduces profits. Only when profits are too small to sustain the news organization—the station, newspaper, or larger corporation—are decisions to subordinate journalism norms to profit norms ethical.[19]

These different points of view illustrate the difficulty in reconciling traditional journalistic values with today's economic realities. As news organizations struggle to define and justify their products, they should remember that objective reporting is still a worthy goal—and, ironically, one that was also born out of economic necessity.

When the Associated Press (AP) of New York (the forerunner to the Associated Press) was formed in 1849, the news it offered to subscribers had to appeal to a wide audience. Thus, the AP developed a factual and condensed style of presenting news that avoided the partisan style of most newspapers of the time and—most important—was salable. The idea caught on, and in 1896, when Adolph Ochs assumed control of the *New York Times,* he made objectivity the guiding principle of the paper, establishing a trend soon followed by others in the media. Ochs's legacy lives on in the form of a credo carved into the *New York Times* building: "To Give the News Impartially . . . Without Fear or Favor."[20]

Media owners and publishers might consider how this principle has affected the ability of the *Times* to grow and prosper. Emphasis on impartiality and fairness lays the foundation for ethical reporting. It also creates a product that has value for its customers and will, therefore, sell.

The Society of Professional Journalists's Code of Ethics states, "Objectivity in reporting the news is [a] goal that serves as the mark of an experienced professional. It is a standard of performance toward which we strive. We honor those who achieve it."

This statement reflects the difficulty of achieving consistent objectivity and underscores the fact that journalists are human beings with human emotions. They are products of their environments and upbringings and have opinions that reflect their life experiences. That alone makes it tough to be objective. When that is coupled with institutional demands to improve ratings and sell newspapers, the goal of objectivity becomes even more elusive.

Those who come closest to achieving the ideals of objectivity recognize that objective reporting requires more than simply offering facts and figures. It requires context—an explanation of the significance and impact of the information reported. It requires balance of the competing interests represented. And it requires independent analysis of the issues discussed.

That independence comes partly from keeping business interests and the news separated. When business pressures influence the quality and content of news, objectivity is lost and the news is distorted.

As Bagdikian points out:

A sacred principle in journalism has been the wall of separation between "church and state," that the reporting, writing and selection of news shall never be influenced by the business side of the news organization. It is considered unethical for any money interest to influence the selection of news. The only legitimate criterion for news is what the journalist perceives to be true and significant in the life of the nation and community, and what may be humanly interesting. It has always been a somewhat porous wall, but is the one principle almost every journalist would agree is central to uncorrupted news.[21]

Avoiding Conflicts

The personal interests of journalists also may influence the news and people's perceptions of it. Because of the important role that journalists play in the process of conveying information to the public, they must be mindful of potential conflicts of interest arising from personal attitudes and activities.

Elite Journalism?

Much like the subtle influence of the corporate presence on journalists' work are class biases that creep into news coverage. Journalists have been criticized for "elitist" reports that reflect a disconnection from readers and viewers and a partisan point of view. *Washington Post* media writer Howard Kurtz observes, "Where once newspapers were at the very heart of the national conversation, they now seem remote, arrogant, part of the governing elite."[22]

Walter Cronkite remembers a different era: "There was a day not far distant, just before World War II, when nearly all of us newspeople, although perhaps white collar by profession, earned blue-collar salaries. We were part of the 'common people.' We suffered the same budgetary restraints, the same bureaucratic indignities, waited in the same lines, suffered the same bad service. We could identify with the average man because we were him."[23]

One example used to show elitism in the press involves Paula Jones and Anita Hill. Although Jones was ridiculed for her allegations of sexual misconduct against President Bill Clinton, Yale-educated law professor Hill received widespread coverage of similar charges against Supreme Court nominee Clarence Thomas. Was Jones virtually ignored by the media because of her lower-class origins? References made by Lynn Rosellini in *U.S. News & World Report* would lead to that conclusion. Rosellini wrote that Jones came from Lonoke, Arkansas, a "land of big hair and tight jeans and girls whose dreams soar no further than a stint at hairdressers school, an early marriage and a baby named Brittany or Tiffany or Brooke."[24]

Such an example deserves thoughtful consideration by reporters and editors who control the flow of information to the public. This example illustrates the need for journalists to be particularly mindful of their own perspectives on the stories they cover and to recognize that their own outlook may differ considerably from that of the audience they serve. Although personal prejudices are inevitable, they should not bias a news report. Intellectual discipline is essential.

Participation in Political and Community Affairs

As citizens, journalists have the right to vote and to express opinions about events and issues that affect their lives. As journalists, they are obligated to keep those opinions to themselves.

CASE: Anchor Suspension

Mike Snyder, news anchor for KXAS-TV in Dallas/Fort Worth, was suspended in 1994 for serving as master of ceremonies at a campaign rally for then-Republican gubernatorial candidate George W. Bush and two prominent GOP officeholders.[25] The station's general manager suspended Snyder for two weeks, saying that Snyder had violated an unwritten station policy regarding any public support of political candidates. News director David Overton said, "[I]f we as journalists are going to pay more than lip service to the idea of fair and balanced reporting, then we can't betray even the slightest hint of our personal and political views."[26]

This example raises the issue of independence and the types of activities in which journalists can participate without being perceived as biased. The SPJ Code of Ethics requires that "responsible journalists possess a single-minded commitment to their audience. Any personal or professional interest that conflicts with the needs of the audience must be avoided or neutralized. Therefore, journalists must . . . search for potential conflicts with the journalistic role and avoid participation in organizations or events they might cover. . . . Where conflicts are unavoidable, disclose the conflict to the public." (See Appendix.)

Under this standard, in what types of political, community, and business activities could journalists participate? Would moonlighting as an annual report copywriter be okay? How about serving as an "expert" commentator on a television talk show? Could the editor of the local newspaper serve on the school board? Any problem with the anchor of the leading network news show heading the United Way drive for the neighborhood? What about journalists marching in front of city hall to protest a new zoning ordinance that affects their homes?

Such questions might lead to the conclusion that journalists must check their opinions at the door of the newsroom before entering. With the exception of those who write op-ed pieces, that's essentially the case. Although strict guidelines on whether and how journalists may express their opinions do intrude into their personal lives, the regulations are necessary to protect the integrity of journalism. This is one of the trade-offs that journalists must live with. People in most other businesses are not faced with this, but journalism is not the same as most other businesses.

Speaking Fees

One conflict of interest issue that has divided the ranks of journalists is speaking fees. Prominent journalists such as Sam Donaldson, Diane Sawyer, Cokie Roberts, David Brinkley, George Will, and others reportedly earn between $10,000 and $30,000 for one speaking engagement. This makes some people uncomfortable and others just plain mad.

In an investigation of what he calls "fee speech," Ken Auletta of *The New Yorker* talked to members of the House Democratic leadership about the practice of journalists taking money for speeches. House members (who have been banned from accepting honoraria since 1991) expressed outrage that Sam Donaldson of ABC's "PrimeTime Live" had delivered a scathing report against the Independent Insurance Agents of America for treating congressional staff members to a Key West junket just a few months after the same insurance group had paid Donaldson a $30,000 lecture fee.

Wisconsin Representative David Obey stated the common view: "What I find most offensive lately is that we get the sanctimonious-Sam defense: 'We're different because we don't write the laws.' Well, they have a hell of a lot more power than I do to affect the laws written."[27]

Others argue that the media should receive the same scrutiny as the people in Congress, including federal regulations that would require journalists to disclose outside income. Despite the questionable constitutionality of any such congressional action, these rumblings demonstrate the need for the media to resolve this issue internally before outside forces, such as the government, get involved.

Those who accept hefty fees say they are perceived as "celebrities" who are invited to speak primarily for entertainment value. Those who decline invitations say the credibility of journalism is compromised by journalist speechmakers who give the appearance of conflict when speaking to groups with a vested interest in news coverage.[28]

Although former executive editor of the *Washington Post* Ben Bradlee readily admits he was paid for speeches while at the *Post,* he now thinks speaking fees are corrupting. "If the Insurance Institute of America, if there is such a thing, pays you $10,000 to make a speech, don't tell me you haven't been corrupted. You can say you haven't and you can say you will attack insurance issues in the same way, but you won't. You can't."[29]

Suggestions for resolving the issue range all the way from not accepting any fees to limiting speeches to nonprofit institutions to just not taking money from people or organizations covered by the journalist/speaker. In the wake of the controversy, ABC reportedly amended its policy to ban paid speeches to trade associations and for-profit corporations. ABC's senior vice president Richard Wald, who initiated the new policy, said the amendment was intended to avoid creating false impressions. "When we report on matters of national interest, we do not want it to appear that folks who have received a fee are in any way beholden to anybody other than our viewers. Even though I do not believe anybody was ever swayed by a speech fee, I do believe that it gives the wrong impression. We deal in impressions."[30]

U.S. News & World Report takes an opposite approach, encouraging its writers to accept speaking engagements. Senior writer Steve Roberts (married to Cokie Roberts) says he is annoyed that some news organizations have been swayed by negative publicity. "This whole issue has been terribly overblown by a few cranks," he said. "As long as journalists behave honorably and use good sense and don't take money from people they cover, I think it's totally legitimate."[31]

The American Society of Newspaper Editors' Code of Ethics requires that "journalists must avoid impropriety and the appearance of impropriety as well as any conflict of interest or the appearance of conflict. They should neither accept anything nor pursue any activity that might compromise or seem to compromise their integrity."

What this means is that journalists should select very carefully the groups they will address and the fees they will accept for speaking. They must be mindful of the perceptions of conflict they create among the people who read and watch and listen to their work.

"Those who frequently lecture make a solid point when they say that lecture fees don't buy favorable coverage," says Auletta. "But corruption can take subtler forms than the quid pro quo, and the fact that journalists see themselves as selling entertainment rather than influence does not wipe the moral slate clean. . . .

Celebrity journalism and the appearance of conflicts unavoidably erode journalism's claim to public trust."[32]

As journalists maneuver around the pressures and conflicts they encounter in their work every day, they should keep one thing in mind: Journalism is more than a business.[33] It is a powerful American institution that provides a "product" needed to safeguard democracy. When making money and serving the public interest collide, the ethical journalist will choose the path that maintains the integrity of that important product.

For Discussion

1. How can the news media best balance profitability and social responsibility?

2. What role should business managers and marketing experts play in deciding what is news?

3. Is news a "product"?

4. Would a government-owned media system (which would eliminate economic pressures) better serve U.S. news consumers' information needs? Why or why not?

5. Should news organizations be legally liable if they withhold important information from the public? Why or why not?

6. Should journalists be allowed to accept fees for giving speeches? Should they be required to disclose outside income?

CHAPTER THREE

Influencing the News

Many of the resources that keep the news media operating come from the public relations and advertising industries. Public relations sources provide a significant portion of the information included on the news agenda, while advertising dollars provide most of the financial revenue that keeps presses running and stations on the air. The potential influences of these industries on the news product create special ethical demands for journalists.

Working with Public Relations Professionals

The news media rely on public relations practitioners to provide what many of them cannot afford to gather on their own: primarily background, explanation, and context. In some cases, the information that reaches the news audience comes directly from public relations sources. Although many journalists accept public relations information with a wary eye, they generally view the material as accurate and often use it in developing stories.

The bridge between journalists and public relations professionals is information, with practitioners in both fields playing important roles in shaping the news received by various audiences. In the process of getting information to the public, journalists are the gatekeepers, and—in most cases—public relations professionals are those who must knock on the gate.[1] Journalists shape the issues agenda—what the public will see and hear—while public relations practitioners try to get their clients' concerns included on that agenda.[2]

A simple analysis of the daily newspaper will show that many of the stories originated from public relations sources. Company announcements regarding personnel changes, earnings reports, and special events are released by corporate communications representatives. Reports on the activities of government agencies come from public information officers. New product/service announcements are often developed by public relations agencies.

Research studies confirm the contribution of public relations to news content. For example, a study by professors Lynne Masel Walters and Timothy Walters found that 86 percent of the news releases distributed from a state agency in 1992 were placed in daily newspapers with a combined circulation of nearly 135 million readers.[3] An earlier report that criticized the *Wall Street Journal* for its use of public relations material brought this response from then-executive editor Frederick Taylor: "Ninety percent of our daily coverage is started by a company making an announcement for the record. We're relaying this information to our readers."[4]

Although the reciprocity inherent in the relationship between the public relations professional and the reporter might suggest a collegial interdependence, history suggests a less-amicable existence. To public relations professionals, the news media are tools, or channels of communication, used to reach targeted audiences. For this reason, journalists are often skeptical of public relations professionals as sources of information. In fact, a 1994 study of newspaper editors found that many journalists expect public relations professionals to be evasive and to withhold information, and they simply accept it as part of the obstacles they face in gathering the news.[5] A comment by one respondent illustrates a typical point of view:

> Public relations people are hired by someone to represent that particular constituency. It comes with the job. . . . Any newsperson worthy of the title recognizes the job of a PR person and

should never assume the PR view of things is necessarily the way it is. . . . I don't like some of the things I've encountered PR people doing over the years, but I accept it as part of the process.[6]

The idea that public relations people will do just about anything to protect their clients from potentially damaging publicity can be traced all the way back to journalism school in some cases. Some of today's journalists were actually taught that public relations is inherently unethical. For example, in writing about what he calls the "non-ethical priorities" of public relations, mass communication professor Dave Berkman says: "The bottom line in PR is to make the client look good. If, in a given instance, it happens that truth and desired image coincide, fine; but that is only a coincidental concern." Is it surprising that research shows that journalists do not view public relations professionals to be their equals in terms of doing their respective jobs ethically?[7]

Journalists' negative attitudes toward public relations professionals may be exacerbated by the fact that many public relations professionals are former journalists. Sometimes viewed as having sold out to a less-worthy profession (which offers considerably higher salaries), these journalists-turned-public relations professionals must suffer the disdain of their former colleagues in the media.[8]

Mobil Oil public relations executive Herbert Schmertz observes that journalists frequently apply a double standard to evaluations of ethical performance: "I have repeatedly found that journalists and editors who work for newspapers and television networks generally don't like to discuss morality with me. To be more precise, they're perfectly happy to discuss morality with me — so long as it's my morality. Their morality, it seems, is off-limits."[9]

Such tensions can distract members of both professions from more specific matters of greater concern. Principal among these matters is the importance of open news channels. The client, be it American Airlines or a local arts organization, should have a fair chance of reaching the public with any newsworthy message.

The ethical task arising in this context is for neither the public relations practitioner nor the journalist to become so caught up in interprofession contentiousness that duties of representation and communication are neglected. Both have responsibilities to the process of conveying information. Goals of the public relations industry's code of ethics include better communication, understanding, and cooperation among the diverse individuals, groups, and institutions of society. These goals correlate well with journalism's obligation to protect and respond to the public's right to know.

Reaching all these goals requires cooperation as well as autonomous action by public relations and journalism professionals. Serving the public interest is a driving force behind journalism and public relations. The majority of public relations professionals are committed to serving the public interest as well as their clients. Excellent public relations is based on principles of social responsibility.

Standards of Conduct

Although journalists' and public relations practitioners' roles in the communication process may differ, a concern for the common good cuts across both disciplines. In their efforts to create an informed public, both groups of communication professionals must thoughtfully consider the ethics of their methods and the outcomes of their work. Just as journalists are guided by their industry's codes of conduct, so, too, are public relations professionals.

The Public Relations Society of America (PRSA), the leading industry association for public relations practitioners, requires members to adhere to the professional norms outlined in the Code of Professional Standards for the Practice of Public Relations. In considering these special ethical mandates of the public relations industry, journalists will quickly realize that their own ethical standards do not exist in isolation. Rather, they must coexist with those of other fields.

For the public relations professional, ethical imperatives are rooted in the responsibility to provide their publics with truthful information. Because journalists are often indispensable links in the information chain, public relations professionals must be cognizant of dual ethical mandates—their own and those of the news business. Similarly, journalists—who are sometimes curtly dismissive of public relations principles—should remain open-minded as they ponder their public relations counterparts' role and standards.

Code of Professional Standards for the Practice of Public Relations*

Public Relations Society of America

This Code was adapted by the PRSA Assembly in 1988. It replaces a Code of Ethics in force since 1950 and revised in 1954, 1959, 1963, 1977, and 1983.

Code of Professional Standards for the Practice of Public Relations

These articles have been adopted by the Public Relations Society of America to promote and maintain high standards of public service and ethical conduct among its members.

1. A member shall conduct his or her professional life in accord with the public interest.
2. A member shall exemplify high standards of honesty and integrity while carrying out dual obligations to a client or employer and to the democratic process.
3. A member shall deal fairly with the public, with past or present clients or employers, and with fellow practitioners, giving due respect to the ideal of free inquiry and to the opinion of others.
4. A member shall adhere to the highest standards of accuracy and truth, avoiding extravagant claims or unfair comparisons and giving credit for ideas and words borrowed from others.
5. A member shall not knowingly disseminate false or misleading information and shall act promptly to correct

---

* PRSA's Code of Ethics reprinted by permission of the Public Relations Society of America.

erroneous communications for which he or she is responsible.

6. A member shall not engage in any practice which has the purpose of corrupting the integrity of channels of communications or the processes of government.

7. A member shall be prepared to identify publicly the name of the client or employer on whose behalf any public communication is made.

8. A member shall not use any individual or organization professing to serve or represent an announced cause, or professing to be independent or unbiased, but actually serving another or undisclosed interest.

9. A member shall not guarantee the achievement of specified results beyond the member's direct control.

10. A member shall not represent conflicting or competing interests without the express consent of those concerned, given after a full disclosure of the facts.

11. A member shall not place himself or herself in a position where the member's personal interest is or may be in conflict with an obligation to an employer or client, or others, without full disclosure of the facts.

12. A member shall not accept fees, commissions, gifts or any other consideration from anyone except clients or employers for whom services are performed without their express consent, given after full disclosure of the facts.

13. A member shall scrupulously safeguard the confidences and privacy rights of present, former, and prospective clients or employers.

14. A member shall not intentionally damage the professional reputation or practice of another practitioner.

15. If a member has evidence that another member has been guilty of unethical, illegal, or unfair practices, including those in violation of this Code, the member is obligated to present the information promptly to the proper authorities of the Society for action in accordance with the procedure set forth in Article XII of the Bylaws.

16. A member called as a witness in a proceeding for enforcement of this Code is obligated to appear, unless excused for sufficient reason by the judicial panel.

17. A member shall, as soon as possible, sever relations with any organization or individual if such relationship requires conduct contrary to the articles of the Code.

Defining Truth

One area in which journalists' and public relations professionals' standards may vary is the accuracy of information disseminated. Ideally, news organizations provide balanced and complete coverage, without spin or emphasis. In a similar way, public relations professionals attempt to serve the public's need for truth while advancing the client's interest. In these efforts, public relations practitioners are often criticized for distributing "selective" truth rather than the "objective" truth expected from journalists.

Journalism professor David Martinson observes that "some journalists see their role as one where they are locked in an eternal struggle to find the truth—while competing against the public relations practitioner whose task it is to do everything possible to prevent them from reaching that goal." Martinson suggests that this view exists primarily because "[t]oo many journalists simply don't understand public relations *as it should be practiced*."[10]

Ideally, as Martinson points out, public relations should attempt to bring about mutual understanding between an organization and its constituents. This can occur if practitioners adopt a policy of substantial completeness and release all the information the public needs to make an informed decision. This policy parallels that of the journalist and illustrates, once again, the common objectives of public relations and journalism. At its best, public relations helps, rather than hinders, journalists in their work.

In contemplating the truthfulness of information received from public relations professionals, journalists should examine their own definition of "truth," says Mary Ann Ramer, a journalist-turned-public relations executive.

Journalists worship accuracy in the church of objectivity and the religion of balance. However, much of my PR life has been taken up with persuading reporters to be accurate by being complete in their stories; to be objective by at least considering the other perspective rather than dismissing it as propaganda, and arguing that balance does not require elevating the-world-is-flat advocates to parity with the overwhelming weight of evidence on an issue or story.

In fact, a great deal of my time in PR has been spent protecting my clients from blatantly bad journalism—you know it as gotcha journalism, as the newspaper or magazine that sells more copies and more ad space when it offers pandering over pondering, as the TV news show that puts entertainment above hard news and sacrifices the truth to good ratings.[11]

The ethical public relations practitioner operates under a "duty to inquire" about the truthfulness of the information released, much like the journalist requires corroboration of a story. Although the fact that both can be held legally liable for reporting false information helps to ensure that the truth-checking process occurs, the ethical mandate under which public relations professionals and journalists operate should also guide their work. The consequence of reporting false or misleading information can be far-reaching.

Consider the "case of the deadly apples," which has been widely reported and criticized as an example of unethical behavior on the part of both public relations professionals and journalists.

CASE: The Alar Scare

In 1988 public relations executive David Fenton was hired by the Natural Resources Defense Council (NRDC) to publicize a scientific study showing that children were being exposed to cancer-causing agents in the pesticide Alar used to preserve apples. Fenton earned his fee. He planned and implemented a media campaign that succeeded in capturing the attention of "60 Minutes," *Time, Newsweek, Consumer Reports,* network talk shows, newscasts, and other media outlets throughout the United States.[12]

The CBS "60 Minutes" report, which kicked off the campaign, began: "The most potent cancer-causing agent in our food supply is a substance sprayed on apples to keep them on trees longer and make them look better. That's the conclusion of a number of scientific experts. And who is most at risk? Children who may someday develop cancer from this one chemical called daminozide."[13] The story was based on an NRDC report that alleged that the risks of eating apples treated with Alar was "intolerable."

Following the "60 Minutes" telecast, the NRDC held news conferences around the nation to warn about the risks of Alar.[14] The resulting news coverage created public panic. School systems banned apples from school menus. Grocery stores began offering "pesticide-free" products. People stopped eating apples.

The apple industry responded by launching a $2 million campaign to counteract the negative impact of the initial reports. Experts were hired to tell the other side of the story. Full-page ads appeared in such publications as the *New York Times*, *Washington Post*, and *USA Today*, asserting that in order to receive a dose of the chemical comparable to that given the mice in the NRDC study, someone would have to eat twenty-eight thousand pounds of Alar-treated apples a day for seventy years. The message also pointed out that Alar was used on only a very small portion of the nation's apple crops.[15]

The U.S. government came to the aid of the apple growers and, in a joint statement by the U.S. Department of Agriculture, the Food and Drug Administration, and the Environmental Protection Agency, declared apples safe. The message said, "Data used by NRDC, which claim cancer risks from Alar are 100 times higher than the Environmental Protection Agency (EPA) estimates, were rejected in 1985 by an independent scientific advisory board created by Congress."[16] The statement noted that the EPA would continue to gather data and would ban the use of Alar if scientific tests warranted such action.

Although apple sales returned to normal within months, the loss to apple growers reached more than $100 million. Some orchards were forced out of business.

Although the NRDC should assume responsibility for its unethical promotion of the misleading report, both public relations professionals and journalists must consider their role in the process of conveying the misleading information. In a lawsuit naming CBS, "60 Minutes," NRDC, Fenton Communications, and others as defendants, a group of apple-grower plaintiffs charged that statements suggesting that Alar was "the most potent cancer-causing agent in the food supply today" were "false, misleading and without proper scientific foundation," as well as made in "reckless disregard of their truth or falsity."[17]

Junket Journalism

Another area of potential conflict involves so-called junket journalism—an issue that has created controversy within both news and public relations organizations. The issue is whether journalists should accept free trips, meals, and entertainment offered by public relations professionals on behalf of their clients. (Of course, the related question is whether public relations professionals should offer them in the first place.) The answer seems clear, according to news industry associations' codes of ethics.

The Society of Professional Journalists (SPJ) Code of Ethics states: "Gifts, favors, free travel, special treatment or privileges can compromise the integrity of journalists and their employers. Nothing of value should be accepted." (See Appendix.)

The American Society of Newspaper Editors Statement of Principles requires that journalists "avoid impropriety and the appearance of impropriety as well as any conflict of interest or the appearance of conflict. They should neither accept anything nor pursue any activity that might compromise or seem to compromise their integrity." (See Appendix.)

The Radio-Television News Directors Association's Code of Broadcast News Ethics states that "[Members will] strive to conduct themselves in a manner that protects them from conflicts of interest, real or perceived. They will decline gifts or favors which would influence or appear to influence their judgments." (See Appendix.)

The SPJ code is pretty clear that nothing should be accepted, but the latter two codes do leave the door open for interpretation.

It is the last phrase of each statement that often creates controversy: "which cloud perception" and "which would influence or appear to influence their judgments." Of course, these are subjective determinations, and history shows that journalists draw the line in different places with regard to the acceptance of "freebies."

Some view free trips as legitimate if they provide the only means to cover a story. Others argue that the acceptance of any "gift" creates the perception that journalists are "on the take" and might be influenced by preferential treatment. Still more suggest that the problem could be resolved if public relations professionals did not compromise their own standards of performance by trying to buy good publicity.

CASE: International Junket

An international oil and gas exploration and production company has headquarters in Dallas and properties in the oil-rich Java Sea off the shore of Indonesia. The headquarters public relations staff arranges a media tour for energy reporters to Indonesia to observe the company's use of new technology that has revolutionized the oil drilling processes used in deep waters. The company offers to provide a complete travel package for reporters willing to accept.

Many of the journalists don't have the financial resources to get there on their own, and they risk losing the opportunity to cover this important story adequately if they stay home. Should they accept? Would you change your mind if a weekend on the island of Bali was thrown in by the company to help the weary travelers recover from jet lag?

This case illustrates the need for public relations professionals to acknowledge journalistic standards of ethics, as well as the need for journalists to resist enticing offers that might compromise the integrity of a story. The journalistic test for determining whether to accept a "freebie" should be whether acceptance creates either a perceived or real bias in coverage and whether the freebie is necessary to get the story. Generally, journalists should pay their own way and avoid questions of impropriety.

Video News Releases

As news-gathering resources dwindle, video news releases (VNRs) and other forms of videotaped information provided by public relations sources have become staples of the television industry—particularly in small markets where news organizations struggle to cover important events. In fact, a 1992 survey by Nielsen Media Research found that every one of the ninety-two television stations surveyed said they regularly use VNRs.[18]

Delivered to stations by either satellite or mail, VNRs have become one of the most controversial forms of public relations-generated material.[19] Although print news releases can easily be revised and incorporated into stories, video presents a troubling ethical dilemma for broadcasters. Using "canned tape" produced by institutions with a vested interest in the information is potentially misleading to viewers, some say.

In a February 1992 cover story about VNRs, *TV Guide* criticized the use of VNRs, calling them "fake news."[20] Others have voiced similar concerns. *Wall Street Journal* reporter Laura Bird asks, "What's news? . . . It's hard to tell sometimes these days as advertiser-produced video news releases—not long ago considered oddities—are increasingly turning up on television news programs. These "news" stories— often perky pieces about recently made commercials—are shrewdly produced by publicists so that stations can seamlessly air them as though they were genuine news, rather than the advertising they are."[21]

In spite of such criticism, VNRs and other footage provide a valuable resource for journalists who cannot afford the time or expense involved in covering many stories. As long as VNRs present information, pictures, and sound that television journalists can rely on for quality, accuracy, and perspective, there should be no problem.[22] The material should be used in the same way that journalists use other source material. If the footage accurately reflects the story being covered and can be incorporated into a balanced, fair report, then the information should not be considered off-limits.

The issue of whether the source of the material should be identified on-screen should turn on whether viewers may be misled if

the identification is left off. Only 55 percent of the television stations surveyed in the Nielsen study said they "always" identify
the source.[23]

Gaining Mutual Respect

Public relations professionals are challenged to devise strategies
that will advance their clients' interests while at the same time
respecting journalistic standards of performance. Journalists are
challenged to work with public relations professionals—who,
don't forget, generate much of the news reported every day—in
a way that allows this mutually dependent relationship to serve
both parties' needs. A relationship based on mutual respect and
a mutual objective—an informed society—will best serve the
interests of public relations and journalism.

That respect may come through journalists' increased understanding of what ethical public relations is. Public relations professionals need to do a better job of explaining their function
within organizations and society, while journalists need to be willing to listen. Although ethical lapses occur in both journalism and
public relations, the recognition that such cases are the exceptions
will go a long way in developing mutual respect between the two
professions.

Advertising Pressures

The news media's reliance on advertising revenue raises concerns
regarding the impact of advertising on the news agenda. Although
mainstream news organizations vehemently argue that the advertising and editorial divisions operate independently, the influence
of advertising is visible in various and often subtle forms, including:

- Control over the editorial content of newspapers, magazines, and television
- Biased editorial opinions that favor the position of the
  advertiser

- Limited or lack of coverage of controversial topics, issues, or stories that would reflect negatively on advertisers
- Positive coverage of advertisers' products, services, or organizations
- Purposely blurred lines between advertising and editorial content [24]

Media attempts to accommodate advertisers range all the way from making no adjustments in editorial decisions, to increasing advertising space, or to killing a story, in order to avoid causing advertisers to pull their ads.

CASE: Ad Boycott by Auto Dealers

When the *San Jose Mercury News* published an eighty-one-inch consumer guide on how to save money when buying a car, unhappy local auto dealers responded by pulling their display advertising. This move reportedly cost the paper at least $1 million in revenue. Complaining that the guide, entitled "A Car Buyer's Guide to Sanity," implied that dealers couldn't be trusted, the dealers continued the ad boycott even after publisher Jay Harris issued an apology for allowing the story to fall "short of what it should have been." [25]

In an effort to win back lost advertising dollars, the *Mercury News* ran a full-page house ad listing "10 reasons why you should buy or lease your next car from a factory-authorized dealer." [26] This widely criticized attempt to curry favor with the dealers illustrates a major concern for the news media: the influence of advertising on editorial content.

The Associated Press Managing Editors Code of Ethics states, "The newspaper should report the news without regard for its own interests. It should not give favored news treatment to advertisers or special-interest groups." [27]

Clearly, the *Mercury News*'s actions violated this standard. This was blatant, but advertising's more subtle effects on the news are even more troubling. In commenting on the auto dealer example, Professor Ronald Collins, who studies advertisers' attempts to shape news coverage, notes that he was surprised that the *Mercury News* ran the piece in the first place. "Usually, the editor will kill that kind of story or the reporter knows certain areas are no-nos."[28] One must wonder how many stories are never told because they fall into the "no-no" category.

According to a study reported in the 1992 *Journal of Advertising,* advertising pressure is a widespread problem. A survey of 250 newspaper editors throughout the country found that "about 90 percent of editors have been pressured by advertisers because of the type and content of stories carried by the paper. Seventy-seven percent said they were pressured to kill stories, and more than 90 percent said advertisers withdrew advertising because of content disputes."[29]

More than one third of the respondents reported that advertisers succeeded in influencing the news at their papers. And more than half said there was pressure from within their newspapers to write stories to please advertisers. The study included major metropolitan papers as well as smaller publications that reported significantly more pressure to please advertisers.[30]

A 1992 survey of selected members of the Society of American Business Editors and Writers (SABEW), which represents print and broadcast media, found that "83 percent consider advertising encroachment a growing threat to editorial integrity; 78 percent believe the threat has increased due to the present economic climate; and 75 percent believe it will not diminish once the economy recovers."[31] These findings should be perceived as an early warning of trouble ahead, according to *Editor & Publisher*. "Editorial integrity is not something that can be turned on and off like a water tap. It should be cherished and not destroyed."[32]

The four-point code of ethics adopted by SABEW outlines the standards for maintaining that integrity:

1. A clear-cut delineation between advertising and editorial matters should be maintained at all times.
2. Material produced by an editorial staff or news service should be used only in sections controlled by editorial departments.

3. Sections controlled by advertising departments should be distinctly different from news sections in typeface, layout, and design.
4. Promising a story in exchange for advertising is unethical.[33]

Of course, an argument can be made that it is the advertisers, rather than news organizations, who need to clean up their ethics. Advertisers who use threats as part of their business strategy should evaluate their standards for dealing with the news media and define specific boundaries that should not be crossed in their attempts to influence editorial content.

They should also contemplate the potential impact that threatening to or actually pulling their ads might have on the media coverage of their businesses. In *The Headline vs. The Bottom Line*, Mike Haggerty and Wallace Rasmussen explain:

> When an advertiser threatens to pull business unless certain news decisions are made, the word filters back to reporters and editors in the newsroom and spreads quickly through the building. Resentment grows against the business exerting such pressure, and that resentment makes it extremely difficult for the news staff to remain objective about the company wielding the money clout.
>
> Some publishers, stung by pressure or cutbacks from disgruntled advertisers, retaliate by eliminating from their news columns any mention of those who don't advertise in their papers. Editors stung by advertiser pressure must also grapple with their ability to make reasonable decisions about legitimate news stories that involve those who have brought such pressure."[34]

The challenge for media gatekeepers is to ensure that their news judgment is not clouded by advertisers' strong-arm tactics to influence editorial content. Although most news organizations make valiant efforts to keep the advertising and editorial divisions separated, the ever-present need to make money may create considerable tension and conflict.

The advice offered by Haggerty and Rasmussen for newspaper editors who must deal with these issues can be applied to other media as well: "[N]ewspapers must resist advertiser pressure, even at the risk of great economic damage—a much easier task for a large newspaper than a small one. And newspapers also have an ethical responsibility not to play the pressure game themselves, refusing to cover a business that doesn't advertise with them. Business people have the right to expect fair and objective treatment from journalists."[35]

Conflicts with public relations and advertising professionals can be avoided by carefully considering the objectives and ethical standards of each industry. Harmonious relationships can be forged and maintained through a shared respect for each other's work and a shared commitment to not compromise the integrity of the news product.

For Discussion

1. Compare the PRSA Code of Professional Standards with the SPJ Code of Ethics included in the Appendix. What common values and principles are evident? Do any standards appear to be in conflict?

2. Would a video news release provided by the oil and gas company referenced in the "junket journalism" case solve the dilemma for journalists contemplating the ethical implications of accepting the free travel package?

3. Should journalists consider public relations practitioners to be "enemies" or friendly sources?

4. How can journalists and public relations professionals develop more-harmonious working relationships?

5. Do advertisers have a "right" to try to influence news coverage because they contribute so much of news organizations' revenue?

6. How far should the news media go to keep advertisers happy?

CHAPTER FOUR

Tabloid Temptations

For those who like sensational news, these are sensational times.

Headline writers are never short of material. Barely does one scandal fade away before another takes its place. As soon as Tonya and Nancy glide out of sight, roaring into view comes O. J. in his Bronco.

Sensationalism is not confined to the supermarket checkout lines or the insomniac's TV schedule. The "flash and trash" approach is insistently pervasive, turning up even in the pages of the *New York Times* and on CBS News's top-rated programs. If it titillates or disgusts (or, ideally, both), it must be news.

Plenty of ethical issues are affected by sensationalism. Perhaps the most important is the never-ending task of defining "newsworthy." What the public purportedly *wants* to know should not automatically be allowed to overwhelm what the public *needs* to know. Sometimes, however, that happens; so much time and effort are spent covering the sensation of the moment that other stories go under or unreported. And even when the sensational story includes some legitimate news, that aspect may be neglected while journalists concentrate on the sordid and spicy.

One British observer of 1994's O. J. Simpson coverage wrote,

The media binge seems to demonstrate nothing more than
America's astonishing capacity for excess and for focusing on relative trivia at the expense of serious matters such as health care

reform, genocide in Rwanda and the threat of nuclear prolifera-
tion that oozes out of North Korea."[1]

Journalists may profess to be merely responding to the public's demands for information about the cause célèbre of the
moment. But news organizations themselves often create the self-
perpetuating messes in which they claim to be trapped. If, for
example, countless hours and pages are devoted to initial reporting of the Simpson case, a sizable portion of the public becomes
addicted not just to the coverage per se but also to the *amount* of
coverage provided.

Sensation junkies need their fix; they are dependent on news—
whether mainstream or tabloid—to provide it. If Tom Brokaw
won't give it to them on "NBC Nightly News," they'll turn to
"Inside Edition" as their supplier. (During Simpson's preliminary hearing, ABC switched for an hour to its usual soap opera
schedule. Its ratings dropped by a third.)[2]

The numbers of sensation fans are too large to be ignored. An
estimated 95 million Americans watched all or part of the
Simpson freeway chase. In the following weeks, the Simpson case
received more coverage than any story since the Gulf War.[3] A
few months before, an audience almost as large followed the daily
saga of Olympic ice-skaters Tonya Harding and Nancy Kerrigan.
When the Simpson verdict was announced in October 1995, the
audience was proclaimed to be the largest in broadcasting history.

The appeal of such tales is not hard to understand. As journalist Molly Ivins wrote about Harding-Kerrigan: "I know a good
story when I see one. Skater-on-skater violence meets all the criteria: It's new, it's different, and while it may not be directly relevant to our lives, it's a lot easier to understand than why Serbs
kill Bosnians."[4]

With plenty of statistical and anecdotal evidence that news consumers want this kind of story, some journalists trample their profession's ethics in the rush to proclaim the next sensation.
Fundamental values, such as fairness, are often neglected.
Mortimer Zuckerman, editor-in-chief of *U.S. News & World Report*,
comments, "The sad fact is that the news cycle works in such a

way that allegations alone, without proof, burst into headlines."
He also says, "The one bandwagon everybody wants to jump onto
is a garbage truck."[5]

Journalists will abandon even their cherished (and valuable)
skepticism if the story promises to be lurid enough. When disbe-
lief is suspended, commitment to accuracy suffers. Fact-checking
happens after the first run of stories, if at all. For instance, of Paula
Jones's accusations that Bill Clinton had propositioned her,
Zuckerman notes: "Can anybody doubt that this suit would not
have been filed if Paula Jones was not counting on the press being
right outside the door, salivating to cover the case and offer her
money? The down-and-dirty tabloids and that new affliction,
tabloid TV, have no qualms about such a story. Digging up dirt, or
manufacturing it, is their business."[6]

The public knows what to expect from print or broadcast
tabloids. When, however, tabloidism spreads into mainstream
journalism, the line between hard news and sensationalized speculation becomes harder to discern.

The Rise of Tabloids

'Tis the Misfortune of the Town to have much News but little
Intelligence. . . . Misrepresentation is, as it were, the Business of
every Writer, and whether they speak of private Persons or of
publick, the character of No Man seems safe, but Scandal and
Slander make havoc of Men's Reputation without Mercy.' [7]

That appraisal of the state of the news business was offered by
the *London Daily Post* in 1719. It was far from the first commentary about scurrilous journalism in the British "pauper press"—
the newspapers aimed at the large audience that preferred
liveliness to accuracy and didn't want to pay much for it. A century later, the publisher of the *Twopenny Dispatch* proposed this
formula to his readers: "It shall abound in Police Intelligence, in
Murders, Rapes, Suicides, Burnings, Maimings, Theatricals, Races,

Pugilism, and all manner of moving 'accidents by flood and field.' In short, it will be stuffed with every sort of devilment that will make it sell."[8]

The American versions of these papers and their publishers were no less aggressive. By the late 1830s James Gordon Bennett had made the *New York Herald* a paper that was "generally read, universally denounced."[9] Bennett attacked the previously sacrosanct, including the clergy and other newspapers' editors.

To Bennett's delight, his targets fought back. Editorials called Bennett a "habitual liar," "contemptible libeler," "pestilential scoundrel," "turkey buzzard," "immoral and blasphemous monstrosity," and other endearments.[10] One editor abandoned verbal jousting and severely beat Bennett with a walking stick. Bennett promptly made the assault the lead story of the day, and readers stood in line to buy the paper.[11]

While visiting the United States in 1842, Charles Dickens got a good look at all this wild journalism. In *Martin Chuzzlewit,* published two years later, Dickens offered his version of New York newsboys peddling their wares: "Here's this morning's New York Sewer! . . . Here's this morning's New York Stabber! Here's the New York Family Spy! Here's the New York Private Listener! Here's the New York Keyhole Reporter! Here's the New York Rowdy Journal! Here's all the New York papers!"[12]

Later in the nineteenth century, Bennett's professional descendants included William Randolph Hearst and Joseph Pulitzer. Hearst, in particular, helped push the United States into the Spanish-American War, using his *New York Journal* to stir up prowar sentiment. Despite being vilified for their "yellow journalism," Hearst and Pulitzer "continued the profitable work begun by Bennett to create a popular press based on the democratic idea that a newspaper must be interesting and, thus, accessible. Sex, crime, scandal and sensationalism created that interest," writes Richard Harwood. "Out of all this," Harwood continues, "came the first real 'investigative reporting' on capitalism, urbanization and their victims."[13]

Harwood's point is important. Sensationalism is not always bad; some stories are sensational and need to be treated as such if the audience is to be shaken awake. For example, the slaughter caused by drunk drivers may deserve "sensational" depiction if that is what it takes to get the public to demand tougher laws. There should be some limits to the goriness of these stories and pictures, but being *too* fastidious may undercut the power of the journalists who are hammering home the importance of this issue.

Modern tabloid journalism tends to feature fewer revelations of injustice and more accusations such as "Aliens Stole My Baby!" Led by the *National Enquirer* and the *Star*—each with more than three million circulation—the supermarket tabloid newspapers offer a mix of Hollywood scandals, miracle diets, and Elvis sightings.

The electronic counterpart of these publications has been on the rise during the 1990s. Tabloid TV has a substantial audience among those watchers of television news who want the lurid details and fact-free guesswork that mainstream newscasts avoid (or claim to avoid). In the selection of content of these shows, entertainment criteria prevail over journalism's public service standards. Philip Weiss of the *Columbia Journalism Review* says that on these programs, "Stories are continually sold as the 'inside look,' 'behind closed doors,' the 'naked truth,' when more often than not the program has nothing to deliver but gossip and speculation."[14]

Also writing about these shows, Yale professor Joshua Gamson says: "Disaster is good stuff, sex and crime and celebrity make terrific news, and famous sex criminals with disastrous impact are the very best. . . . Production techniques have also increasingly begun to mimic tabloids: the point-of-view and slow-motion shots, the choppy MTV editing, the bold graphics, the high-emotion music."[15]

Tabloids Leading Nontabloids

Sometimes the tabloids' topics cross over into the presumed realm of "mainstream" journalism, such as when the *Star* in 1992 published a story about Bill Clinton's alleged marital infidelity. The more-mainstream tabloids then jumped in: the *New York Post* headline was "Wild Bill," and the *New York Daily News* used "I'm No Gary Hart."[16] Meanwhile, the traditional press fidgeted self-righteously for a while before rising above principle and publishing their versions of the story, which often were not much more substantive than the tabloids' accounts.

Clinton aide George Stephanopoulos says, "The tabloids don't set the standards, but I think they weaken the resistance of the mainstream media." Concerning reporters' even raising the question about a Clinton-Gennifer Flowers relationship, he says, "Once it's in play, it's more or less fair game for the mainstream media to answer it one way or the other, so that by putting accusations in play in a way they wouldn't otherwise be, you get a hook, whether it's the denial or the damage control efforts. . . ."[17]

The story takes this form: "The candidate was asked today if he had done anything wrong. He said no. Here are the rumors he is denying." Some journalists may say, "We can't report a denial without explaining the accusation." Backing into the story this way ensures that the accusation, even if unsubstantiated, reaches the public.

The growing tabloid influence has an economic basis. Lesley Stahl, a reporter on CBS's "60 Minutes," says: "One of the reasons why there's so much 'tabloid news' in the mainstream is because the public wants it. News judgments are being made on the basis of polls. For the last 20 years, we've been heading more and more in that direction, and not just the networks. *Time, Newsweek,* the newspapers: Everybody is asking, 'What does the public want?'"[18]

ABC News senior vice president Richard Wald has said that covering topics in which people are interested is "the business of mass daily journalism" and that objections to this are rooted in "an elitist attitude."[19] This reflects the special economic imperatives of the television industry. TV news is expected to make money and to compete with entertainment programming for audiences and advertising.[20]

Those who run the tabloid shows believe that their work is on the cutting edge of journalism. Mike Watkiss, Los Angeles bureau chief for "A Current Affair," says: "We don't cover the water board. We go after stories of human drama that have heartbeat, passion. The fact is, the networks had lost their way, and now they're falling in behind us."[21]

Marvin Kalb, a veteran television journalist who moved to Harvard's Barone Center on the Press, Politics and Public Policy, is one of many traditional journalists who have little use for the tabloids' news standards. He says, "There is a perversion of news values when a presidential visit to Eastern Europe and a presidential visit to a G7 summit cannot get . . . the same amount of time as a pretrial hearing of a former football player."[22]

Along these lines, columnist Carl Hiassen said: "I shudder to think of the fortune being spent covering the Simpson spectacle, money that could generate other stories more vital to the average reader's health and well-being. Problem is, the average reader wants to know about O. J."[23]

The Simpson story was perfect for the tabloids: a celebrity murder case with truth in such short supply that speculation could be broadcast with little fear of it being contradicted. Everette Dennis of the Freedom Forum Media Studies Center wrote:

> What's more, these reports are produced against the backdrop of the courthouse, a place known more for slow, predictable procedure than for fast-breaking events. As a result, this kind of moment-by-moment reactive reporting has done more to trivialize the story than to elucidate it. Both the prosecution and the defense also have played a hand in this trivialization by producing various "outrage of the day" elements — often in the form of juicy tidbits about Mr. Simpson or about the two victims in the case.[24]

At one point before the trial, the *National Enquirer* said a sheriff's deputy overheard Simpson exclaiming to a jail visitor, "I did it!" The *Chicago Tribune* and the *New York Times* were among the news organizations that referred to the *Enquirer* article in their own Simpson story. The *Tribune* noted that the *Enquirer* is known for its sensationalism and for paying some of its sources; the *Times* did not. *Times* executive editor Joseph Lelyveld said, "We're not subcontracting our editorial judgment in the Simpson case to a supermarket tabloid," but the *Times* still received some criticism for apparently relying on the *Enquirer* and for not reminding readers that the source's reliability was questionable.[25]

During jury selection in the Simpson case, Judge Lance Ito asked the networks to delay broadcasting a story about an inflammatory book about Nicole Simpson. When CBS disregarded the judge's request and aired an interview with the book's author, CBS News president Eric Ober said this was "consistent with responsible journalism." Media critic Jonathan Alter of *Newsweek* responded, "A more honest statement would have called it consistent with ratings journalism."[26]

Yale's Joshua Gamson makes the case that even the prime-time news magazine programs have become "often indistinguishable from sensational tabloid melodrama." He offers examples:

> "Turning Point" debuted on ABC this year [1994], very successfully, with a much-hyped interview with has-been murder guru Charles Manson. Jeffrey Dahmer's father read from his book and hugged his serial-killer son on NBC's "Dateline." CBS News sent Connie Chung to Oregon (for more than a week) and then to Norway to secure an interview with Tonya Harding, a world-class figure skater but not exactly a world figure. ABC News flew a "PrimeTime Live" producer to Manila in a bid to land an interview for Diane Sawyer (she of the $7 million salary) with Michael Jackson's former housekeepers. . . . Not long after "A Current Affair" asked Gennifer Flowers to rate Bill Clinton on a one-to-ten love-maker scale, ABC News's Sawyer was asking Marla Maples if Donald Trump really provided the best sex she'd ever had. [27]

Among the most egregious examples of tabloid television is Miami station WSVN. Jonathan Cohn of *The American Prospect* described one of the station's evening newscasts in 1994:

> It's July 18—the day of a visit by President Clinton to Miami—and WSVN . . . is leading its ten o'clock newscast with yet another lurid murder story. "Let me let you take a look at the body of Carmen Rodriguez, still laying next to her car," reporter Glenn

Milberg says as the camera zooms in on a white, body-shaped shroud with a pool of blood at one end. "That's exactly where she was shot a few hours ago." WSVN cuts from Milberg to film of the victim's son arriving at the scene and bursting into tears, then to taped footage of the body that shows the arm of Carmen Rodriguez extending out from under the canvas.

WSVN manages to get five more bodies on screen within the next seven minutes, including the partially uncovered corpses of four teenagers killed in a car accident. . . . Nine minutes, six car wrecks, and one beating into the broadcast, the words "ROAD-SIDE RAPE" swoop on screen like a spacecraft.

This is followed by a reenactment, using actors, of women being attacked while driving through the city.[28]

This is standard fare on WSVN, a highly profitable Fox affiliate. Cohn comments:

With every broadcast, WSVN tests the limits of decency, feeding Miami's social divisions and caustic political atmosphere along the way. . . . What's most worrisome here is not the lack of taste or judgment at one television station but the reaction of the audience. While 69 percent of South Floridians think local news contributes to a "climate of fear," more than three-quarters say they still rely on it as their primary source of community information.[29]

This is an important point. To dismiss tabloid journalism as inconsequential—to assume that it is so tastelessly trashy that it has no impact—is to underestimate its addictive appeal. Tabloid stories usually are easy to understand, and their naughtiness makes them entertaining. As supplement to mainstream coverage, the tabloid adds spice to the information stew.

But suppose the tabloids are relied on as more than mere supplements to other news sources. The news consumer who finds the *National Enquirer* or "A Current Affair" enthralling may not be balancing that material with information from *The Economist* or "Nightline."

With other news media responding to the influence of tabloids and indulging more frequently in sensationalism themselves, tabloid publications or broadcasts might not be so far outside the mainstream. The genres may not seem all that different.

For example, during the 1992 presidential campaign, rumors about George Bush having had extramarital affairs received front-page treatment from the tabloid *New York Post*. The major television networks then promptly did the story (which was basically Bush's vehement denial). A CBS producer said, "We wish we didn't have to deal with this, but if our viewers are hearing it all day . . . we sort of have a responsibility to address it."[30]

"If our viewers are hearing it all day" from whatever the source, we'll give it to them again. That next step puts the imprimatur of CBS or some other "respectable" news organization on the tabloid's report. This gives much more support to a potentially damaging story built on a shaky factual foundation. That is how the "tabloidization" of journalism takes place.

Clear lines between responsible and sensational coverage are often hard to draw. Consider, for example, the prospect of a televised execution of a state prison inmate. The 1990 lawsuit seeking this right to cover was filed not by a tabloid show, but by KQED, San Francisco's highly respected Public Broadcasting station.

KQED lawyers argued, "It is appropriate in a democratic society for citizens to be able to observe—not filtered through the unaided, faulted or biased memories of witnesses hand-picked by government—the ultimate sanction of our criminal justice system." The station proposed videotaping an execution—not carrying it live—and judiciously choosing any excerpts it wanted to run.[31]

The KQED position met with disapproval from some in the news business. Among their comments: "There's nothing newsworthy in it." "Except for the macabre interest in watching someone die on television, what is the news value?" "This is not something we feel needs to be shared, it is not something that is under any public 'need to know.'"[32]

Executions by the state may be newsworthy *and* their coverage may be sensational. The two are not always mutually exclusive.

Elusive Standards

Standards can collapse quickly, and soon the mainstream news organizations may find themselves not just matching but outdoing the tabloids. In 1991, when a woman accused William Kennedy Smith of raping her at a Kennedy family home in Palm Beach, Florida, "NBC Nightly News" disclosed the woman's name. The next day, the *New York Times* (in a rumor- and innuendo-filled profile of the woman) followed NBC's lead. The major tabloids, meanwhile, had not used the name, and the editor of the *National Enquirer* found himself in the unusual (although presumably not unpleasant) position of being able to criticize the *Times*'s behavior. He said, "I think we took a more ethical standard than they did."[33]

Much rhetoric is devoted to praise of "standards" without ever building a philosophical foundation that will have some permanence. In her *Newsweek* column, Meg Greenfield observed:

> When we do give exceptional coverage to something like the Simpson case we will invariably explain, with more ingenuity than persuasiveness, that it is beneficial to the public for some medicinal type reason; in this instance it has been that the public will now learn a lot about legal procedure, trials and so forth. Oh, yes.[34]

This stumbling by the news media reflects the moral ambiguities pervading American society. When Paula Jones charged that she had been sexually harassed by Bill Clinton, one commentator noted, "The culture that permits her to advance that claim—the culture that regards the conduct she says took place as worthy of public exposure and condemnation—is also the culture that finds nothing too intimate or too embarrassing to broadcast on the evening news. . . . We apparently find this stuff so offensive that we cannot get enough of it."[35]

This is not to say that the news media may escape responsibility by claiming, "We only give the public what they want; they—not we—are the prurient slobs." If a profession collectively embraces ethics, its members implicitly accept a leadership role in setting and maintaining standards. For example, journalists should acknowledge their influence in the public's determination of what is and is not "tasteful."

This definition evolves gradually, shaped in part by personal standards but certainly affected by the news media's decisions about what to cover and how to cover it. For instance, the language used to describe crimes may desensitize news consumers. Paula LaRocque, writing coach of the *Dallas Morning News,* said, "Crime, police, or trial stories often invite loaded language or sensationalism." She offered some examples:

- A reporter describes a man charged with child abuse as wearing a "sardonic smile" when he's escorted to the courtroom.
- A reporter refers to the victim in a rape trial as "voluptuous."
- A reporter says of a man found guilty of murdering his girlfriend that he "loved his girlfriend to death."

Of this last item, LaRocque wrote: "Anyone whose life has been touched by murder knows that murder is not really Damon Runyon or *True Detective* territory. A woman is dead, and she wasn't loved to death."[36]

By no means is crime the only topic that inspires sensationalism. For example, some alternative religions may be classified offhandedly as "cults," and a major religion may be denigrated by using a term such as "extremists" when a writer refers to a handful of its followers.[37] The men who bombed New York's World Trade Center were consistently labeled "Muslim extremists," but the Branch Davidian followers of David Koresh in the 1993 Waco siege were not called "Christian extremists."

In this context, sensationalism includes dismissing as "nuts" those who embrace nonmainstream religions. In the Branch Davidian case, disdain for the intensity of faith of Koresh's followers contributed to the news media's and law enforcement's failure to anticipate the group's collective suicide.[38]

One reason for sensationalism's pervasiveness is journalists' failure to inform themselves about what they're covering. Dismissing the nonconformist as a nut is the easy way out, as is

THE POWER OF PICTURES *69*

describing people with sincere but uncommon religious beliefs as cultists. Nancy Bernhard of the Harvard Divinity School wrote: "The press should grant religious knowledge and experience a greater measure of respect. . . . Of course David Koresh was mad. But if you never consulted the Book of Revelation you missed a big part of the story. And if you think everyone who believes in the Book of Revelation is mad, you may well miss the next one."[39]

Sensationalism will fill the vacuum created by the absence of substantive information. If journalists were to do a better job of providing substance, sensationalism might lose some (but certainly not all) of its appeal.

The Power of Pictures

Sensationalism often magnifies the mundane, exaggerating an event's importance regardless of its lack of intrinsic newsworthiness. This problem arises frequently when news organizations use dramatic pictures (still photographs or video) based solely on the emotional power of the pictures.

Sometimes, however, a story may be sensational *and* newsworthy. When that is the case, ethical questions usually concern limits on how far to go with using the pictures. Even newsworthiness does not provide unlimited license for sensationalism.

CASE: Gulf War

As the 1991 Gulf War drew to its rapid close, American-led forces pounded the retreating Iraqi army. Photographer Ken Jarecke captured the fate of an anonymous Iraqi soldier, burned to death while trying to escape his flaming truck. The decision by some newspapers to play this photograph prominently provoked protest from those who thought the image too gruesome. Photographer Jarecke argued in response, "If we are big enough to fight a war, we should be big enough to look at it."[40]

Although some news organizations chose not to use the photo because of its gruesomeness, others thought the public needed to

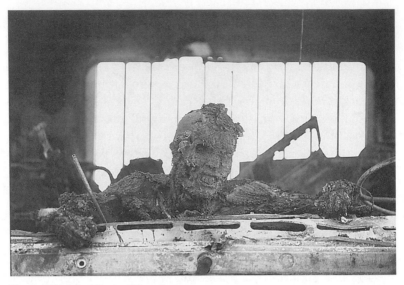

Kenneth Jarecke/Contact Press Images

see it. Phillip Greer, the *Chicago Tribune*'s director of photography, said: "We ran it because it's important that the horror of wars be shown. It's not sensationalism for sensationalism's sake. But it brings the story home and wakes the readers up."[41]

Along the same lines, Harold Evans, former editor of *The Times* of London, defended the editors of a British newspaper— London's *Observer*—that had published the Jarecke photo:

> The photograph met both the tests I suggested some years ago for the intrusion of images of violence on our peace of mind: Is the event portrayed of such social and historic significance that the shock is justified? Is the objectionable detail necessary for a proper understanding of the event? I recoiled from the picture the moment I saw it, as most people surely did. In part that was an elemental human sympathy. Then I was forced to recognize that I had willed this man's death. I believe the Gulf War was a just war, and perhaps the dead Iraqi believed he was fighting a holy war, but here, inescapably, was the consequence of our convictions. It is right that we should contemplate the results of our

beliefs. No action can be moral if we close our eyes to its consequences. Here, in charred flesh and grinning skull, was the price of patriotism. That was the service that publication of this photograph performed.[42]

Evans's argument illustrates the depth of ethical considerations that publication of a photograph may entail. The image is grotesque and horrifying, but war is grotesque and horrifying. Journalists have a responsibility to report the truth, and this photograph captures the essence of the truth about war.

This was particularly important during the Gulf War because television audiences had been treated to Pentagon-supplied footage of "smart bombs" zipping toward their military targets. Such images, however, reduced the war to a video game, sanitized for living room viewing. For a news organization to withhold photos such as Jarecke's would be to put journalism's stamp of approval on this distortion.

On the other hand, those who object to the use of such pictures may say that the public knows what war is and doesn't need to be gratuitously horrified by news organizations' pandering to the ghouls in their audience. As a matter of basic humaneness, reporting the agony of death—even in the course of a newsworthy event such as a war—should be kept within bounds of decency. This reasoning can be taken further by citing the dead soldier's privacy. Even though his name was unknown and he was "the enemy," he was still a human being whose final agony should not have been presented for the world to view.

Arguments for publishing and for withholding are compelling. At their heart is the debate about how much license accompanies newsworthiness.

CASE: Budd Dwyer Suicide

In 1986 Pennsylvania State Treasurer R. Budd Dwyer was convicted of conspiracy, mail fraud, and racketeering as a result of a kickback scheme involving a state contract. On January 22, 1987, the day before he was to be sentenced (he faced a term of up to fifty-five years), Dwyer called a news conference at his office in

AP/Wide World

Harrisburg. Many politicians and journalists assumed he was going to announce his resignation from office.

Instead, he began reading a rambling, twenty-five-minute denunciation of fellow politicians, the FBI, the judge in his case, the news media, and others. He then pulled a .357 magnum revolver from a large envelope, put the barrel into his mouth, and pulled the trigger.

Still and video cameras recorded every instant. The newsworthiness of what happened is indisputable. The pictures of what happened are horrifying. If you're a Pennsylvania newspaper editor or television news director, what do you do?

On the noon news that day in Philadelphia, the state's largest city, only one of three network affiliates—WPVI (ABC)—used the moment of suicide. KYW (NBC) and WCAU (CBS) halted their footage before Dwyer fired.

The news directors of the latter two stations approached their decisions differently. Discussing the case on a Society of Professional Journalists panel several months later, Randy Covington of KYW said, "This was an easy call . . . [the videotape was] far worse than I ever imagined" and was unsuitable, particularly on a day when a snowstorm had closed schools and many children would be home watching television. On the other hand, WCAU's Jay Newman said: "This was not an easy call at all. I have always operated on the basis that we're not in the business of censoring news." Newman added that he felt the reality of the story could be conveyed without showing the entire tape. (WPVI chose not to participate in the panel.)[43]

On the print side, decisions also varied about which photographs to publish. In Allentown, Pennsylvania, an initial decision to use the gun-in-mouth photo was reversed. *Morning Call* executive editor Lawrence Hymans said: "We came 180 degrees. After first feeling the pictures should run because they were shown to a wide television audience, we didn't think it was necessary to show people how to commit suicide."[44]

Similarly, the *Pittsburgh Press* decided to use just a file photo in its first run. Of the suicide photos, managing editor Madelyn Ross said: "The word image we had in our story of Dwyer putting the gun in his mouth and pulling the trigger was simple enough." (In later editions, the *Press* ran the picture of Dwyer brandishing the pistol.)[45]

The *Daily Times*, a tabloid published near Philadelphia, published three photos on page one, including one of Dwyer with the revolver in his mouth and one taken a split second after he pulled the trigger, with an apparent explosion of blood behind his head.

The *Philadelphia Inquirer,* considered to be one of the nation's best newspapers, ran two pictures on page one: Dwyer with gun in hand warning people to stand back (five by four inches) and the gun-in-mouth photo (five by eight inches). Inside, on page 16, the *Inquirer* ran a large photo of Dwyer lying on the floor a few seconds after the shooting.

The *Daily Times* received three hundred calls the day the photos were published. This led to some introspection at the paper. *Daily Times* editor Stuart Rose, in an editorial published two days later, wrote: "The next time a news decision with the same type of violent impact is presented to us, more than the news value alone will capture our attention. The impact on our readers will also be discussed."[46]

Elaborating on this for a Society of Professional Journalists publication, Rose noted that parents made a compelling argument about not wanting their young children to see such graphic photos. Placement on the front page made parental supervision difficult. Rose said the pictures should have been run inside.

But to those who said words alone would have sufficed in telling this story, Rose wrote:

> If the story had concerned an obscure state official elsewhere, I might have given this argument more weight. But to us Budd Dwyer was an important man, and he'd been on our front pages off and on for three years. His public suicide was unquestionably one of the leading political stories of the year here. And photographs provided the most compelling, most effective summary of that story.[47]

The *Inquirer*'s coverage also elicited public reaction. In a column about the Dwyer photos, editor Edwin Guthman wrote: "Some readers were sickened. Some were appalled. Some were outraged." Nevertheless, said Guthman, using the photos was essential. Dwyer, he wrote, "had confronted society with a very public, horrifying act. We felt that we had an obligation to our readers to portray the story for what it was; that if we published only the photo of him holding the gun while warning others to stay away, we would not really convey what had happened."[48]

That is the essence of the case for publishing. As with the Gulf War photograph of the dead Iraqi soldier, depicting reality, however gruesome, is of paramount importance.

But one element of the *Inquirer's* rationale raises another issue. Guthman wrote, "In agony, Dwyer was trying to make an appalling statement, and however deranged he may have been, we did not want to tamper with the force of what he was attempting to convey."[49] Dwyer chose to die in this way; Dwyer chose to shock the public. But journalists, as gatekeepers, have the right—and the obligation—to "tamper with the force" of what is being conveyed when that message is clearly designed to manipulate. (Analogous to this is the manipulation of media by terrorists who stage an event such as a hostage-taking to compel news organizations to cover them. Not "tampering with the force" of their action means ceding partial editorial control to them.)

Joanne Dwyer, Budd Dwyer's widow, later said her husband's choice of a news conference for his suicide "was a statement to the press and only to the press about how they treated an individual and what they had done to help convict that individual."[50] Dwyer knew that he would be covered and presumably believed that the press would look bloodthirsty by covering his death the way he expected they would.

Journalists should not surrender editorial control to the subjects of coverage, regardless of how spectacular their attention-getting actions may be. In such instances, decision making about coverage should not be shared between journalists and those they cover.

When newsroom managers are confronted with decisions such as those surrounding the Dwyer photographs, a sliding scale is used: the greater the newsworthiness, the more leeway for "sensational" aspects of the story. The Dwyer case makes this more complicated by raising an ancillary question: When does a newsworthy photograph become *too* sensational to merit publication?

CASE: Paul Broussard Suicide

The role of gatekeeper becomes more difficult as live television coverage becomes more common.

On September 15, 1994, deputy sheriff Paul Broussard murdered his wife in downtown Alexandria, Louisiana, and then ran across the street to the courtyard of a bank. He sat on a bench for more than two hours, talking to a priest. Then he put his pistol to his head and killed himself.

This case differs from the Dwyer story in two principal ways: The Broussard suicide was televised live, and the level of this event's newsworthiness was questionable.

The camera's focus on Broussard was so tight that viewers could see splattering blood and even the bullet hole. Jack Frost, news director of KALB, said: "We did not televise a suicide. The incident we televised was a situation that put the downtown area in danger, and our public needed to be aware of that. We didn't know if he was going to erupt again into violence. We prayed—I prayed—that would not happen. Unfortunately, it did."[51]

That justification may have been sincere, but it also is flimsy. Alerting the public to danger through live coverage did not require a tight camera shot of the distraught Broussard. Particularly because this station did not have tape-delay capability, this coverage decision carried with it an implicit surrender of editorial decision making. Whatever happened—no matter how horrendous—would be presented instantaneously to the public.

Live journalism carries with it extraordinary ethical responsibilities. Sensationalism, even if inadvertent, is much more likely to prevail when editorial deliberation is removed from the news delivery process. If a story is carried live, decisions must be made in advance about all foreseeable contingencies. In the Broussard case, his suicide was certainly one of those contingencies.

Also, determination of an event's newsworthiness should not be made solely on journalists' access to that event. Just because a camera could be placed where it could watch Broussard does not in itself mean this was an event the public needed to see unfold in such minute detail. The story was newsworthy, but probably not that newsworthy.

In considering this case, Roy Peter Clark, a senior scholar at the Poynter Institute for Media Studies, raises a sometimes overlooked but always important issue: public opinion about journalists' news judgment. Having appeared on a radio talk show to discuss the Broussard coverage, Clark cites callers who believed that the Alexandria TV station's managers were hoping for a bloodily dramatic conclusion to the event. "They assume," said Clark, "we would celebrate a death for a good story." He then asks, "How can a public so deeply cynical about journalists depend on us for the essential needs of the community?"[52]

The television pictures of Paul Broussard's death have impact that transcends the power of words. They possess an innate sensationalism that may exceed their news value. These images affect not only people's understanding of this one event, but also their opinions about what is news and their perceptions of the news business. That underscores the need for high ethical standards among the journalists who are being scrutinized.

CASE: Intruding into Private Tragedy

In the Broussard case, at least some argument could be made that the public needed to know what was going on. A law enforcement officer had committed a murder and efforts to capture him were underway in the city's downtown. The public needed information about this, even if that need did not extend to seeing Broussard kill himself.

Sometimes, however, this threshold of public need to know might not be reached. Consider the photograph of Jamie Peterson that ran in newspapers around the country in March 1985. This was the caption as it appeared in the *Dallas Morning News*:

> Jamie Peterson watches in horror as her family's apartment in Lexington, N.C., burns with her 4-year-old son trapped inside. Matthew Peterson was listed in serious but stable condition Friday. His father, Scott, and younger brother, Daniel, were in satisfactory condition. The fire Thursday apparently started in a closet in Matthew's bedroom. Matthew was burned over most of his body.

In Lexington, perhaps this was news. But elsewhere, certainly not. A nonfatal apartment fire in a distant city is simply not newsworthy. The only part of this story that made it news was the photograph

H. Scott Hoffmann

that captured Peterson's anguish and awakened in all who saw it the dread that something similar could happen to them.

From a photographer's standpoint, it is a great picture, possessing a rare and frightening vividness. Because it so grippingly depicts a slice of life, the public ought to see it. Also, it may remind those who see it of the importance of smoke detectors and family fire escape plans.

On the other hand, what right do we have to intrude on what is probably the most horrible moment of this woman's life? She is not a public figure, she has done nothing wrong, and she has not willingly surrendered her privacy. She is merely the victim of terrible circumstance.

Given all that, the actual decision making comes down to this: You're the editor determining what goes into tomorrow morning's newspaper (your community's only paper). This picture comes over the Associated Press wire. It is stunning. Do you put it in the paper or throw it into the trash can? Those are your only choices. Let your readers see it and think about it, or keep them from seeing it. Which choice is the more ethical?

Creating Standards

In November 1993, in Springfield, Oregon, Allen McGuire smothered his two-year-old daughter, Shelby, in a plastic bag and then used gasoline to set himself on fire. Police arrived and tried, unsuccessfully, to save both lives. Journalists arrived at the same time and recorded the events on film and videotape.

After intense discussion among staff members, a daily newspaper and a television station ran the pictures. A few viewers called the TV station to complain; many readers called the newspaper. News managers at both organizations defended the pictures as being newsworthy.[53]

With some time to think about these matters, another local newspaper came up with a different way to submit the pictures to the public. This paper, the semiweekly *Springfield News*, used a half-page wraparound to cover its front page pictures and to tell readers what they would find in the *News*'s coverage of the McGuire case. The text on the wraparound read:

> Caution to readers. Some people may be disturbed or offended by photographs on pages 1A and 3A of today's newspaper. Please use discretion with children.
>
> An explanation: The Springfield News believes it is important to confront the horror of domestic violence and abuse. We hope our community will be moved to act. See editorials. . . .
>
> Complete coverage: Police and neighbors react to the tragic events. . . .

A call to action: Many agencies in this community can help
people involved in domestic violence. If you need help, or if you
want to find out how you can give help, please see the directory
on the left side of this page.[54]

This approach illustrates how ethical goals can sometimes be
met by presenting the news in a thoughtful way. Careful presentation lets news consumers know what they are getting and gives
them an opportunity to be selective about the words and pictures
they will read and see.

Whether a picture depicts violence or intrudes on someone's privacy at a time of tragedy, journalists should appreciate the power of
the visual image. More than words, pictures open their subjects to
public scrutiny. In some instances—such as war photographs—
that may be an essential part of the journalist's duty. Sometimes,
however, a picture may be sensational and nothing more.

Lou Gelfand of the *Minneapolis Star Tribune* suggested that local
journalists take their community's standards into account and
declare a moratorium on "broken-heart" photos—those such as of
a parent grieving over a dead child. The thesis behind such self-
policing is that "there may be something innately dehumanizing
and prurient in peering too often into the abyss of someone else's
grief."[55]

No ironclad rule can be created; the standard will have to be
flexible enough to fit the different circumstances of different news
stories. Human reaction to tragedy is sometimes an essential part
of a story. The news should not be sanitized by ridding it of all
unpleasantness. But, as Gelfand wrote about one case in which
he thought a photo should have been withheld: "Newspapers can
show compassion without compromising their mission. Denying
the readers this view of someone's grief would not have short-
changed the news report."[56]

Curiosity versus Privacy

How should journalists respond to someone's desire to be left
alone by the news media? Does the answer change if this someone

is involved in a newsworthy event? Should public figures be treated differently than people who have come into public view by chance?

These are all parts of a larger question: Can journalists ethically justify virtually every intrusion on privacy as being legitimized by the public's right to know, or in some cases should public curiosity be left unsatisfied unless it meets a *need*-to-know test?

Answers to such questions are difficult to formulate partly because the public speaks with different voices about these issues. People who profess to be outraged when a famous former athlete is pressured by the press to reveal that he has AIDS may also read everything about the story that they can get their hands on.

Finding a path through this morass requires guideposts in the form of definitions of what is private and what is not.

CASE: Public Figures

People who thrust themselves into public view—such as political candidates, entertainers, and professional athletes—are generally assumed to have waived some of their privacy rights. After all, the reasoning goes, their livelihood depends in large part on their visibility. They know that, and because they benefit from news coverage they should not expect to be able to control that coverage.

Even that premise has its limits. Consider the case of tennis star Arthur Ashe. After an outstanding career, Ashe had to give up playing because of a heart condition. He remained in public view as a tennis coach and commentator and as a champion of numerous political causes. Ashe contracted the HIV virus through a blood transfusion and developed AIDS. This was known among some sports journalists, but the information was not published out of respect for Ashe's privacy.

This respect for privacy did not last. After Ashe received queries from *USA Today* in April 1992 that led him to believe that a story about his condition was about to be published, he called a news conference and announced that he did indeed have AIDS. He said he had wanted to withhold this information until his five-year-old daughter could better understand it and deal with the stigma that unfairly plagues AIDS victims and their families.

News professionals split in their opinions about coverage of the Ashe story. Peter Prichard of *USA Today* said, "Journalists serve the public by reporting news, not by hiding it." Taking the opposite view, the *Washington Post*'s Jonathan Yardley wrote: "No public issues were at stake. No journalistic 'rights' were threatened. The fight against AIDS will in no way be hastened or strengthened by the exposure to which Ashe has been subjected."[57]

Ashe himself asked: "Are you going to be cold, hard, crass purveyors of the facts just for the sake of people's right to know, under the guise of freedom of the press? Or are you going to show a little sensitivity about some things?"[58]

Even public figures are human beings. Like other people, they deserve compassion, especially when their situation does not affect the public's welfare. A difference exists between the Ashe story and a report about the health problems of an elected official whose job performance is being affected to the detriment of the public.

Debate tips one way, then another. Most news managers say they will publish private material about public figures only when the material can be verified and can be shown to affect the individual's public performance. Others in the news business, however, say that almost any private information (about, for instance, alcohol abuse or sexual misconduct) tells something about that person's character and therefore is of public interest.[59]

The principal ethical issue to be resolved in such cases is this: Does a public figure surrender *all* right to privacy?

CASE: Private Persons

Sometimes chance pushes the media spotlight in such a way that it suddenly illuminates—with its full, garish intensity—the life of a person who neither wants nor deserves to be stripped of privacy.

Such situations raise challenging ethical questions. For instance, should extraordinary care be used in defining "newsworthy" when a private person is involved? Should the "public's right to know" include everything within the realm of the public's curiosity? Should journalists help to shield victims of tragedy, disease, and crime from public view?

Journalists as gatekeepers control the flow of information to the public. The ethical gatekeeper knows when to open and close the gate. Simply leaving it permanently open is an abdication from responsibility, but so, too, is being too quick to slam it shut.

Consider this case. A woman is driving to work when she comes upon a car wreck. She recognizes the car as her husband's. She stops and rushes to a police officer, who tells her that her husband has been killed. At that instant, a photographer snaps her picture. A California newspaper ran this picture. The paper's ombudsman defended this decision, saying, "It did not, in my view, hold the woman up to ridicule."[60]

Should "absence of ridicule" be the standard? If so, news organizations need only wrap invasions of privacy in a gauze of respectfulness (genuine or feigned) to justify publication.

Sensationalism and privacy cannot coexist. One witness to journalists' pursuit of a victim of tragedy said that one reporter had asked a question "only to get (the victim) to cry on camera." She added, "I know the media has a job to do, but too often all they really want is to show people crying and sobbing, and that's cruel and wrong."[61]

Sometimes, however, journalists do show restraint, even when the story in question continues for years. This was the case with David, who came to be known in news stories as the "bubble boy." He was born in 1971 with a serious immune deficiency and lived his entire life—he died in 1984—in a sterile bubble in his Houston home. The story of his medical care and survival was covered by more than two hundred reporters from five continents. Not one published David's family name or his address. It can be done. [62]

Defining a "reasonable right to privacy"—particularly in the face of sensationalist pressure—requires a healthy dose of compassion. Journalists searching for an ethical course to follow might try putting themselves in the place of the subject of coverage. Would the reporters want to subject themselves or their families to the invasive techniques that are so common in the news business? Is the damage caused by trampling on privacy really outweighed by the public's being given whatever information is gathered this way? Would journalists fail in meeting their responsibility to inform the public if they were more respectful of privacy?

Another View of Tabloids

Tabloid news is still news, and as such it should be considered within the scope of journalistic ethics. Because of its influence and pervasiveness, it merits rigorous critiquing.

But this medium should not be overly denigrated by journalism purists. Print and broadcast tabloids not only have large audiences, they also may provide access to the public for persons whose stories are ignored or undercovered by mainstream news organizations.

Describing the case of a rape victim whose story was not getting a hearing, Minnesota writer Louise Mengelkoch said:

> The tabloids' greatest virtue . . . is exactly that which makes people sneer at them. . . . As gatekeepers they're lousy, and that's often fortunate for those who need them most. They will listen to your story when nobody else will, if it has the elements and angles they're looking for. If we truly believe in access, that journalists should be dedicated to comforting the afflicted and afflicting the comfortable, the tabloids must be recognized as sharing that mission. [63]

Kind words about tabloids are not heard often. And even occasional praiseworthy reporting by tabloids does not excuse other instances of the sensationalism that overwhelms truth and fairness. But a substantial portion of the public is certain to retain its loyalty to tabloid-style news. Journalists should recognize this and work to keep the minimalist ethics of tabloidism from having too much influence on the standards of mainstream news.

For Discussion

1. Why is tabloid journalism so popular?

2. What is the difference between sensational *news* and sensational trash?

3. How much privacy—if any—should public figures be allowed by the news media?

4. When a private citizen is accidentally and innocently thrust into the public spotlight, how much privacy should he or she be allowed by the news media?

5. Why should journalists treat pictures with greater care than they do words?

6. What guidelines should news organizations adopt when covering inherently sensational events such as the O. J. Simpson trial?

CHAPTER FIVE

Tricks of the Trade

Gathering news sometimes is easy: attend a news conference or read through a press release and turn the information into something publishable.

Much news is readily obtainable in this way. But much other information that the public has a right and a need to know is not simply handed to journalists. It is gathered through painstaking research and investigation. This process can be long and tortuous, and sometimes just when the end is in sight and only one more confirmation is needed, the journalist runs smack into the brick wall of "No comment" or missing documents or vanished sources. Then he or she must look for another route or perhaps even abandon the quest.

News gathering is, for the most part, straightforward. Correspondents observe events and describe them. If facts cannot be gathered firsthand, reporters identify human sources or repositories such as libraries and archives that may have useful information. Then they ask for interviews or access to the material. Sometimes the requests are granted; sometimes legal help—such as is provided by the Freedom of Information Act—is needed to open closed doors.

On occasion, journalists have to be particularly aggressive and imaginative as they pursue stories. Their tradecraft—the tactics they employ in news gathering—may raise ethical concerns. The principal questions arising in such instances are these: Does the public's right to and need for the information outweigh ethically questionable methods in getting it? Does the newsworthy end justify the reportorial means?

Deception and Misrepresentation

Misleading their sources, using hidden cameras and tape recorders, conducting ambush interviews, re-creating events, and even breaking the law are in the repertoire of some news organizations. Such measures may be condemned, but the counterargument is that they produce accurate stories that the public has a right and a need to know about. This debate is often fierce and often hard to resolve definitively.

CASE: Undercover Reporting

Consider these two cases:

- As a reporter for a big city television station, you want to call your viewers' attention to the harsh life endured by homeless persons living in your community. You decide that the best way to get a large and attentive audience is to spend a week posing as a homeless person, living on the streets with a camera crew hidden in a van, recording whatever you encounter. You plan to talk with real homeless persons, social workers, police officers, and others you meet on the street, but you will tell none of them that you are a reporter. Instead you will use a story you have invented about being down on your luck and having nowhere to go.
- As a newspaper editor, you hear reports that local real estate agencies are steering African-American home buyers away from houses that are for sale in any areas except those that already have high concentrations of black residents. So far, all you have is anecdotal evidence—not enough corroboration to publish. To get solid proof, you send two of your African-American reporters to visit realtors, posing as a couple wanting to buy a house. You then send a pair of

white reporters to the same realtors to compare the treatment the couples receive. At no time do any of these reporters reveal their true identities to the real estate agents.

Deception, misrepresentation, undercover reporting. Whatever the label, tactics such as these have one common characteristic: The reporters portray themselves as something other than journalists while they gather the news.

The people with whom they deal have no idea they are speaking to reporters. Presumably, the resulting stories are truthful renditions of their undercover experiences. But is it ethically acceptable—is it honest?—to pose as someone you are not even though you believe "the public interest" will be served by the reporting that your ploy produces?

Such questions elicit diverse opinions from people in the news business. Don Hewitt, executive producer of CBS's "60 Minutes," has defended misrepresentation in specific cases, such as posing as a street person to convey the grim realities of homelessness.[1] One of the leading opponents of misrepresentation is former *Washington Post* executive editor Ben Bradlee, who barred the practice at the *Post.* "In a day in which we are spending thousands of hours uncovering deception," said Bradlee, "we simply cannot deceive. How can newspapers fight for honesty and integrity when they themselves are less than honest in getting a story?"[2]

Another prominent newspaper editor, Eugene Patterson, agreed with Bradlee's position: "Hard work and shoe leather could have unearthed the sources necessary" to do most undercover stories. "The press as a whole pays a price in credibility when a newspaper that editorially calls for government in the sunshine and candor in business shows itself disposed to shade the truth or mask its motives in its own method of operation. . . . "[3]

Bradlee and Patterson were instrumental in denying a Pulitzer Prize in 1979 to the *Chicago Sun-Times,* which had run an undercover sting operation that documented government corruption. For four months, the paper operated the aptly named Mirage Bar—complete with reporters as bartenders—and found that city inspectors and other officials solicited payoffs to disregard health and safety hazards. The journalists were careful not to entrap the

officials and had ample photographic and written documentation of the corrupt practices.[4] The resulting stories exposed the
illegal activity and helped law enforcement agencies respond to it.
Such results are what news organizations are supposed to produce. Praising the *Sun-Times*'s effort, Joseph Soquist of the
Milwaukee Journal said, "This was a worthy subject that needed a
dramatic presentation to capture the public's attention."[5]

Nevertheless, the principal objection to the *Sun-Times*'s tactics
was that the deception was unnecessary. Bradlee, Patterson, and
others argued that the same results could have been achieved
without reporters posing as anyone else. By contacting other bar
owners who were victims of the city inspectors' shakedowns, a
good story could have been written. It may have lacked the dramatic impact of the Mirage sting, but drama, said the *Sun-Times*'s
critics, is not an acceptable criterion for going undercover.

From the Mirage case and similar incidents emerge two guidelines about deception and misrepresentation:

- Undercover efforts should be undertaken only as a last resort,
  when conventional reporting techniques have been tried and
  have failed. Using deception merely because it will produce a
  more sensational version of the story is inappropriate.
- The story should be of vital public interest. For instance, if a
  journalist has reason to believe that residents of a nursing
  home are being abused and if standard reporting has hit a
  dead end, an undercover effort may be called for. In this
  case, innocent people may be in jeopardy; this should offset
  some of the reluctance to use deception. On the other hand,
  if the story is less crucial—such as finding out factory workers' attitudes toward their employer—standard, undis-
  guised reporting techniques should suffice. Using deception
  to get a job in the factory may be going too far.

Some other issues are also worth considering:

- Before an undercover reporting operation is launched, reasonable certainty should exist that it is being targeted at people who have done something wrong. In a case involving

real estate steering (as in the hypothetical mentioned earlier), an editor was hesitant about using misrepresentation
while picking real estate agents at random. He asked,
"Should there be a threshold of presumed bad conduct
before a newspaper unleashes this sort of thing on unsus-
pecting people?"[6] Sending reporters as reporters to talk to
realtors would be acceptable; targeting a random sample for
undercover work might not be.

- A difference exists between active and passive deception. A
  Washington Post reporter traveled on a bus carrying visitors
  to a prison. She sat quietly and listened as her fellow passengers talked about smuggling drugs in to the inmates.
  Apparently, those on the bus thought she was just another
  relative of a prisoner. She never said she was, and had anyone asked her, she would have said she was a reporter. Her
  editor, Ben Bradlee, who had criticized the Mirage reporting, said: "I see a really seminal distinction between planning any kind of deception, however much the end might
  seem to justify the means, and embarking on a project
  where your occupation as a journalist is not advertised. In
  the first instance the journalist is actually posing as someone else, be it a bartender . . . or whatever. In the second
  instance there is no pose." There may have been no sign
  around his reporter's neck, he added, but at no time did she
  lie to any of her fellow passengers.[7]

During the Pulitzer deliberations about the Mirage story, board
member James Reston of the *New York Times* "reportedly drew a
distinction between 'pretense' and 'deception' at the board meeting. Pretense, in this scheme, is a passive act: the reporter allows
someone to draw the wrong conclusion about who he is or what
he knows. Deception, however, is active: the reporter intends to
mislead."[8]

"Active" versus "passive." "Pretense" versus "deception." These
might seem to be finely drawn semantic points, but this issue has
fueled much serious debate. Harvard ethicist Sissela Bok notes that
undercover reporting may increase public mistrust of journalists:

The press and other news media rightly stand for openness in public discourse. But until they give equally firm support to openness in their own practices, their stance will be inconsistent and lend credence to charges of unfairness. It is now a stance that challenges every collective rationale for secrecy save the media's own. Yet the media serve commercial and partisan interests in addition to public ones; and media practices of secrecy, selective disclosure, and probing should not be exempt from scrutiny.[9]

CASE: Hidden Cameras and Tape Recorders

Among the tools sometimes used in undercover reporting are hidden cameras and tape recorders. Again, this is unarguably deceptive, so finding a rationale for its being ethical can be challenging. (In some states such tactics—especially audio recording without the other party's permission—are illegal. For the sake of this discussion, assume that the examples occur in states where there are no legal barriers to the measures discussed.)

The hidden camera has become a popular element of television news gathering, particularly on magazine programs such as ABC's "PrimeTime Live" and CBS's "60 Minutes." Some of the resulting stories have been both dramatic and important, providing evidence of patients being neglected in a Veterans' Administration hospital, children being mistreated in a day-care center, and bad meat being disguised and sold to consumers by a major grocery store chain.

In this latter instance, a "PrimeTime" producer was hired as a meat wrapper by Food Lion (after lying on her job application) and surreptitiously wielded a small camera that captured store employees rewrapping and relabeling old meat that should have been thrown away. Other footage featured a counterman saying, "Sell the bad stuff first." Such video was the foundation of a report that was supported by more than seventy interviews with Food Lion employees.[10]

Ira Rosen, another "PrimeTime" producer, made a case for this kind of reporting: "You can discredit whistleblowers. You can't discredit the video. It's a very compelling way to show wrongdoing, to show abuses, to show criminality."[11] An NBC producer agreed: "Seeing is believing. That's why television has higher credibility with the public than print."[12]

Not surprisingly, Food Lion executives took a different view. Vincent Watkins, a vice president of the chain, said: "It's an invasion of privacy. . . . It's like being violated in some way."[13]

Also, some journalists and others who were not necessarily sympathetic to Food Lion's complaints still had concerns about the way this story and others like it were put together. *Washington Post* columnist Colman McCarthy didn't care much for the argument that violating "Thou shalt not lie" is less bad than violating "Thou shalt not steal." McCarthy called that rationale a "conveniently self-serving exoneration of what is, in essence, lazy journalism, not aggressive reporting." He added, "It's possible to uncover the truth by being untruthful, but where do television news people secure the right to legitimize their deceits?"[14]

Veteran "60 Minutes" correspondent Mike Wallace was more sanguine about using hidden cameras: "It really depends on your motive. Are you doing it for drama, or are you doing it for illumination? Each one has to be weighed separately as to the cost-benefit."[15] Veteran investigative reporter Pam Zekman noted that hidden camera footage can offset wrongdoers' lies or "amnesia." She said, "The good thing about the hidden camera is it allows no wiggle room."[16]

Regardless of which side of the debate seems more convincing, some basic questions should be pondered before a news organization embarks on a hidden camera project:

- When does investigating become spying, and is spying always wrong?[17]
- Is it unfair to record the words of someone who is unaware that he or she is being filmed?[18]

Although the results may be less dramatic, similar questions apply to the use of undisclosed audiotape recorders, whether in person or on the telephone. If the person knows that he or she is participating in an on-the-record interview, some reporters look at recording or not recording as an administrative matter, not an ethical issue. Why, they ask, should the source care whether his or her words are being recorded on tape instead of being written down in a notebook?[19] Reporters also may claim that recording an interview ensures greater accuracy (which is true).

These positions both avoid the question of ethics (or simple good manners). Why not ask the person being interviewed for permission to record? In most instances, interviewees will realize that improved accuracy is in their interest, and they will grant permission. If they don't, reporters can scribble notes as they always have.

In some cases, however, the newsworthiness of the story may be such that purist ethics take second place to pragmatic reporting. When the Lexington, Kentucky, *Herald-Leader* was investigating boosters' payments to University of Kentucky basketball players, editors decided to tape interviews surreptitiously to guard against future lawsuits. The sources knew that the interviews were on the record and that they could expect to be quoted.

Sure enough, when the stories appeared, some of the people who had been interviewed denied they had said what they had been quoted as saying. They were informed by the newspaper that tapes of their comments were secure in a bank vault. The paper's editors are convinced that they would have faced a number of lawsuits had they not been holding this evidence.[20]

Would the people being interviewed in this case have been as forthcoming had they known they were being recorded? Perhaps not, which would have hindered the *Herald-Leader*'s investigation. But failure to tell the sources that they were being recorded is deception. Is that breach of ethics outweighed by the stories' newsworthiness? Some leading journalists apparently thought so; these articles won the Pulitzer Prize for investigative reporting.

Some news organizations address these issues in their own ethics codes. The *Detroit Free Press* uses this guideline:

> Except in rare and justifiable instances, we do not tape anyone without that person's knowledge. To do otherwise violates a general policy of treating people as we would want to be treated. An exception may be made only if we are convinced the recording is

necessary to protect us in a legal action or for some other compelling reason, and if other approaches won't work. Such instances require a managing editor's approval in advance.[21]

CASE: Ambush Interviews

Normal practice for a reporter seeking information from a source is to request an interview. In the majority of cases, the request is granted. In the cases when it is turned down, the reporter usually accepts the fact that the would-be source is exercising his or her right not to talk.

But suppose that an interview with this source is crucial to the story. Does that give the journalist an acceptable reason to track down the source and ambush him or her with camera rolling?

This is an especially important issue for television reporters because the camera is an intrinsically unfair weapon. The surprised source saying, "I don't want to answer your questions" while backing away or perhaps putting a hand over the lens is likely to look guilty, apparently hiding some dark secret, even if there is no guilt and no secret. Years of sensationalized reporting (particularly on the tabloid news shows) have conditioned much of the television audience to view this kind of news gathering as a battle between good and evil, with journalists assiduously cultivating their image as the champions of good.

Some of journalism's more thoughtful practitioners don't see it that way. Former CBS News president Fred Friendly called ambush interviewing "the dirtiest trick department of broadcast journalism," and he pointed out that refusing a television interview is everyone's constitutional right.[22]

Journalists may apply different standards according to the experience of the person being interviewed. Ambushing a politician who has been indicted for accepting bribes may be less of a transgression than confronting a private citizen who has had no experience in dealing with the news media.

Also, a modified version of the ambush may cause fewer ethical problems: Confront the source with the camera remaining at a distance and ask permission to do an interview on the spot. If the source declines, the reporter has a long shot of the source declining to talk. That can be used in the story.[23]

Another variation on the ambush approach (and one that print as well as television reporters use) is to get the source's agreement to be interviewed by telling him or her that you want to talk about uncontroversial Topic A. Then—after a few soft questions about A—start asking about controversial Topic B. The source might end the interview right there, but with the interview underway the reporter has at least some chance to get comments concerning the real issue.

As with many examples of borderline ethics, journalists' defense is often based on the "greater good" or "lesser evil" rationale. For example, a TV news crew walked into a home for mentally ill and mentally retarded persons with camera running to get the facility director's comments about alleged mistreatment of the home's residents. The journalist supervising this project said that the tactic was appropriate to "correct a greater harm"—the abuse of the residents.[24]

An argument certainly can be made that the welfare of innocent, helpless people is more important than are esoteric standards of journalistic behavior. On the other hand, being too quick to use that rationale can lead to pushing aside almost all ethical concerns while pursuing "noble" stories. At some point, that practice itself may become the "greater harm."

CASE: Reenactments and Staged Events

Consider this case: A recent story that attracted media attention concerns an American diplomat, Felix Bloch, who was allegedly a spy for the Soviet Union. The FBI, which kept Bloch under surveillance, reportedly had a videotape showing him passing a briefcase to a Soviet agent. ABC's "World News Tonight" showed what appeared to be this FBI video. Actually, viewers saw two ABC employees posing as Bloch and the agent. The "simulation" label was accidentally left off the screen.[25]

Even if this label had appeared, would this reenactment have been ethical? Such segments are "good TV"—they entertain and engross the audience. But that does not necessarily make them good journalism. A television newscast implicitly promises its viewers pictures of reality. Because the FBI would not make its tape available for airing by the news media, ABC was left with two ways to do the story: show the reenactment or simply have its anchor or reporter say, "The FBI reportedly has videotaped evidence of Bloch passing a briefcase to a Soviet contact." The latter lacks the few seconds of pictures that the reenactment provided, so maybe it is not "good TV." But it is real.

Edward R. Murrow warned against such lapses: "There will always be some errors in news gathering, but the tricks that microphones, cameras, and film make possible must never be contrived to pass off as news events that were fabricated to document an event that we missed or which may never have happened."[26]

Newspapers encounter similar problems with posed photographs. For a story about teenagers smoking, a photographer was dispatched to a local high school to shoot some pictures of students smoking in the school parking lot, as was known to happen regularly. When the photographer arrived, no smokers were there, so he gave several students cigarettes and asked them to light up and take a few puffs while he shot his pictures.[27] The specific content of the photo was unreal, but it accurately depicted a more general reality. Given the firm evidence that students often did smoke there, was it wrong to use this staged picture?

One response to such questions is to look at the issue as a matter of truth in packaging. If the video or still photo is clearly labeled as a simulation or re-creation, then the public is not being deceived and, in fact, may be getting a better understanding of the story by being able to see what is being described. That has a certain logic to it, but it may be too facile a dismissal of the importance of reality. For one thing, should news consumers always have to be on their guard, uncertain about whether what they are seeing is real? Television news viewers are particularly vulnerable because they may be doing other things while watching the news and may miss seeing the label on a simulation.

Most news organizations give their audience news that they gather, not news that they miss and re-create. The ethical standard of truth does not have much flexibility.

CASE: Breaking the Law

Should you ever break the law in pursuit of a story? The answer seems obvious: of course not.

That takes care of the basic rule. But as with much else in ethics, exceptions can be found. Differentiating this from other ethical issues is not just the seriousness of the principle involved. It also may open the door to the criminal justice system's intervention in the news business.

Consider this hypothetical case: You are a reporter, and after several months of investigating you are convinced that the mayor of your city is involved in major corruption, including taking kickbacks from contractors whose substandard work on highway bridges endangers the public. You do not have enough evidence to publish the story. A source whom you have found to be highly reliable in the past tells you that in the mayor's office files are documents linking him to these contractors and to the payoffs. You know your way around city hall, so you are sure you could break into the mayor's office late at night, find the documents, and take them for use in your story.

Should you do it? Most ethics decisions involve selecting a course from a variety of possibilities, some less palatable than others, but all of them legal. In this instance, you would be breaking the law. Maybe you will find the documents, dethrone the mayor, and be a hero, and your lawbreaking will be overlooked. But consider this scenario: You break into the office, go through the files, find nothing . . . and then the police arrive. The First Amendment does not give journalists the right to commit burglary.

Regardless of whether you find the documents, and regardless of whether you are caught, you have committed a serious crime. Despite the eloquent case you might make for the public's right and need to know about the mayor's corruption, whenever you place yourself above the law you have climbed onto a morally flimsy structure. "The public interest" will have to be strong indeed to reinforce that construction.

Inevitably, some chipping away occurs even if the rule at hand is "Don't break the law." For instance, if you are racing to cover a story, you run a red light when no traffic is in sight. Or, when photographing a major fire—and staying well out of the way of firefighters and other rescuers—you are ordered by the property owner to leave; you refuse, becoming a trespasser. In such cases, an argument might be made that there is some logic-based flex in the law, as there is in ethics. But whenever a journalist breaks any law, he or she had best be prepared to be punished for it. If pursuit of the story really takes place on the moral high ground, willingness to be prosecuted should be part of the reporter's ethical stance.

Another side of this issue appears when journalists benefit from the illegal acts of others. Perhaps the most famous instance of this was the Pentagon Papers case of 1971. Defense Department analyst Daniel Ellsberg presented the *New York Times* with a highly classified forty-seven-volume study of American involvement in Vietnam, filled with material certain to embarrass political leaders and to undercut their arguments for waging the Vietnam War. Ellsberg had copied the documents on his own, without contacting the *Times* until he was ready to offer them to the paper.

Editors at the *Times* knew that the documents were ill-gotten. The editors were initially advised by their lawyers that publishing stories based on the papers might lead to legal action against the *Times* by the federal government under provisions of the Espionage Act. The lawyers' advice was rejected (the lawyers then resigned and were replaced by others) because the newspaper's management judged that the papers were so important and so vital to the public's understanding of the war that it would be irresponsible not to accept them. In response to the question: What right do you have to receive stolen property?, the *Times* implicitly answered: What right do we have to suppress such material?

Besides arguing the ethical appropriateness of providing the public with essential information, news organizations that published excerpts from the Pentagon Papers found that they had constitutional support as well. When the U.S. Supreme Court considered the government's effort to suppress publication of the excerpts, a majority of the justices sided with the *Times* and other papers that used Ellsberg's material. Justice Hugo Black wrote, "In revealing the workings of government that led to the Vietnam war, the newspapers nobly did precisely that which the Founders hoped and trusted they would do."[28]

In all of these matters related to deception and misrepresentation, journalists should resist the temptation to consider themselves a special class with license to make and break rules based on their own needs and convenience. Even if deception is sometimes necessary, it should be accompanied by cautious introspection.

Some news organizations' ethics codes address this. The *Orange County* (CA) *Register*'s code says:

> In the course of our reporting, staff members will not knowingly engage in criminal activity, or encourage or induce any person to commit a crime. Any exception will be undertaken with the approval of the editor and in consultation with legal counsel, and an exception will not be undertaken lightly. Some issues may require the commission of acts technically in violation of criminal statutes, but never will reporting allow for acts that may result in physical injury to another person. . . .[29]

Harvard ethicist Sissela Bok considered the *Washington Post*'s tactics in pursuing the Watergate story, as described by reporters Carl Bernstein and Bob Woodward in their book *All the President's Men.* She wrote:

> It is certain that the reporters deserve great credit for exposing the misdeeds of the Watergate scandal. It can be argued that, in order for this exposure to be possible, deception was needed; but what is more troubling in the book than the lies themselves is the absence of any acknowledgment of a moral dilemma. No one seems to have stopped to think that there was a problem in using deceptive means. No one weighed the reasons for and against doing so. There was no reported effort to search for honest alternatives, or to distinguish among different forms and degrees of

deception, or to consider whether some circumstances warranted it more than others.

The absence of such reflection may well result in countless young reporters unthinkingly adopting some of these methods. And those who used them successfully at a time of national crisis may do so again with lesser provocation. The impression gained by the reading public is that such standards are taken for granted among journalists. The results, therefore, are severe, both in terms of risks to the personal professional standards of those directly involved, the public view of the profession, and to many within it or about to enter it.[30]

Sources

In many cases, reporters' stories are only as good as their sources. In few instances can a journalist develop a story totally by himself or herself; very seldom will even the most comprehensive paper trail lead to a publishable product without supplemental material from sources.

How reporters get sources, how they work with them, and how they decide whether to reveal or withhold the identities of those sources raise numerous ethical questions.

Relationships with Sources

The simple definition of the reporter-source connection is this: an arm's-length relationship exclusively for the purpose of receiving information.

As with most simple definitions, this one crumbles quickly under the weight of real-life complexities. Neither reporters nor their sources are robots; they have feelings about the subject at hand. Information is not merely package goods; it is part of someone's life.

Journalists' independence can be compromised if they become too friendly with people whom they use as sources or who are subjects of their coverage. For example, suppose you are a

Washington reporter, and you frequently call on a particular senator for comments about legislation and politics. This senator invites you to her home for a dinner party. The guest list includes many prominent politicians. Should you go? On the one hand, you are wary of becoming too friendly with this source. She is, after all, a politician about whom you are expected to report objectively. On the other hand, you may pick up lots of useful information at the party, and if the senator herself is well disposed toward you, she may provide you with material that she does not give to your competition.

Many journalists believe that this kind of socializing is part of their job. Others refuse to have anything to do with their sources when they are not working. This issue becomes complicated when ground rules and motive come into play.

Suppose when you are invited to a party hosted by a source, you are told that everything that happens will be off the record; you must not use anything you hear or see at the party, except perhaps as a lead to pursue elsewhere. You are a news gatherer, and you will be in the midst of news makers. Should you be "off duty"?

Also, why are you being invited? Is it because the host enjoys your company or because he or she recognizes (and wants to take advantage of) your influence?

New York Times columnist William Safire wrote about an invitation he received from Ronald Reagan during the president's 1984 reelection campaign. He was invited to attend a small reception at the White House for about ten journalists, off the record. Safire wrote a column about his response to the invitation. He said, in part:

> Like everybody else, I'd love to have a drink with the President in the Oval Office. But the purpose of this well-meant and beautifully engraved invitation is not social, it is political and influential, and I have found that in the world of political journalism, good fences make good neighbors. Therefore, I respond . . . with a respectful regret. I want my questions answered by an alert and experienced politician, prepared to be grilled and quoted—not my hand held by an old smoothie.[31]

The counterargument to Safire's position is that even an off-the-record session can offer useful insights about the president's thinking and demeanor that might not be available in his carefully scripted public appearances. In this example, Reagan's age was a campaign issue, so firsthand observation in an intimate setting might provide valuable background information about his apparent ability to do the job for another four years.

Variations on this kind of reporter-source link come up from time to time. Occasionally a reporter becomes romantically involved with his or her source. That creates a significant conflict of interest that can be resolved only by ending the personal relationship or ending the journalistic relationship.

Another conflict arises when the reporter and source enter into a business relationship. In one instance, a newspaper reporter secured the book and movie rights to the life story of someone she was covering. This created a number of conflicts: The reporter was no longer an independent observer; she had an interest in hyping the story to make it more appealing to publishers and moviemakers; she might have been tempted to withhold some information from her newspaper and save it for her later ventures. None of these problems would have arisen had she kept her distance and stayed simply a reporter, not a business partner.[32]

The *Philadelphia Inquirer* addresses this issue in its ethics code: "A staff member should not write about, photograph or make news judgments about any individual related by blood or marriage or with whom the staff member has a close personal, financial or romantic relationship."[33]

Despite the case that can be made for reporters keeping their distance from sources, carrying this too far can prove counterproductive. Sources are not forced to talk to a reporter. Their motivation may be altruistic or selfish, but it is always their choice. Often they agree to talk or are more forthcoming because they trust and like the reporter. Being too standoffish removes an incentive for openness.

Still another source-related problem may occur when reporters become too comfortable with and too reliant on a single or small number of sources. No matter how knowledgeable they seem, sources usually have their own agendas that might conflict with journalists' need for honest information. Also, if a heavily relied-upon source turns out to merit being the subject of a tough story, a reporter overly dependent on that source's goodwill might soften the story. The public, of course, knows nothing about these relationships and ends up receiving watered-down journalism.

Also, using a narrow range of sources is likely to produce a narrow range of viewpoints. News consumers deserve to hear from as many sides of an issue as is possible. For example, if you are writing a story about local police officers demanding a pay raise, your source list should not be limited to police officers, who quite probably have nothing but good things to say about the raise. Elected officials might have concerns about tax implications, and employees of other municipal departments might have complaints about not getting comparable raises. All these voices—and perhaps others—are worth including in this story.

Limited range of sources is a problem not only for the individual reporter, but also for journalism collectively. A 1994 study found that

> the mainstream media cover issues with often striking similarity. Whether it is domestic issues, foreign policy, or political scandal, the media follow each other's lead as they "converge" on the same topics and interpretations, often limiting the range of views on important policy debates. Indeed, considering that thousands of journalists cover such "media events" as economic summits, political conventions, and most recently, the Persian Gulf War, remarkably few divergent points of view emerge. . . . By relying on a common and often narrow network of sources—newsmakers, experts, and commentators, in other words—the news media contribute to this systemic convergence on the conventional wisdom, the largely unquestioned consensus views held by journalists, power-holders, and many audience members.[34]

Confidential Sources

Whenever a journalist uses information from an unidentified source, the news consumer is being deprived of the ability to make an independent judgment about the information's credibility. The journalist is saying, "You don't need to know who this is. Trust me; I've checked out the source's reliability."

Lots of news consumers quite rightly don't want to turn over total evaluation of information to journalists. They want to make up their own minds, and that requires knowing where the information came from.

Nevertheless, rarely if ever does a day go by without news stories citing sources "who declined to be identified," "spoke only on condition of confidentiality," or who are described by some other formulaic phrase that tells the reader, viewer, or listener, "We're not going to tell you who said this." Journalists protest mightily that they don't like any of this, but the great majority of news organizations still rely—often heavily—on anonymous sources.

Even journalists are confused about what their own code words mean. For the December 1994 issue of the *American Journalism Review,* writer Alicia Shepard asked a number of newspeople to define "off the record," "on background," and "on deep background" and to explain the differences among them. Journalists came up with different answers or said they didn't know. For example, Michael Gartner, former NBC News president and editor of the Ames, Iowa, *Daily Tribune,* said of "on background": "It means different things to different people. I've never understood it."[35]

Depending on whom you ask, "off the record" means either you can't use the information at all or you can't use it unless you get it elsewhere as well. In a book that discusses manipulating the press, Marvin Kalb, television correspondent-turned-Harvard professor, offers these definitions: "Background" means "it can be used, even with quotes, but the source is not to be identified by name, only by organization or government, as in 'U.S. officials said today.'" "Deep background" means that neither the source's name nor his country or organization can be identified," forcing the reporter to use "such awkward phraseology as 'Yeltsin is said to believe' or 'It has come to light here that,' or not using it at all."[36]

No wonder journalists and the public get confused.

The debate about unidentified sources stirs considerable passion within the news business in part because of the frustration the topic engenders. Many journalists decry the use of such sources, but then proceed to use them, citing competitive pressures and the inability to gather enough on-the-record material.

Among the defenders of confidential sourcing is the *Washington Post*'s Bob Woodward, whose rise to fame was aided by "Deep Throat"—the famous confidential source during the Watergate investigation. Woodward said, "When you are reporting on inside the White House, the Supreme Court, the CIA or the Pentagon, you tell me how you're going to get stuff on the record. Look at the good reporting out of any of those institutions—it's not on the record." He also pointed out that just because something is on the record doesn't mean it's true, and he says a confidential source may be more accurate because he or she doesn't have to worry about losing a job or being reprimanded.[37]

Another *Washington Post* writer, David Broder, has said that readers should place some trust in reporters who use unnamed sources "because I can tell you things that way, which otherwise I could not." The process, according to Broder, works this way: "You get as much on the record as you can, and then you pump them for more, with a guarantee that it won't be directly attributed. Everything you learn from one person you use to gain more information from the next. And eventually you may have a fairly clear idea of the story."[38]

Looking at the other side of the issue is former NBC News president Michael Gartner: "Beware anonymous sources. They can lie without accountability. They can fudge without responsibility. They can hide behind anonymity. They can strain readers' credulity and damage journalists' credibility."[39] Along the same lines, Associated Press managing editor Darrell Christian said: "There's a legitimate concern on the part of newspapers that they want their readers to believe what they're writing. The best way to do that is to put names with the facts."[40]

In practice, many news organizations find middle ground. When the *Seattle Times* published allegations of sexual misconduct by Senator Brock Adams, it relied on information from eight women who said they had been harassed or attacked by Adams over a twenty-year period. None of the eight would allow her name to be used in the story, but all signed affidavits pledging to testify if Adams sued the paper. (He didn't.) Although the *Times* was initially criticized for publishing such a devastating story without named sources, the paper clearly had handled its investigation carefully. *Times* executive editor Michael Fancher said: "The choice we faced was publishing a story we believed to be true and knew to be important with anonymous sources, or publishing nothing at all. Given that choice, I still think we did the right thing."[41]

Some news organizations have established rules to limit, or at least to impose standards on, the use of unnamed sources. Gene Foreman, as managing editor of the *Philadelphia Inquirer,* developed guidelines and this checklist of questions to be asked before using a confidential source:

- Is there any way to get the statement on the record?
- Does the source seeking anonymity really stand in jeopardy if identified?
- Is the information really important?
- Can we give the readers some idea of how qualified the source is?
- Is the information derogatory to any individual and, if so, have we gone extra lengths to make sure we are being fair?[42]

This is not a foolproof plan, but using it—or some variation of it—is likely to reduce reliance on unnamed sources.

Reporters making pledges of confidentiality are not doing so as independent operators; they are acting as agents of their news organizations. They should make clear to the source that a supervisor is in on the arrangement; the editor, executive producer, or whoever is in charge will be told the source's identity. One reason for this is libel insurers' insistence that top news executives be part of this decision making.[43]

Anonymous sources' charges can precipitate libel suits that are particularly hard to defend because the origin of the information cannot be revealed. Of course, as a practical matter reporters must have considerable discretion when dealing with their sources. As one veteran journalist notes, "A reporter can't stop a source who's offering an anonymous tip or an off-the-record interview to say, 'Hold it, I've got to call an editor for permission.'"[44]

After the pledge of confidentiality is made by the journalist, it must be taken seriously by all parties. Reporters have sometimes gone to jail rather than reveal a source's name. The principle of maintaining confidentiality is important in part because whenever a pledge is broken, it may scare off other potential sources.

On occasion, however, journalists decide to break the pledge. The reasons vary. If, for example, a source has been pledged total anonymity but then reveals to the reporter that he or she is planning to commit a serious crime, the journalist's responsibility to the public transcends the obligation to the source.

Traditionally, journalists were the arbiters in deciding how sacrosanct the promise to a source should be. They chose whether to keep it or break it. That changed in the aftermath of a story published in Minnesota in 1982. Dan Cohen, a supporter of the Republican candidate for lieutenant governor, contacted several reporters offering—in exchange for confidentiality—information about the arrest record of the Democratic candidate. The reporters agreed, making the promise. The information turned out to be of little consequence: a misdemeanor shoplifting conviction twelve years previously. Regardless of the quality of the material, the reporters considered themselves bound by their pledge.

Their editors, however, decided that the public had a right to know the origin of this smear attempt, and—over the reporters' objections—reneged on the promise, identifying Cohen as the source. (One paper also criticized Cohen in an editorial and ran a cartoon depicting him as a garbage can.)[45] As a result of this publicity, Cohen lost his job and sued the papers.

In 1991 the U.S. Supreme Court held that the papers could not break their promise with impunity and that the First Amendment did not bar Cohen from claiming that the journalists had made and then broken a contract. He had performed his end of the deal—delivering the information—but the journalists had broken their binding promise of confidentiality, causing him financial damage for which the newspapers were liable.[46]

The Cohen case signalled news organizations that they should be far more careful when promising confidentiality. If they make the pledge and then decide that it was a mistake, they might find that breaking it is very costly.

Professional standards reinforce the sanctity of promises of confidentiality. For example, the Code of Ethics of the Radio-Television News Directors Association says its members will "recognize the need to protect confidential sources. They will promise confidentiality only with the intention of keeping that promise."[47]

In theory, controversies such as the Cohen case should diminish reliance on confidential sources. In practice, however, the legacy of "Deep Throat" remains intact. A reader perusing news stories will still find many anonymous sources.

Checkbook Journalism

Journalists see their job as finding information, putting it into understandable and useful form, and delivering it to the public. Good reporters know enough about investigating, researching, and writing to do this well.

Some news organizations, however, buy information rather than dig it up on their own. This is "checkbook journalism." It raises serious ethical questions.

The practice has its defenders. Bill O'Reilly, while anchor of the tabloid news program "Inside Edition," claimed that paying for news was necessary, particularly for programs such as his that compete with network news organizations. He wrote: "Research tells us that readers and viewers want information, regardless of whether someone is paying for it. . . . Big money has changed the news and information industry just as it's changed professional sports. Few journalists like it, but there's nothing we can do about it."[48]

That may be a rather superficial defense. Digging for facts might require more effort than writing a check, but it is more honest.

Buying news will create a marketplace for untruths in which the more lurid the story, the higher the payment. Money-hungry sources will be likely to embellish and fabricate to drive their prices higher. Also, this practice is likely to damage even further the public's opinion of how journalists do their job.

When the sources are selling information related to a court case, the legal process suffers as much as journalism does. In the O. J. Simpson case, some witnesses were discredited when attorneys found that they had sold their stories to news organizations such as the *National Enquirer* or "Hard Copy." In the Simpson case, *Enquirer* general editor Mike Walker appeared on "Larry King Live" holding a million-dollar check that he offered to Simpson's friend Al Cowlings to tell what had gone on during the famous Bronco ride on the Los Angeles freeways.[49] For the Simpson story or for scandals involving celebrities such as Michael Jackson, print and TV tabloids often engage in high-stakes bidding wars.[50]

Not just the tabloids participate in news buying. "60 Minutes" paid Watergate scandal figures H. R. Haldeman and G. Gordon Liddy for interviews.[51] A producer with a mainstream TV news magazine complained: "We're paying people who are players in the story and calling them consultants. We're buying off local reporters to get their sources. We're acting like the tabloid shows. And what's really distressing is that no one feels bad about it."[52]

Even when news organizations refuse to buy stories that the tabloids are pursuing, they still are not above using the purchased material as the basis for their own reports. This happened during the 1992 presidential campaign when Gennifer Flowers's allegations about having had an affair with Bill Clinton appeared in the weekly tabloid, *The Star*. Flowers reportedly had been paid at least $40,000 for exclusive rights to her story. Mainstream news organizations faced a difficult choice: Absent proof that they gathered themselves, they could ignore the story that was greeting shoppers in grocery store checkout lines around the country, or they could do articles based on the *Star*'s version. Many followed the latter course (but some pointed out the inconsistencies in Flowers's story).

Although most journalists are unimpressed by the tabloids' rationale of buying stories as merely a form of entrepreneurial journalism, some defend the practice. When "Hard Copy" paid a rape victim $3,000 to tell her story, which she felt had not been fairly reported by mainstream media, one writer commented, "For the powerless in our culture who knowingly open themselves up to very personal stories that should be told—that have a real message for the public—it seems only fair that they should be compensated for their willingness to go public."[53]

In some cases, such an argument might seem acceptable. But that does not offset the systemic damage that checkbook journalism does. When the expectation of payment exists, all reporters encounter problems. More and more journalists have stories to tell about approaching sources and being asked for payment. The temptation to pay is great, but every time a reporter succumbs to that temptation, the more firmly entrenched checkbook journalism becomes.

The Importance of Accuracy

One of the journalist's principal responsibilities is to make sure that the information he or she provides to the public is accurate. News consumers have every right to expect this.

Inaccuracy is not merely an esoteric failing. The public relies on journalism to tell it about everything from baseball scores to medical advances to political change. That reliance creates for journalists the ethical obligation to be accurate. Of course, *accuracy* in some cases may be a relative term. The ideal must coexist with the pragmatic.

Defining "Truth"

Are "truth" and "news" always the same? If not, should the journalist's primary responsibility be to deliver the news or the truth?

In *Public Opinion*, Walter Lippmann wrote: "News and truth are not the same thing and must be clearly distinguished. The function of news is to signalize an event, the function of truth is to bring to light the hidden facts, to set them into relation with each other, and make a picture of reality on which men can act."[54]

Here is how this takes shape in practice: The White House press secretary tells reporters, "The president is delighted to be working with members of both parties in Congress to revise the budget he submitted last week." This official statement from the White House is news, but the whole story may be more complex. Perhaps the president has to revise the budget because he found that he did not have enough support in Congress to pass it, and he has told White House staff members in a meeting, "I can't stand working with those jerks who are opposing me." *That* is the truth.

Should journalists be satisfied to report just the *news*, or should their stories be based on the *truth?* The *news* is not untrue; it actually happened, and the public has a right and a need to know what the press secretary said. That version is just not as complete as the *truth* is.

To make this more complicated, suppose that reporters suspect that what the White House press secretary has told them is just part of the story—the news—but that they cannot immediately uncover the rest of the information—the truth. Should they hold their stories until they are satisfied they have everything? Also, suppose a reporter is told by one White House staff member what the president said in the meeting. Is that adequate, or should the reporter get corroboration from more sources? If so, how many more? One? Two? Ten?

These questions underscore the elusiveness of certainty in journalism. Unless the president himself confirms what he said (about the "jerks"), reporters will have to decide when a level of truth has been reached that merits being published. In most cases, "absolute truth" may never be determined. So, unless you want to publish monthly, you accept "the best obtainable version" of the truth. Defining "best obtainable" presents another series of hurdles. News organizations often have general guidelines about verification. After those are met, the information may be passed on to the public. Being sloppy about this means you might deliver bad information; being too stringent means you might not deliver enough. Journalists look for the middle ground.

None of this diminishes the importance of precision in reporting. The words, pictures, and sounds that are provided to news consumers should mirror reality. For instance, if a newspaper story includes a direct quote from someone, the reader should be able to assume that these were the words actually spoken.

That is solid theory, but in practice things don't always work out quite that way. How should this example be handled? You are covering a ten-car wreck on the local freeway. When you arrive at the scene, you find a witness who agrees to answer your questions. Here is his description of what happened: "I was standing, you know, right over there, like ten yards from where the uh, uh, pileup started, and, you know, what I mean is, I seen the guy in the first car like swerve to avoid—is that the right word?—a box or somethin' that sorta was laying in, you know, the middle, uh, of the road, and he almost like ran me over before, you know, the car hit somethin' or other and stopped."

Assume that this is the most articulate witness you can find, so you must use his information or do without a firsthand account. You have some choices. You can paraphrase him: "A witness said the driver of the first car swerved to avoid a box on the highway." You can quote him exactly, as was just done. Or you can clean up his quote: "I was standing ten yards from where the pileup started, and I saw the guy in the first car swerve to avoid a box or something that was lying in the middle of the road. He almost ran over me before the car hit something and stopped."

Many journalists would select the third option. A direct quote is more vivid than a paraphrase, but the witness's actual statement is incoherent, too long, and includes grammatical errors. The reader need not be forced to wade through all those superfluous words to find out what happened, and the witness—perhaps flustered by seeing the accident and by being interviewed—need not be depicted as inarticulate.

Although "quote cleaning" is a common practice, news organizations that formally address the issue in their in-house codes of ethics are likely to ban it, endorsing a policy such as, "If words appear within quotation marks, they should be what the person actually said." Many news organizations, however, decide to keep their guidelines fuzzy, allowing changes such as those in the example given.[55]

As a matter of law, the quotation mark does not guarantee that the speaker's exact words have been used. In *Masson v. New Yorker Magazine, Inc.*, the Supreme Court held that altered quotes are actionable if "the alteration results in material change in the meaning conveyed by the statement." That gives journalists considerable leeway.[56]

Using a flexible standard is appealing because it benefits the news consumer. The report is more understandable, and nothing is lost by doing repair work on the quote. In some circumstances, however, the structure of the quote may itself be newsworthy, as when a major political figure babbles excitedly at a time when composure is important. Then the public should be given the opportunity to pass judgment.

This issue illustrates the appeal of flexibility in some ethical guidelines. An absolute ban on quote cleaning probably would produce significantly diminished use of direct quotes. This may not deprive the news consumer of much information—paraphrasing usually gets the same message across—but the copy will be less lively. The issue was summed up well by journalism professor Norman Sims: "Everybody does it. Journalism would look more like an oral history report if that weren't the case."[57]

Correcting Errors

Given the tremendous volume of journalism that is produced every day, mistakes will inevitably be made, regardless of the care taken to prevent them. When this happens, ethical responsibility moves from prevention to correction.

Two basic guidelines apply:

• Corrections should be made as soon as the error is discovered, whether that is the next day, the next month, the next

year, or even longer.
- Corrections should be presented in the way most likely to offset whatever damage was done by the error. This involves the thoroughness and placement of the correction. For example, if a detailed story was thoroughly wrong, the correction should say more than, "Our story was in error." The accurate version should be printed. Also, an erroneous front-page headline deserves more than a correction buried at the bottom of page 20. Many newspapers now run a "Corrections and Clarifications" box in the same prominent spot every day, so readers are likely to see it.

The print media are far more diligent about making corrections than are the broadcast media. The excuse often offered is that the format of a television or radio newscast does not lend itself to making corrections. On network news programs, mistakes are made—TV journalists are not so much wiser than their print colleagues that their work is error-free—but think of the last time you saw an on-air correction. If a lawsuit has been threatened, then the format might suddenly be adjusted to allow time for a correction. When NBC's "Dateline" presented its dramatic report about "dangerous" General Motors pickup trucks, it neglected to mention that remote-control incendiary devices had been used to trigger a fire on the pickup used in the story. General Motors threatened to sue, and NBC broadcast a four-and-a-half-minute correction/apology.

Such instances are rare. Televised mistakes are apparently assumed to vanish into the ether along with the rest of what was aired.

Format or any other excuse is flimsy when compared to journalists' fundamental obligation to provide accurate information. Even when the matter seems trivial, the correction is important at least as a matter of principle. (A perusal of "Corrections" boxes in newspapers will frequently find items such as, "Richie Ashburn's 1954 batting average was .313, not .312 as was reported in yesterday's Sports section.")

Regardless of the topic at hand, the basic rule is this: Get it right, but if you get it wrong, fix it.

As they gather news and get it in shape for public consumption, journalists might be tempted to "do whatever it takes" to get the story. But even when championing the "right to know," people in the news business should not lapse into an end-justifies-the-means rationale. The industry's standing in American society depends in large part on the public's belief in the good faith of journalists. Resorting to questionable tactics may not only be unethical, but also may prove self-defeating.

For Discussion

1. If no harm is caused by a journalist's going undercover to get a story, why might this tactic be ethically questionable?

2. Did the *Chicago Sun-Times* do the right thing by setting up a sting operation when doing the Mirage Bar story?

3. As a reporter investigating allegations about a hospital mistreating mentally ill patients, would you take a hidden camera with you on a visit to the hospital?

4. As a newspaper editor, would you have accepted the Pentagon Papers, knowing that they had been taken illegally?

5. As a reporter, what tests would you apply before agreeing not to identify a source?

6. If a politician gives a speech attacking an opponent, but journalists are not sure if the charges are true, should the story be reported immediately or held until the material in the speech can be verified?

CHAPTER SIX

Journalist as Watchdog

The average citizen rarely has the time or the access to ask government officials or political candidates what their policy positions are or to challenge them about possible wrongdoing. Journalists, however, can do that. They are the public's surrogates, monitoring the workings of government and politics, giving people information they need to cast an informed ballot, and helping to keep players in the political process accountable to the people they are supposed to serve.

This clout has led to the news media being called "the fourth branch of government." That is a convenient label, but it should be used with care. Certainly, the press pulls the public's attention to issues and scrutinizes government and politics. But this influence has its limits: For the most part, the news media have no statutory authority to make politicians do anything. (Exceptions to this are open meetings laws and freedom of information regulations that ensure press and public access to certain government functions.)

The press can alert the public to what is going on, but then the more formal, institutional processes of democracy must come into play. Even in one of the most famous cases of the press investigating the government—the Watergate scandal of 1972–1974—news organizations could only apply heat to the Nixon White House and arouse public anger, which then stimulated governmental and political responses. Ultimately the judicial and legislative branches had to use their authority to compel answers from administration officials and, through Congress's use of the impeachment process, to push Richard Nixon into resigning the presidency.

The claim that the press chased Nixon from office is an over-simplification, as are notions that the press makes policy. The news media played an influential role, but the *real* branches of government—executive, legislative, and judicial—exercised the real power.

This system was explained well by Walter Lippmann: "The press is no substitute for institutions. It is like the beam of a searchlight that moves restlessly about, bringing one episode and then another out of darkness into vision."[1]

Deciding where to point that spotlight is one of the most important decisions that journalists make. Complicating this is the conflict that sometimes arises between being a good journalist and being a good citizen. To what extent should journalists cooperate with governmental bodies such as the armed forces or the police when doing so might compromise news gathering? Should responsibilities of citizenship transcend the duties of journalism? Who should define "the public interest"—government or press?

CASE: Wartime—On the Team?

During the Vietnam War, Associated Press reporter Malcolm Browne, whose tough coverage from Saigon had won him few friends within the Pentagon establishment, was asked by a U.S. Navy admiral, "Why don't you get on the team?"

In other words, why don't you support your government—your country—in its war against its enemy? This was not an uncommon sentiment among American military and diplomatic officials. Critical journalists found their visas not renewed or pressure brought to bear on their bosses to reassign them. Browne's colleague Peter Arnett wrote, "The authorities could not understand why we didn't champion the war effort as reporters had done in World War II and Korea."[2]

Press attitudes had changed in the decade between the end of the Korean War and the first years of accelerating American involvement in Vietnam. Journalists did not see their job as requiring—or even allowing—that they take *any* side. If problems existed in America's Vietnam War effort, they would be covered. Longtime White House correspondent James Deakin offered this response to the "get on the team" exhortation: "If the journalists are on the team, who will report the game?"[3]

This is another instance in which the power of the press may have been overrated. As was to happen in the Watergate scandal, it wasn't the press but rather the substance of what the press reported and the response of formal governmental institutions that shaped events. Johns Hopkins professor Simon Serfaty wrote about the impact of Vietnam coverage:

> In the end it was not an adversarial press that precipitated the U.S. failure in Vietnam. Rather, the mounting evidence of failure precipitated and exacerbated the hostility of the press whose coverage grew in intensity and improved in organization *after* American opinion began to shift against the war. To be sure, because it was the conduit for such evidence the press played an important role in facilitating that shift. The conduit was especially decisive in the case of television, whose images of the war—from the rice paddies of Vietnam to the streets of Chicago—had unprecedented impact on public perceptions. But opposition to the war found its catalyst elsewhere: in the open criticism of the administration's policies by congressional leaders and former officials.[4]

Underlying the controversy about the press's role in wartime is the theory that patriotism and honesty are not always compatible and that the ethical course is to give the former precedence over the latter. Most journalists would say that this is nonsense, that patriotism in a democracy embraces honesty, even when the honesty is unpleasant.

In practice, covering a war is more complex than the "on the team" debate would indicate. Aside from political concerns about the effect of coverage on public opinion, real security issues arise. Although unfettered by law, a free country's journalists should feel constrained from revealing information that would put the nation at military risk. This means not divulging facts that would benefit the enemy in combat. Negligence about this would endanger military personnel and civilians of this country and of its allies.

In this era of "real-time news"—live coverage—this issue is particularly important. During the Persian Gulf War of 1991, for instance, new broadcast technology gave television journalists the capability to report live from the battlefield. (This had not been possible during the Vietnam War.) But possessing technical capability does not in itself justify such reporting. In fact, it mandates extraordinary care in deciding what and how to cover wartime events.

Consider this scenario: An Iraqi Scud missile has just slammed into downtown Tel Aviv. Within instants, correspondents for CNN and other worldwide television services are doing live reports just a few blocks from where the missile exploded. As they do their on-camera stand-ups, the skyline of Tel Aviv is visible behind them, as is the smoke rising from where the warhead exploded. Meanwhile, back in Baghdad, Iraqi military intelligence officers are watching. They see the skyline and smoke and so can identify precisely where their missile struck. If they were a bit off target, they can adjust before the next launch. The television reporters have served as the equivalent of artillery spotters.

During the first days of the Gulf War, this happened, not as the product of any malevolence on the part of reporters but rather because of the naivete that accompanied this unprecedented coverage. The Israelis quickly imposed guidelines that all television networks wanting to do live reports had to agree to follow. Basically, the rules eliminated any pictures or graphics that would divulge precise location of missile strikes and also any wording that might tell the Iraqis how effective their attack had been. All live coverage was then supervised by Israeli officials who could literally "pull the plug" if anyone violated the rules (as happened at least once).

Censorship? Of course. But journalists would not even need the threat of enforcement to adhere to the guidelines. They knew a nation's existence was at stake, and no journalist with a conscience would want his or her reports to endanger the Israeli soldiers and civilians at risk from Iraqi attacks.

Similarly, no American general could allow a correspondent to report live that "a U.S. tank column has just left its base in Saudi Arabia and is moving north toward Kuwait." But again, the military probably would not need to impose formal restrictions. American journalists would not purposely jeopardize the American troops.

This is not being "on the team" in the sense that news media become vehicles for government propaganda. At another level, however, the American journalist and the American soldier *are* on the same team. In situations such as this, responsibilities of citizenship may transcend the (perceived) journalistic imperative of delivering news as quickly as possible.

Live wartime coverage involves ethical issues beyond military security matters. For instance, suppose that during the retaking of Kuwait a firefight between American and Iraqi forces was covered live. Consider the horrific effect on the families of soldiers killed in the battle if they saw it happening on their televisions at home. News about casualties is always terrible, no matter how gently it is delivered. But if television reports from the battlefield were to include "live death," that news would be even more excruciatingly traumatic.

Sometimes being ethical requires merely the thoughtful exercise of common sense. The still-evolving technology of live wartime coverage underscores this.

CASE: Police—Covering or Helping?

News gathering by journalists and evidence gathering by police have much in common. In both pursuits, facts are assembled, witnesses interviewed, pictures taken. So when law enforcement agencies need help in protecting the community's safety, why shouldn't journalists contribute their efforts to supplement those of the police?

Consider this case. After a controversial court decision, rioting erupts in a major U.S. city. The police are quickly overwhelmed and pull back, opting to let the riot burn itself out rather than seeking to suppress it with harsh action certain to cause considerable loss of life. After the police retreat, widespread looting breaks out. Local journalists cover the story intensively and, for the most part, the rioters let them do their work. As part of their coverage, TV crews videotape some of the looting, collecting much footage of people carrying television sets and other goods from stores. Some of this appears on the air during newscasts, but many of the tapes are set aside.

A month after the riot, the district attorney's office decides to prosecute as many looters as it can find. Because the police were not present, the D.A. requests help in identifying the looters. Prosecutors taped news shows during the riots and have been able to use these tapes in locating some alleged looters. Now the D.A. asks local TV news departments to provide all the tapes shot during the riots so further arrests can be made.

You are the news director of one of the local stations. Would you help the prosecutors? Note that this is a *request,* not a subpoena, from the D.A. You are not being ordered to deliver the tapes. That would raise complicated legal issues, but as presented this is purely an ethical decision.

The "good citizen" response might be: "Sure; use our tapes. We're not pro-looter here. If we can help you lock up criminals, we'll be glad to do so."

That reply sounds noble, but it contains a significant problem. Journalists were able to do their reporting after police had left the riot area because the rioters were angry with the police but not with the news media, and they distinguished between the two. If, however, the news gatherers turn out to have been evidence gatherers, the next time a similar event occurs the public may not treat police and reporters differently. The journalists might not be able to cover the event from the vantage points they previously enjoyed, and they may even find themselves in danger.

So, as news director you have another answer to consider: "Sorry; we don't approve of looting, but we're in the news business, not the police business. You'll have to build your case against the looters yourselves. The separation between journalism and law enforcement must be maintained."

Many journalists taking this latter position would not treat it as an absolute rule. If, for example, in the course of the riot the TV crew had taped someone committing murder, the station might turn the tape over to the police without even being asked for it. Circumstances may dictate a temporary lowering of the barrier between press and law enforcement.

The similarities of news gathering and evidence gathering can create other ethical dilemmas. Journalists covering crime and police sometimes face difficult decisions about publishing or withholding information, as in this case:

Six young women have been murdered in your community, apparently by the same person. The police report no progress in finding the killer. You are a reporter for a local newspaper, and in the course of doing your stories about these crimes, you learn that several of the victims' cars were found in shopping mall parking lots with flat tires. You also interview a woman who, after shopping and discovering her car had a flat tire, was approached by a man who offered to drive her to a service station. She was frightened by him and ran away. Your theory is that the killer spotted his potential victims as they entered the mall, flattened a tire, and waited for them. Before publishing a story about this, you take this idea to the police, and they tell you they have come to the same conclusion.

But police officials ask that you print nothing, saying that they plan to stake out some shopping malls and don't want your story to tip off the killer that they know how he operates. They do not indicate that they suspect any particular person or know where he is most likely to strike next.

Would you hold the story or publish it immediately? Should you cooperate with the police and hope they make an arrest, or alert the public so women will be aware of the murderer's tactics?

A reporter who faced such a decision described the choice this way: "What if we didn't report the story and a woman was killed in the ensuing days? What if we ran the story and ruined any chance the police had of catching the killer?"[5]

The paper ran the story. The killings stopped. No one was ever arrested for the murders.

Looking back on this case, the reporter wrote:

> It's unclear whether our decision was a good one, whether it saved lives or merely forced a killer to new killing fields. But the story illustrates the difficulties faced by journalists caught between the public's right to know and the sometimes legitimate need of officials for secrecy. . . . On the other hand, if we had not insisted on reporting the story and another young woman's body had surfaced . . . I think I would have felt like an accessory to murder.[6]

When the police say, "Help us convict looters" or "Don't keep us from catching a killer," those in the news business should carefully consider not only the obvious appeal of complying, but also the less-obvious but still very real danger to journalistic integrity when autonomy is superseded by cooperation. In the long run, carefully maintained independence may prove more valuable than the short-term benefits of joint ventures.

Covering the Courts

Ninety-five million Americans sat glued to their television sets during the evening of June 17, 1994, as football hero O. J. Simpson led the police on a slow-speed chase down a Los Angeles free way.[7] The story of Simpson's impending arrest for the murder of his ex-wife Nicole Brown Simpson and her friend Ronald Goldman captured the attention of the public and kept it for months on end.

The nation was fascinated by this true crime story, and the news media were intent on making the most of that interest. Networks preempted regular daytime programming to cover the Simpson proceedings. News magazine shows earned record ratings when they featured Simpson-related segments.[8]

Although other sensational crime stories were reported while the Simpson case plodded onward, none received the same amount of coverage. A *USA Today* study found that the Simpson saga averaged 742 stories per week, followed by Rodney King with 218, Michael Jackson with 101, and Tonya Harding with 88.[9] This massive coverage of the Simpson case led a Los Angeles judge to take the unprecedented action of abandoning a grand jury investigation into the murders because members of the panel had "become aware of potentially prejudicial matters."[10]

That judge was not the only one who was less than happy about the incessant and not always accurate coverage. Many people believed that the news media had tried and convicted Simpson even before he was arrested. According to the *New York Times:* "Sooner or later, the case of The People of California v. O. J. Simpson will be played out in a courthouse. But first, as inevitably occurs in today's world of big cases, big lawyers and big media, Simpson v. People will be tried in the court of public opinion."[11]

As the "trial by media" continued, the question of whether Simpson could receive a fair trial despite the relentless news coverage was debated nationwide. Public opinion polls showed that the majority of Americans believed that it would be difficult for Simpson to receive a fair trial because of the pervasive publicity.[12] Studies also found that many people considered the coverage to be irresponsible.[13] Perceptions became increasingly negative as time passed. Just before the trial itself began in January 1995, an ABC survey found that when people were asked how they felt about the continuing coverage, more than 80 percent said they were "sick of it."[14] But, as the ratings indicated, not so sick of it that they wouldn't watch.

Journalists themselves questioned the media's responsibility in reporting the Simpson story. *New York Times* columnist A. M. Rosenthal asked: "Are we journalists or garbage collectors? If some other journal or broadcast distributes unverified rumors—the equivalent of journalistic garbage—do we just pick it up and peddle it ourselves?" And finally, "Do we recognize any ethical press obligation not to imply guilt before the accused is convicted?"[15]

Fort Worth Star-Telegram columnist Bill Thompson says the reason the media were so quick to imply guilt in the Simpson case is "cynical and self-serving, perhaps, but simple: People keep feeding us information. What are we supposed to do with it— put it in a time capsule and dig it up 200 years from now? We're in the news business, for heaven's sake. The problem is, we no longer seem to know the difference between news gathering and rumor mongering, between legitimate information and wide-eyed speculation."[16]

Writing in *Nieman Reports,* Jerome Berger argued that the new "gotcha" journalism has left a long list of victims who were all found guilty in the "court of journalistic opinion" before ever finding their way into a courtroom. "A basic premise now seems to rule the media," Berger wrote. "People are guilty until proven innocent."[17]

Admittedly, the Simpson story was exceptional because of the extraordinary public interest in a fallen American hero. It was compelling journalism—or, perhaps, as an ABC News vice president put it, "certainly compelling television. Whether it was compelling journalism or not, I'm not sure."[18]

Either way, this and other high-profile cases raise an important ethical challenge for journalists who cover the courts: Can the media provide accurate and appropriate coverage without undermining the integrity of judicial process and interfering with trial participants' rights?

Ethics Questions

The sheer volume of news coverage dedicated to the Simpson case posed an ethical dilemma for media gatekeepers. How long should editors and producers have allowed this story to consume so many newspaper pages and broadcast minutes while other important matters went un- or at least under reported? Although sensational crime stories make good drama and generate good ratings, such coverage pushes aside less sensational, but often more significant, news.

Breadth of coverage is an ethical issue. Article One of the Society of Professional Journalists Code of Ethics states: "The public's right to know of events of public importance and interest is the overriding mission of the mass media. The purpose of distributing news and enlightened opinion is to serve the general welfare." The American Society of Newspaper Editors code mirrors this: "The primary purpose of gathering and distributing news and opinion is to serve the general welfare by informing the people and enabling them to make judgments on the issues of the time.[19]

Consider another high-profile case. In 1991 William Kennedy Smith—nephew of Senator Edward Kennedy—was accused of rape. The case was one of the first judicial proceedings to be broadcast in its entirety from the courtroom. Reporter Peter Levin noted that the trial's TV coverage—a ratings bonanza for CNN— gave the American people a chance to see the justice system at work: "Viewers had the opportunity to learn about the admissibility of evidence, the rules of procedure, courtroom decorum, expert testimony, credibility of witnesses, burden of proof and reasonable doubt."[20] That's the good news.

The bad news is that once again a "celebrity crime" got disproportionate attention. As Levin commented, "While these criminal cases received heavy coverage, I would venture to say that important cases on employment discrimination, sexual harassment, product liability, surrogate parents, right to die, prayer in school, abortion and prison overcrowding—civil cases all—were being ignored."[21]

Excess coverage of celebrity cases is not a problem simply because there is so much of it. Members of the public can decide how much is too much and then simply turn away from it when they reach their limit. *Washington Post* ombudsman Joann Byrd, writing about the public and the Simpson story, said: "I'm not going to worry about them. I'm going to worry instead about how the media can ever again sell the idea that we are guided primarily by such high-minded goals as public service and informing the populace of the critical issues of the day."[22]

Free Press and Fair Trial

Another issue of concern in covering the courts is the potential impact of news reports on a defendant's ability to receive a fair trial. The U.S. Supreme Court has held that "due process requires that the accused receive a fair trial by an impartial jury free from outside influences."[23] "Outside influences" generally means publicity generated by the news media.

The free press–fair trial debate has been long and heated. The issue is how the courts can balance a defendant's Sixth Amendment right to receive a fair trial with the press's First Amendment right to report the news. The question surfaced in the Simpson case, just as it does in every high-profile trial.

A review of the research in this area finds mixed reports but little proof that pervasive publicity prejudices the outcome of a case. One recent study concluded that "despite widespread fears of prejudicial coverage, the conditions necessary for media coverage to prejudice jurors to the extent that they are unable to decide a case based on courtroom evidence are likely to occur in only one of every 10,000 cases."[24]

Of course, the Simpson case was unique. Never before had the media focused so much attention on one case. Never before had a grand jury been suspended because of prejudicial publicity. And never before in such a high-profile murder case were the media allowed such expansive access to pretrial proceedings and information.

Does this mean the case was prejudiced by the news coverage? Maybe. Although actual prejudice may never be proved, there is another issue equally important from a journalistic perspective. In covering the courts, journalists should consider their role in maintaining public confidence in the judicial process.

When examining the news media's role as a watchdog of the judiciary, it is important to remember the Supreme Court's reason for establishing the media's right to cover judicial proceedings. In an early access case, the Court stated:

> The value of openness lies in the fact that people not actually
> attending trials can have confidence that standards of fairness are

being observed; the sure knowledge that anyone is free to attend gives assurance that established procedures are being followed and that deviations will become known. Openness thus enhances both the basic fairness of the criminal trial and the appearance of fairness so essential to public confidence in the system."[25]

In other opinions, the Court observed that the media play a crucial role both in contributing to public understanding of the court system and in helping to prevent potential abuses in judicial process.[26]

Litigation Journalism

When investigating charges of unlawful activity, journalists must determine what the public should know about allegations that may or may not be true. Given the ability of the news media to mold public opinion quickly, journalists must be careful not to report—intentionally or unintentionally—information that might interfere with due process.

The news media have come under fire recently for allowing trial participants to use the media in an attempt to influence outcomes of cases. Names like Michael Jackson, the Menendez brothers, and Timothy McVeigh come to mind.

Journalism professor Carole Gorney charges that in a practice called "litigation journalism," reporters allow lawyers to schedule media interviews for clients in an effort to win public sympathy:

> The role of the courts is being pre-empted and their procedures undermined as more cases are tried in the public arena long before official hearings take place. The arguments are mostly one-sided, devoid of cross-examination, evidence or witness.
>
> It is not the function of the press, or of those who disseminate news and information on the fringes of journalism—like talk shows—to allow the merits of individual cases to be argued or promoted outside due process.[27]

Gorney also noted that those who use the First Amendment to defend litigation journalism should remember the ethical requirements of fairness, balance, and responsible reporting.

Harvard Law School professor Archibald Cox echoed those thoughts. "The ideal of justice dictates that court decisions be rendered by a judge, jury, or appellate bench that is not only impartial but governed solely by reasoned deliberation upon the evidence and . . . that the litigants and public perceive it to be so. Public pressure on the tribunal arising from editorials and other public discussions of pending cases runs counter to this interest."[28]

Despite the importance of maintaining the integrity of the judicial process, if allegations have been made public, the accused should be able to defend himself or herself in the court of public opinion. When addressing such issues, journalists should consider their own judiciousness and be sensitive to the rights of the accused as well as of the victims. Decisions about what to publish should not be based on whether the information is titillating or provides good cocktail party chatter.

Sometimes even the traditional objective approach to reporting raises ethical questions in the context of covering the courts. Professor John Merrill illustrates the dilemma with the story of an alleged rape: "Reporters may worry about the victim and thereby omit the name while at the same time giving almost no thought to printing the name of the accused or arrested rapist. In other words, the report contains the name of the 'suspected' attacker (who may well be innocent) but omits the name of the confirmed victim. Good reporting? No. Ethical reporting? Maybe."[29]

Consider the following excerpts of the explanation provided by NBC News president Michael Gartner in an in-house memo after the network broke ranks with tradition by reporting the name of the alleged victim in the William Kennedy Smith rape case without her consent. This decision, and the reasoning behind it, created considerable controversy within and outside the news business.

> Why did NBC News name the woman who says she was raped at the Kennedy compound in Florida over the Easter weekend. How was that decision made? . . .
>
> Here is my reasoning:
>
> First, we are in the business of disseminating news, not suppressing it. Names and facts are news. They add credibility, they

round out the story, they give the viewer or reader information he or she needs to understand issues, to make up his or her own mind about what's going on. So my prejudice is always toward telling the viewer all the germane facts that we know.

Second, producers and editors and news directors should make editorial decisions; editorial decisions should not be made in courtrooms, or legislatures, or briefing rooms. . . . In no other category of news do we give the newsmaker the option of being named. . . .

Third, by not naming rape victims we are part of a conspiracy of silence, and that silence is bad for viewers and readers. It reinforces the idea that somehow there is something shameful about being raped. . . . One role of the press is to inform, and one way of informing is to destroy incorrect impressions and stereotypes.

Fourth, and finally, there is an issue of fairness. I heard no debate in our newsroom . . . on whether we should name the suspect, William Smith. . . . Yet we dragged his name and his reputation into this without thought, without regard to what might happen to him should he not be guilty. . . . We are reporters; we don't take sides, we don't pass judgment.[30]

Journalists who allow themselves to be swept away by stories that are sure to sell newspapers and make ratings soar should consider the article in the Society of Professional Journalists Code of Ethics that states, "The media should not pander to morbid curiosity about details of vice and crime." Although the Simpson and Smith cases, as well as many other sensational crime stories, played out like "made for television" movies, journalists should remember the presumed innocence of those accused and the privacy rights of victims.

In no other context do the news media have a greater obligation to report fairly and accurately than in covering the courts. Information presented by journalists influences opinions and judgments. Although perceptions created by pretrial publicity are examined during the jury selection process and so do not proceed unchecked into the courtroom, news reports can compromise witness testimony or other forms of evidence. They might also cause irreparable damage to trial participants and to public trust in the media.

When news coverage fosters a presumption of guilt that turns out to be wrong, says news executive Al Neuharth, "that public which reflects on such cases wonders how it could have been so misled or misinformed."[31]

Although the news media have done much in this field to deserve being castigated, they still can be an invaluable force to fortify the integrity of the justice system. As veteran legal affairs writer Lyle Denniston has noted, "truth is the common pursuit of the professions of law and journalism."[32]

Politics—Coverage Techniques

In political journalism, reporters generally try to maintain an adversarial but civil relationship with those whom they cover. That is how it should be if the public is to get the information needed to make intelligent decisions about voting and about the merits of important issues. Politicians know how important news coverage is and never stop trying to make that reporting more favorable to themselves and to the policies and ideas they champion. This leads to a perpetual tug-of-war about who really determines the content and tone of the news stories on which the public relies.

For journalists covering campaigns, ethical questions arise about process as well as about content. The following sampler of these matters addresses three principal topics: pack journalism, horse-race journalism, and the use of polls and projections.

Pack Journalism

Watch candidates in presidential and many other campaigns and you'll see them being trailed by a pack of journalists, sometimes snarling, sometimes panting, always close by. A symbiotic relationship exists between politician and pack: Candidates rely on the news coverage to get their messages to the public, and the press corps relies on the candidates to generate stories for them to put in print or on the air.

The pack at its largest is truly huge. For instance, the 1992 Democratic National Convention was attended by 4,928 delegates and alternates, while about 15,000 persons received press credentials. Size itself creates problems, mostly logistical. But it is the way the pack works that affects the product that the news consumer receives.

The issue is sameness—the dominance of a conventional wisdom within the pack that is easy to subscribe to and that smothers initiative. In *The Boys on the Bus,* Tim Crouse's classic book about campaign news coverage, the reporters' work habits are described this way: "After a while they began to believe the same rumors, subscribe to the same theories, and write the same stories."[33]

Reporters' reliance on the pack's collective thesis limits the range of ideas presented to the public. If, for example, the pack's conventional wisdom is that only two out of a field of eight candidates are really worthy of coverage, many voters will be deprived of the chance to evaluate the other six. And sometimes the pack is dead wrong.

An example: The pack initially covered the 1984 campaign for the Democratic presidential nomination as a two-man race between Walter Mondale and John Glenn. Reporters didn't notice that Glenn's campaign was disorganized and had little hard-core support. They also didn't notice that Gary Hart—one of the candidates who they decided wasn't worth covering—was organizing efficiently and winning support for his vague but appealing commitment to "new ideas." To the press corps's great surprise, Hart walloped Mondale in the New Hampshire primary and within weeks came close to knocking Mondale (who eventually was nominated) out of the race. Because coverage of Hart had been so skimpy, voters in the early primary states had little on which to base judgments of the candidate.

Defining the pack's tunnel vision in such cases is a screening process. Reporters look at the candidates' standing in the polls, the amounts of money they've raised, and the organizations they've built and then make judgments about who does and who does not have a chance of winning the election. The few who are considered to have realistic prospects to win get the coverage.

This is enormously frustrating for candidates who run into a devastating Catch-22: Without voter support you can't get coverage, but without coverage, you can't get voter support. In practical terms this means that many voters—those who pay some but not much attention to politics—will never even consider some of the candidates.

Journalists respond by arguing that they must make these choices because the air time and column inches available for political stories are limited. Reporters also point out that some candidates simply are not realistic contenders: the candidate, for instance, whose platform consists of a proposed alliance between the United States and Mars.

But between the frontrunners and the oddities may be candidates who are saying interesting things that voters might want to ponder even if not eventually endorse. The Libertarian Party, for example, regularly fields presidential and other candidates who just as regularly get ignored by the press. Maybe none of them would be elected, and maybe the Libertarian message about minimalizing government would not win much support. But should journalists ensure that Libertarian candidates won't be elected and ensure that their views won't win support by making them virtually invisible?

Such questions underscore the intrinsic power of the screening process. Some form of it may be necessary because of the compression of news, especially on television. But the journalists who use it have a responsibility to do so thoughtfully, recognizing how much power they wield.

Horse-Race Journalism

Much political reporting, in its jargon and emphasis, treats campaigns as if they were sports events. Polls and analysts are heavily relied on to keep the public apprised—sometimes day by day—about who is ahead in the race for the presidency or other office.

Up to a point, that is fine. Problems arise, however, when these stories become so numerous and dominant that they smother reports about issues, candidates' qualifications, and other matters that voters should know about before casting their ballots. Journalists are not supposed to be bookies, but they sometimes seem to be as they tout the latest speculation and prognostication about the campaign's eventual outcome.

Perhaps this keeps people interested enough in the campaign that they will also pay attention to more substantive matters. But news organizations should watch themselves carefully to make certain that their coverage maintains balance between contest and content. This involves matters such as story placement—not consistently leading newscasts or front pages with horse-race stories while relegating issues pieces to less-visible spots.

This is one of those issues that is on the periphery of ethical concerns. Horse-race journalism should not be deemed unethical; that is a simplistic overreaction. But sustaining overall high quality in political coverage *is* an ethical responsibility because of the vital role that the news media play as the link between political process and public.

Polls and Projections

A big part of horse-race journalism is the use of public opinion polls commissioned by news organizations or candidates. The art of polling has come a long way since the *Harrisburg Pennsylvanian* published results of a local straw poll that showed Andrew Jackson ahead in the 1824 presidential campaign. Today, the methodology of survey research has become so sound that a properly designed and administered poll is likely to be accurate and insightful.

But poll results are limited in what they reveal. Most offer just a snapshot of respondents' thinking at the moment; comparative analysis is needed to pull more from the data. And if a poll was taken this morning, a story on this evening's newscast might change the opinion that was so fervently expressed just a few hours before.

Also, polls can be manipulated to produce desired results. This is most likely to happen when the poll has been commissioned by politicians. For example, suppose that during the 1992 presidential race the George Bush campaign had released results of its latest survey that showed Bush leading Bill Clinton 60 percent to 40 percent. Before reporting that, journalists should ask questions such as these: How big was the sample? How was the sample selected? What was the precise wording of the questions?

Suppose it turns out that the sample was one hundred persons who all live in heavily Republican areas, and that the question about voting preference was phrased, "If the election were today, would you vote for the distinguished world leader George Bush or the adulterous draft-dodger Bill Clinton?" That poll clearly was designed to produce pro-Bush results that might convince voters that he held a commanding lead in the campaign, and it might create a helpful bandwagon effect. News organizations should ignore this poll. Reporting it would be merely transmitting propaganda.

This hypothetical example is extreme; most real cases of tainted polling are more subtly corrupt. But even honest mistakes by pollsters produce misleading information. Journalists should exercise great care in reporting polling data, recognizing how even a slightly skewed sample or a badly worded question can affect the poll's results and, when those results are published, shape the public's perception of political reality. To guard against misleading reports, news organizations might devise guidelines to govern their use of polls. The sample, questions, timing, and other elements of the poll should meet these in-house tests. If they don't, the poll results probably should not be used in news stories.

Exit polling—questioning voters as they leave their voting places—is the foundation of the election night projections that broadcast media love to flaunt. The quest to be first to declare the winner drives this competition among networks. Sometimes this competitiveness tramples on the political process itself.

The issue is the impact of these projections on people who have not yet voted. When the network anchors pronounce a presidential winner at 8:00 P.M. eastern time, millions of West Coast voters have yet to cast their ballots. If the broadcast sages say it's over, why bother voting?

Of course, maybe the sages are wrong. And even if they're right about the presidential outcome, plenty of other races are on the ballot awaiting the voters' decisions. But if news reports deter voting in this country, where voter participation is consistently dismal, news organizations might consider the virtues of self-restraint.

Withholding news is a step never to be taken lightly. In testimony to Congress about this in 1981, CBS News president William Leonard said: "We believe our responsibility is that of any news organization: to report accurately the information we have, and its significance, as soon as it becomes available. . . . We cannot patronize our audience by withholding from them what we know. To do so would be a violation of trust and would seriously jeopardize our credibility."[34]

That statement is a bit patronizing itself. All news organizations exercise editorial discretion about when and what they report. The First Amendment would not be threatened and probably the public would not be upset if news executives decided to delay reporting election results until all the polls had closed.

On the other hand, being coy about projecting outcomes can sometimes be ridiculous. In 1984, for example, it became clear early on election day—and certainly by the time the first East Coast returns were reported—that Ronald Reagan was on his way to a landslide victory. (He carried forty-nine states.) The only way not to project his victory at least implicitly would be to carry no election returns at all.

In 1992 the networks waited until about 11:00 P.M. eastern time to declare Bill Clinton the winner, even though Ross Perot had publicly congratulated Clinton a half-hour earlier. Noble self-restraint? Some thought so, others didn't. Among the critics was Michael Kinsley, writing in *Time*: "The drama that had you glued to your TV was a fraud. . . . The networks generated false tension while suppressing the very information that would dissipate it."[35]

So the debate bounces back and forth. Responsible news organizations continue to search for the elusive middle ground: deliver accurate information and beat the competition, without infringing on voters' prerogatives.

Politics—Topics for Coverage

In addition to the way political journalists work, the topics they cover may raise ethical questions. Voters rely on the news media to identify and explain the most important issues. News organizations must decide what those issues are and what aspects of them merit coverage.

"Issues" can mean different things: policies about tax reform, gun control, abortion, national defense, environmental protection, and so on. Or, the issue can be more purely political—about the nature of the candidate or the campaign.

The latter category means difficult choices for journalists. Two topics that have received increased coverage during recent campaigns are candidates' character and their advertising.

"Character"

Voters want to know about issues, particularly those that they believe affect them directly. In national elections, the dominant issues are often economic ones—inflation, unemployment, cost of living, and the like. In local campaigns, the concerns are even closer to home—ambulance response time, trash pickup, pothole filling. Relatively cosmic matters such as foreign policy or federal-state relations often evoke more yawns than interest.

In most elections, issues are not on the ballot; people are. And in many campaigns, the principal question the voter ponders is not "Which candidate has the best issues positions?" Instead it is "Which candidate do I like or trust most?"

This is character as issue. Writer Gail Sheehy defined *character* this way: "A perceived combination of those traits—together with the values he or she represents—that set a person apart, and motivate his or her behavior." [36]

The candidates themselves recognize the importance of this issue to voters. During the first months of the 1992 presidential campaign, character was the dominant issue, as Bill Clinton's marital fidelity and his efforts to avoid being drafted to fight in the Vietnam War were extensively scrutinized by journalists. Later in the campaign, George Bush, knowing that economic issues were working against him, tried to make character decisive. In the first presidential debate, he attacked Clinton for demonstrating against the Vietnam War while a student at Oxford University, saying it was "a question of character and judgment."[37] Bush consistently argued that he, not his rivals, possessed the character a president should have.

Many candidates eagerly use the character issue as a way to depict themselves as heroes or their opponents as scoundrels. Ultimately, journalists themselves must decide which character strengths and weaknesses are worth covering. Answering the following questions might help in establishing context for reporting about character:

- Is the character-related matter germane? Might it affect the candidate's ability to perform the duties of the office that he or she is seeking? If Bill Clinton smoked marijuana while in college (regardless of whether he inhaled), would that affect his presidency twenty years later?
- Is the politician's behavior hypocritical, making a minor transgression more significant? When Pat Robertson ran for president in 1988 as a zealous advocate of high moral standards, should the press have reported that his first child was born just ten weeks after he and his wife married?
- Does the information about the politician's character come from a reliable source willing to go on the record? Are reporters being manipulated by a political rival using anonymity as a shield?[38]

On the germaneness issue in particular, journalists' views vary. For instance, when allegations arose in 1992 about Bill Clinton committing adultery, some journalists thought the story had to be covered because there were voters—even if not a large percentage—who felt that such behavior should disqualify a person from becoming president. The journalists' own judgment didn't matter.[39]

Others argued that without proof of the impact of private behavior on public performance, the story should be left alone. Of course, that approach probably will not work because of the pervasiveness of tabloid media that will jump on a lurid story regardless of germaneness.[40]

What does the public think about all this? An ABC poll of New Hampshire voters during the peak of the Clinton adultery coverage found that 80 percent of respondents thought the press should not poke into Clinton's private conduct.[41] Another indication of some voters' unhappiness with news coverage of this topic was seen when Phil Donahue interviewed Clinton, focusing on adultery and marijuana. The audience of the Donahue show began jeering the host, and one woman stood up to tell Donahue: "Given the pathetic state of most of the United States at this point . . . I can't believe you spent half an hour of air time attacking this man's character. I'm not even a Bill Clinton supporter, but I think this is ridiculous."[42]

With all this contentiousness about covering character, journalists look for standards. Germaneness remains the most relevant test. Even candidates deserve some privacy—perhaps not much, but some. So the question that journalists should ask themselves as they delve into a politician's character should be not merely "What does the public have a *right* to know?" but also "What does the public have a right and a *need* to know?"

Answers to such questions will affect the tone and substance of American political life. As newspaper editor Davis Merritt observes: "The relentless search for the next Watergate necessarily turned politicians into stereotyped targets in the minds of many journalists. Increasing numbers of people inclined to enter public life, particularly politics, decided it was not worth the grief imposed by cynical and suspicious journalists."[43]

Advertising

Until recently, campaign advertising was outside the purview of political reporting. No rule enforced this; most ads simply were considered gimmick-laden puffery and not newsworthy.

Within the past decade, that view has changed. Advertising is a part of campaign discourse. Although survey research shows that voters rely far more heavily on news than on ads for information about candidates and issues, the advertising must have some effect or else campaigners would not put so much money and effort into it. So it should be covered.[44]

Reporting about advertising has to be done thoughtfully. Otherwise, news organizations end up providing free extra exposure for the ads. Media critic Mark Crispin Miller cited "passive collusion" between press and politicians in news stories about the 1988 Bush-Quayle ads because the reporters rarely did "what journalists ought to do with any piece of propaganda: expose its sly half-truths and outright lies, and then correct them."[45]

In 1990 and more widely in 1992, news organizations became more sophisticated in their coverage of ads and began "truth-testing" candidates' TV spots. This kind of story is rooted in news organizations' role as voters' surrogates, removing smoke screens that hide the truth.

Not all ads lend themselves to truth-testing. Those that state opinions rather than hard facts are difficult to challenge. Suppose, for instance, the 1992 Bush campaign had run an ad saying that "Bill Clinton was a terrible governor of Arkansas" and that "unemployment in the state rose 20 percent during his tenure." The first statement may or may not be true, but it is opinion, not fact. The second claim, however, should be checked out by reporters, and if it is not true, voters should be told so and given the accurate figure.

When newspapers truth-test TV ads, they generally run the script of the spot followed by an analysis of its accuracy. Television journalists face a trickier task because they do not want to reinforce the candidate's message, particularly if it is false, by giving it free air time. Viewers might pay more attention to the ad—especially if its visual content is strong—than to the critique. To avoid this, broadcast news organizations might develop a special format for their truth tests, shrinking the ad images to fill only part of the screen while using electronic graphics to show viewers questionable phrases. Some truth tests forego subtlety and slap the word "False!" on the ad as it appears on the screen.[46]

The more aggressive coverage of ads has led to some changes in the way politicians use advertising. They are more careful about blatant lies because they know that they may not be attacked just by their opponents. Reporters-as-referees might also criticize them in news stories. Also, campaigns more frequently accompany their ads with documentation, which is given to reporters when the ads first air.

That sounds to be all to the good: increased accountability and accuracy. But journalists should be cautious when taking on expanded responsibilities in political coverage. As media critic Tom Rosenstiel said after the 1992 campaign:

> Policing what candidates said changed the relationship between reporter and politician. By labeling a candidate's statement as distorted or false, the press went from being a color commentator up in the booth to being a referee down on the field. Implicitly, this role acknowledged that the press not only reflected political events, it shaped them.[47]

What the Public Wants, Needs, and Expects

Thorough news coverage of government and politics is essential if a democracy is to work. Even though the United States is more a republic than a pure democracy, the public still must know what is going on if it is to place its trust and authority in the hands of those it elects to govern.

The universe of information sources is expanding and changing shape. The number of newspapers continues to shrink, but the electronic gathering and dissemination of news is growing rapidly. Satellites and cable bring distant and varied events into the living room with unprecedented speed. Computer networks mean that a trip to the keyboard can often replace a trip to the library.

An assumption behind this expansion is that the public wants to be well informed, wants to put all this information to work. Perhaps. Voter participation in the United States remains dismal. Little evidence exists that the information age is bringing about a renaissance in political activity.

Journalists and news consumers should think about this and ask themselves if they are doing their respective jobs adequately. News organizations might try harder to find out what voters are interested in and then do better at providing that information. James Boylan, founding editor of the *Columbia Journalism Review*, wrote about this in 1991, urging that journalism not be "like a panel discussion in which those in the audience never get to ask a question."[48]

For their part, voters might avail themselves of more news sources. Watching a television newscast once or twice a week is not enough. No matter how many magazine subscriptions, TV sets, or computer terminals a household may amass, the information they offer must be taken advantage of. That requires affirmative acts by the news consumer.

The politicians also have important obligations to make information available to the public either directly or—as will happen most of the time—through the news media. Candidates and government officials who are deceptive or secretive undermine democracy. Persistent journalists and voters might finally dig up the truth, but forcing an endless battle about what the public has a right to know ultimately aids no one.

In the realm of politics and government, ethical responsibility is shared by those who govern, those who are governed, and those who report what is going on. Quantifying whose burden is the heaviest is neither possible nor necessary. We're all in this together.

For Discussion

1. During wartime, should journalists do stories that might damage morale, such as reporting about incompetent officers or defective weapons, or should their stories emphasize positive aspects of "our" side?

2. If journalists witness even a minor crime while they are gathering news, should they voluntarily provide information to the police that will help in arresting and prosecuting the offenders?

3. What guidelines should govern the scope and content of news coverage of trials?

4. What are the pros and cons of allowing television cameras in courtrooms?

5. Are journalists too intrusive when reporting about politicians' private lives?

6. Does political journalism give voters the information they need to cast informed ballots, or does coverage focus on personalities and tactics rather than on issues? What are political journalists' principal ethical responsibilities?

CHAPTER SEVEN

The Compassionate Journalist

The extent of news media influence can be debated endlessly. It can be discussed as a lofty esoteric issue or as a matter of gritty pragmatism. Whatever the approach, a basic fact remains: Journalists wield power. When they shine their searchlight on a person, institution, or event, the world—at least part of the world—takes note.

If the subject of a story is a person, a life becomes public. An audience of strangers may suddenly be examining something that once was private, learning about something that once was secret.

Assume that a particular item of "news" is truly newsworthy. It is not merely sensational or trivial; it is something that the public has a right and a need to know. After that test is met, are journalists' responsibilities fulfilled? Or is there yet another level of ethical duty?

Finding a place for compassion in news judgment can be difficult. The prototypical hard-bitten editor or news director chases stories relentlessly and heartlessly. If the honest pursuit of news produces information useful to the public, nothing else matters. Sure, there may be casualties along the way. Privacy may be battered, if not shattered. The grotesque underside of life may be revealed. Words and pictures may shock not just the general public, but also those who are the subjects of those stories and photographs. That's unfortunate, but in many cases unavoidable.

To a certain extent, a cold-blooded approach is necessary. A story about a violent crime or a disaster cannot be sanitized to the point of distortion just to spare the feelings of victims. But an argument can be made that middle ground exists, that dispassion can be balanced with compassion.

Benefits and Detriments of Compassion

Being compassionate sounds like a nice idea, especially if you aspire to sainthood. But if your aspirations are secular and journalistic, nice ideas may seem inconsequential unless they provide professional benefit. Along these lines, compassion can help produce better reporting.

Underlying this premise is the reality of the reporter-source relationship: No one ever *has* to talk to the news media. If sources think they will be dealt with unfairly or rudely, they may decide to say nothing. This is particularly true when the story is about a sensitive matter. A brusque journalist may be shut out, while a compassionate reporter gets a great story.

Journalistic advantages of compassion were illustrated in a Pulitzer Prize-winning series by *Des Moines Register* reporter Jane Schorer about the rape of a Grinnell, Iowa, woman. The stories, published in 1990, were made possible in part by the sympathetic relationship that Schorer had with the rape victim, Nancy Ziegenmeyer. *Register* editor Geneva Overholser had written an op-ed column about the widespread policy of withholding victims' names in stories about rape. She argued that speaking honestly and openly about rape might help break down some of the stigma surrounding it. Ziegenmeyer read the column and contacted the paper. Schorer was assigned to write the story.

Being compassionate does not mean being coopted. Writing later about how she approached the story, Schorer said: "Several times a week, after her children were off to school, she would call me. . . . The conversations became like those of two girlfriends—we chatted about kids, politics, dinner menus, hair-styles and rape."[1]

Schorer also took care to maintain Ziegenmeyer's trust. Because only a few people in Grinnell knew about the assault, Schorer put limits on her background investigating: "I knew if a reporter from *The Des Moines Register* walked into Grinnell and started asking questions, the story would be all over town by noon. I was not willing to betray the privacy she was still guarding."[2] Schorer did quietly gather some background information, but she was extraordinarily willing to agree to Ziegenmeyer's requests about keeping parts of it out of print. After all, Ziegenmeyer had come forward on her own and had been extremely open about details of the rape.

The relationship between Schorer and Ziegenmeyer was that between reporter and source. But Schorer's empathy certainly made her news gathering easier and enhanced the power of the stories she wrote.

Backed by her editors and with Ziegenmeyer's cooperation, Schorer produced a detailed, explicit story about rape. She held back on no major aspects of the story.

Sometimes, however, compassion might threaten to overwhelm journalistic imperatives. Suppose, for example, in a story similar to the one about Ziegenmeyer, that the victim told the reporter everything but then asked that key elements of her story be withheld because she considered them too embarrassing. The compassionate thing to do would be to accede to the victim's wishes. But does the public have a right and need to know? What should the journalist do?

The larger question is this: To whom does the journalist owe his or her principal loyalty—source or public? Remove all sympathy, and the answer is easy: the public. But many journalists believe that they should not strip their work of compassion. Thus, the dilemma.

Occasionally, news organizations go overboard with compassion. The genre is familiar; its stories feature the child whose Christmas presents were stolen, the amputee who lost his or her wheelchair, the destitute widow who can't afford a coffin for her late husband. These stories are rich in human drama, designed to bring tears to the audience's eyes and to elicit an outpouring of goodness: buy new presents, replace the wheelchair, donate a coffin. Everyone ends up feeling virtuous—the journalists for bringing the story to the public's attention and the responding news consumers for helping out someone in need.

All this is wonderful, but beneath the surface are other, larger difficulties. Critics of this kind of journalism say "even the most generous outpouring of support for individuals does not address the systemic problems that often underlie personal tragedies."[3] Everette Dennis of the Freedom Forum Media Studies Center says: "It's hard to complain if one single individual is helped. That's good, God knows. But certainly there's a lack of fairness and equity when the media perform an anointing function for those rare individuals who come to their attention."[4]

For instance, a newspaper may publish an occasional series about families coping with poverty. After each installment, readers flood the paper with offers to help that particular family. But when that flurry ends, the public turns its attention elsewhere, while plenty of other families face equally hard times. The long-term complexities of the issue get lost in the pursuit of an illusory quick fix.

Some news organizations take on the role of a social service organization. They appeal for public support for in-house charities and provide direct assistance. They operate job hot lines to help persons who are out of work. They publish social services directories.

Usually the motive behind such efforts of individual news stories is pure: the desire to help someone in need. But sometimes the rationale is considerably less noble—news organizations may manipulate human drama as a self-promotion tool to boost circulation or ratings.

Generally, journalists will be most effective in combatting social injustice if they focus on systemic issues as well as on dramatic examples. This approach may not be as audience-grabbing as the tear-jerking tale of woe, but in the long run it truly is at least as compassionate because it might help alleviate the root causes of problems.

When journalists become intent on displaying their compassion, they run the risk of shortchanging news consumers. After a fraternity house fire killed five students at Bloomsburg University in Pennsylvania, editors of the student newspaper, the *Campus Voice*, criticized "the hordes of media that flashed photos and assaulted us for an interview." The editors proudly said that in their coverage they had "backed off from the university community as much as possible." Compassionate? Certainly, but at what cost?

Jim Sachetti, editor of Bloomsburg's *Press-Enterprise*, wondered if the student editors were softening their journalistic values. He wrote:

> Do we tell [student journalists] that the information we gather is essential to the community's understanding of a tragedy? . . . Do we assure them that readers who rely on our work don't really want us to "back off" even when they say they do? . . . We teach young journalists how to cover fires and borough council meetings, but not how to handle the hostility they are likely to encounter when they get too close or dig too deep.[5]

Aggressive reporting and civility are not mutually exclusive, nor are good journalism and compassion. The challenge is to find the appropriate balance.

News Makers as Human Beings

When unsolicited celebrity suddenly arrives, the recipient may find his or her life turned upside down. News stories are not just consumed and forgotten—they may have lingering, magnifying effects.

If the news is good—winning a multimillion-dollar sweepstakes, for example—your fame probably will be tolerable. Strangers staring at you, stopping you on the street to congratulate you, irritating you with bad jokes and nosy queries about your new wealth—all this happens not just because you won the prize but also (perhaps primarily) because now you are "news." When your story enters the public domain, so do you, like it or not.

Journalists generally justify their intrusion on the life of the sweepstakes winner by inferring a willing surrender of some privacy. If you entered the contest, you hoped to win, and you must have known that if you won you'd get news coverage. That makes sense, so this news maker has little basis for complaint about being covered.

But suppose the news is bad and the celebrity unsolicited. Consider the case of families of American military personnel killed during the Persian Gulf War of 1991. The war is the biggest story of the year; American casualties are unquestionably newsworthy. Given that, should journalists feel ethically constrained when gathering news about those killed? Should they go to the families' homes to ask background questions for news stories? Should television crews go to the cemetery to record the burial?

This issue is not just about "news"; it is about people. Journalists too often lose sight of that and fail to consider how their coverage might worsen the trauma those people have suffered because of the loss of their family members.

After the 1995 bombing of the Oklahoma City federal building, *Daily Oklahoman* managing editor Ed Kelley addressed these issues in a letter to newspaper employees. He noted that some staff members wondered "whether the burden of reporting the details of this crime to satisfy the desires of a reading public was trafficking in the misery of the victims' families." He defended the coverage, arguing that "responsible newspapering is a noble craft, and never more noble than in times of great tragedy." The paper's journalists, he continued, "could, in depth, make sense of what happened, and why, and explain what lies ahead."[6]

The choice is not between intrusive coverage and no coverage. Middle ground exists. In this instance, reporters might ask a friend of the family to act as intermediary to provide background information. Television stations might use pool coverage to report the funerals. The public will get plenty of news about this important story, but the impact of the coverage on the families will be minimized. After the Oklahoma City bombing, the *Daily Oklahoman* decided not to cover funerals. "We decided they were too predictable," wrote Kelley. "Preachers preach and people cry." The families of the victims did not need to have their privacy invaded further. The story could be told in other, better ways.[7]

Such situations present journalists with difficult questions: Just how much is the news worth? Is "the public's right to know" reason enough to add to an innocent person's anguish? To go a step further, is it reason enough to jeopardize the life of even a not-so-innocent person?

Consider this case (a hypothetical based on fact). In 1996 you—a reporter for a major newspaper—find out that during the 1970s a prominent scientist working for a defense contractor in your community was a spy for the Soviet Union. He passed on many military secrets, doing considerable harm to this country. He was caught by the FBI, and a deal was made: If he would become a double agent and send material provided by the U.S. government to the Soviets, he would not be charged with any crime. The scientist agreed and for several years served as a double agent. Eventually, the Soviets dropped him; whether they thought he had been compromised or they no longer needed him was never known. The American officials were true to their word; the scientist was never prosecuted, and his story remained secret.

You have uncovered all this and piece together the story. Before you publish it, you contact the scientist, who is now retired and lives in another state. He confirms all your information.

The day before your story is to run, the scientist calls you. He is distraught and tells you that not even his wife or his children—who are now adults and live near him—know anything about his years as a spy and double agent. He says that if you publish this story about his treason, he will kill himself.

You know your story—which apparently no other news organization has—is true and important, deserving publication. If you disguise the identity of the scientist, you will water down the story significantly. Also, this man was a traitor. You do not believe that he deserves to have his secret protected.

On the other hand, his spying happened more than twenty years ago, the Soviet Union no longer exists, and he did cooperate with American intelligence agencies after he was caught.

What should you do?

In the real case on which this example is based, the newspaper published the story. The scientist then killed himself.

An argument can be made that the journalists could have found a way to be more compassionate without backing off from the story. Particularly because there was no competitive pressure from other news organizations working on the same story, the newspaper's editors could have afforded to delay publication. They could have called the scientist's wife or his children, explained the nature of the story and his suicide threat, and given them two or three days to intervene. The editors could have made clear that the story *would* appear but that the family would be given time to get the scientist admitted to a hospital or otherwise cared for beforehand.

This was a story that the public had a right and a need to know, but no compelling reason existed for the public to know today as opposed to three days from now. Showing some compassion would not have damaged the journalistic product and might have saved a life.

Interviewing

A major part of a reporter's job is interviewing. This is a sophisticated craft, involving careful phrasing of individual questions and thoughtful planning of the entire interview as a logical progression that will elicit the maximum amount of useful information.

Often the interviewee is a public figure wise in the ways of the interview, skilled at shaping answers and at ducking tough questions. Watch the give-and-take between an experienced reporter and a veteran politician during a televised news conference or an interview show. You'll see two professionals matching well-honed skills.

Many other times, however, the person being interviewed is not experienced at being questioned for the public record and has no self-serving reason for doing the interview. He or she may have witnessed a newsworthy event or otherwise have information that the reporter believes the public should know about.

In these interviews, the journalist has the upper hand. Questions can be loaded, interviewees can be pushed, the television reporter can use lighting and camera angle to make the respondent look saintly or devilish. The inexperienced interviewee might not even realize what is happening. If the reporter decides to treat the interview as a contest, he or she will win almost every time.

Jousting with a politician is one thing. Taking advantage of a frightened or otherwise vulnerable source is something very different. For interviews in this latter category, the ethical journalist should restrain competitive urges and add a touch of compassion to his or her interviewing technique.

This may be particularly important when a story requires prolonged interviewing during weeks or even months. In such cases, reporter and source may become friends. That carries its own dangers, perhaps blurring the lines of objectivity. But in these instances it may be appropriate for the journalist to remind the interviewee occasionally that he or she is *not* talking to "a friend" but rather to the public. Jane Schorer made this point when describing her relationship with Nancy Ziegenmeyer while writing the rape story discussed earlier in this chapter. Noting the informality of their telephone conversations, Schorer said, "But every now and then, I reminded her that on my end of the line I was writing down everything she said, filling page after page of yellowed scrap copy paper with her thoughts and feelings."[8]

Some reporters might argue, "Look, this source is an adult, knows what journalism is, and doesn't have to be coddled. Anything said may be published." Legally, yes. Ethically, maybe.

In most cases involving an inexperienced interviewee, the following may be a helpful guideline: If the person being interviewed does not understand the rules of the game, such as what is on or off the record, the reporter should explain them. If the source is nervous or upset, reminders during the interview might help. Even asking, "Do you really want me to use that?" may be proper, depending on the interviewee's state of mind. After the journalist is confident that the source comprehends all this, anything said may fairly be published at the journalist's discretion.

CASE: Beyond Publication

The intricate ground rules of journalism are concerned principally with the narrow definition of the journalist's job: Gather the news and deliver it; side effects of the gathering and aftereffects of the delivering are not the journalist's concern.

Such narrowness may be convenient, but it can create ethical problems. Does a news professional's responsibility encompass even aspects of a story that do not appear on the page or on the air? A good example of how this question may arise was seen in the aftermath of one of the most notorious cases of bad journalism.

On Sunday, September 28, 1980, the *Washington Post* ran a front-page story headlined, "Jimmy's World." In gut-wrenching detail, it described the life of Jimmy, an eight-year-old who had been turned into a heroin addict by his junkie mother and her pusher friends. The story included graphic descriptions of adults "plunging a needle into his bony arm, sending the fourth grader into a hypnotic nod." *Post* reporter Janet Cooke told her editors that she had witnessed Jimmy's dismal life. When pressed for details, Cooke said her sources had threatened to kill her if she revealed their names. Her editors accepted that.

The story created a huge sensation in Washington. The mayor and police department pleaded with the *Post* to give them Jimmy's address. The *Post,* however, refused to cooperate, citing the importance of keeping promises of confidentiality. This was traditional hard-boiled journalism: "We got the story; you find the kid."

The following spring, Cooke and the *Post* were awarded the Pulitzer Prize—newspaper journalism's highest honor—for "Jimmy's World." The spotlight of celebrity now shined on Janet Cooke and her story, revealing hitherto overlooked facts. Within a few days, Cooke had resigned and the *Post* had returned the Pulitzer. "Jimmy's World" was a fabrication; Jimmy didn't exist.

This scandal produced much self-recrimination within the *Post.* After all, this was one of the world's greatest newspapers, driving force behind the Watergate story, beneficiary of confidences from the most famous of anonymous sources, "Deep Throat." Bill Green, the *Post*'s ombudsman, wrote an exhaustive analysis of failures in the *Post*'s editing (which the *Post* published in full).

Compassion becomes an issue in this case because it was *not* an issue at the *Post*. At no time when Cooke was readying her story for publication did her editors say, "What about Jimmy?" Even in Green's postmortem, the principal questions were about why editors did not push Cooke harder about the identity of her sources. In Green's lengthy report—which was based on forty-seven interviews, primarily with *Post* staff members—no evidence is found of anyone having been concerned about Jimmy.

Taking the *Post* to task about this was retired *Post* ombudsman Charles Seib. In an essay in *Presstime* magazine, Seib made the point that "What was at issue in the Jimmy story was something quite different from source disclosure. What was at issue was a callous disregard for a human being on the part of the *Post*'s editors." After all, wrote Seib, the *Post*'s reporter had witnessed (or so her editors believed) "a crime, a terrible crime—the injection of heroin into the arm of a little boy."[9] Anyone with the slightest amount of sense knows that shooting heroin into an eight-year-old is tantamount to murder. If these editors had cared about Jimmy, wrote Seib, "things might have turned out differently": The *Post* might have discovered on its own that Cooke had written a phony story and been spared the embarrassment of losing the Pulitzer it should not have won.

In a private conversation with Seib after "Jimmy's World" had been published and had precipitated the D.C. government's search for the child, but before the story had been exposed as a hoax, one *Post* editor said that if he had to do it over again, he would act differently. "Before publishing the story," wrote Seib, "he would put pressure on Jimmy's mother to get the child into treatment. The *Post* could have footed the bill, he said. There would have been no need to bring in the authorities,"[10] so the source's identity could still have been protected.

Of this editor's second thoughts, Seib wrote:

> The irony here, of course, is that if he had done that—if he had
> allowed a humanitarian instinct to rise briefly above his enthusiasm

for a smashing story—there is a good possibility that he would have uncovered the deception and the story would have died aborning. Had the compassionate course been followed (assuming, of course, that the story had been true), the result would have been just as effective a piece of journalism; perhaps it would even have benefited from an upbeat ending—the saving of Jimmy.[11]

The message here is that journalism and compassion *can* coexist. Subjects of coverage are not mere "news makers." They also are human beings.

Journalists as Human Beings

Just as journalists sometimes treat subjects of news stories as dehumanized objects, so, too, do news professionals sometimes try to strip themselves of feelings. This is done in the name of "objectivity," the notion being that emotions get in the way of news judgment. In theory, this cold-blooded objectivity may seem both attainable and ethical. In practice, it might prove to be neither. Traci Cone, a police reporter-turned-features-writer, says of her former beat: "Every day your whole job was to interview people on the absolute worst days of their lives and write about the absolute saddest things that happened to them in their lives. . . . People think reporters don't care, but how can you listen to all of these stories of tragedy and sadness and not be worried about it?"[12]

CASE: The Photographer's Dilemma

You're a news photographer, and you've just arrived at the scene of a terrible highway accident. The wreckage of cars and bodies is everywhere. As you survey the scene, you know that this is a newsworthy story, but you also realize that much of what you see is too bloodily graphic to be published. You start taking pictures. Should you avoid taking the shots that you think your editors will decide are unsuitable for publication?

Photographers often operate on the premise of shoot first and think later. Professors Gene Goodwin and Ron Smith write: "Not all photographers are enslaved by this convention, but many still see their job as 'get the pictures, let the editors decide what to do with them later.' If photographers worry too much about the ethics or propriety of taking this or that picture, they're apt to come back with no pictures, this convention holds."[13]

This illustrates a quintessential clash between ethical deportment and news gathering. Urging a news professional to suspend ethical judgment is risky, but so, too, is making a snap decision to back away from collecting newsworthy information (in this case, taking a photograph).

From the photographer's standpoint, perhaps the best way to reconcile this is to look at ethics as a function of the news *system.* With this systemic approach, *who* makes ethical decisions does not matter, as long as the ethical decision is made before the news process delivers its product to the news consumer.

This does not mean, however, that the on-site news gatherer is released from ethical responsibility. Decisions still must be made about intruding on privacy, for instance.

And somewhere in the morass is a standard of decency that should be observed. War photographer Eddie Adams took a famous picture of a South Vietnamese general executing a Viet Cong prisoner. As Adams took the photo, he thought that the general had pulled his pistol just to threaten the prisoner. When the general fired and Adams snapped his shutter, the resulting picture was of the prisoner's head taking the impact of the gunshot before the bullet left his head. Adams did not take a second photo. "There was no blood," he wrote, "until he was on the ground— whoosh. That's when I turned my back and wouldn't take a picture. There's a limit, certain times you don't take pictures."[14]

Defining that limit is a difficult ethical task.

CASE: Witnessing Horror

While photographer Steve Lehman was covering the war in Chechnya in 1994, a bomb dropped by a Russian aircraft exploded near him, knocking him off his feet. He rose to find that his colleague, Cynthia Elbaum, had been killed, as had many Chechen civilians around them. He wrote: "There is a fine line in this work, as to when watching someone else's tragedy starts becoming your own. That day, we crossed the line."[15] The outside observer had moved deeper into the grisly reality he was covering.

Part of the journalist's job is to cover the world's horrors, large and small. From the single death in a senseless robbery to the thousands dying in a famine, the journalist observes and describes. Veteran journalist Jim Wooten says he learned that to endure reporting about the madness of humankind he had to "create some psychological workspace between the truth and how I felt about it."[16]

But when in Zaire in 1994 to cover the exodus of refugees from the war in neighboring Rwanda, Wooten was overwhelmed; the psychological workspace evaporated. He described it this way:

> No distance was possible. And no escape either. . . . For seven days human beings were constantly falling all around us. In many cases, we and the lenses of our cameras were the very last things they saw in the very last moments of their lives. It was an excruciating dilemma: at last, a reality so wretched it demanded some degree of personal involvement; and yet a story whose wretchedness was of such epic proportions that any personal involvement was useless.[17]

Wooten tells of interviewing Yves, a young refugee working as a volunteer among his cholera-infected countrymen and women. As he talks to Yves, says Wooten, "I cannot help but notice over his left shoulder, just a few feet behind him, a young man about his age lying on his side. Our eyes meet for a moment, then his slowly close. He coughs weakly and dies. Yves finishes his answer and I ask another question."[18]

Put yourself in Wooten's place. Would your journalistic detachment and objectivity survive in such circumstances?

Another journalist reporting about the Rwandan refugees not only was emotionally overwhelmed, as Wooten had been, but also was able to intervene in the story he was covering. Bob Arnot, a physician and CBS News medical correspondent, saw a little boy—perhaps seven years old—lying near death by the side of a road. Arnot checked his pulse, gave him some water, and took him to a refugee camp's tent hospital, where 250 people had died of cholera the night before. Arnot returned hourly throughout the day, pouring fluids into the boy. By the next day, the child was well enough to be sent on to an orphanage. Arnot's intervention saved the child, but four days later Arnot himself was hospitalized with cholera, due in part, he assumed, to his exposure to the sick boy.

Arnot recovered his physical health, but he admitted that his emotions had not fared well. "It was just one of those situations," he said, "where you gave up trying to cope. . . . You just grieved."[19]

A standard rule in journalism is "Don't become part of the story." Keep your distance, report what happens, and let your coverage have its effect. As a general rule, that makes sense, but few would criticize Arnot's violation of it. (And, of course, Arnot, as a physician as well as a journalist, had other professional ethical standards to meet.)

Even in stories of less-epic proportions than the Rwanda war, circumstances occasionally test the reporter's resolve to remain an observer. Consider this hypothetical: A heavily armed man is barricaded inside his house. You are a reporter covering the standoff. The gunman threatens to kill any police officer who approaches him and then to kill himself. But he says he will talk to a reporter. Assuming that you put aside concern about your personal safety, would you become part of the story and talk to the man (with police approval)? Or should you let the police deal with him while you simply cover events as they develop?

Change the scenario: The gunman is holding two children hostage. He threatens to kill them if anyone other than a reporter approaches. In this instance, would you become involved?

These situations do arise, not every day, but often enough to make it worthwhile for journalists to ponder their role in events that they cover.

Here is another hypothetical. You are a reporter writing a story about child prostitution around the world. Your assignment takes you to a distant country where you encounter the buying and selling of children on a downtown street. You watch what is going

on, taking notes for your story. As you do so you see a little girl—
she cannot be more than ten years old—being sold by one man to
another. The little girl looks at you. You look at her.

What should you do? Slug the buyer, grab the child, and run?
Outbid the buyer yourself and take the child to some orphanage
or other agency that will care for her? If you rescue her, what
about the hundred other children being sold on this same street?
(And forget about calling for police help; they've been paid off
by the sellers.)

Or should you just watch, take notes, and write a story that you
hope will create public awareness of these horrible facts and perhaps bring about change? Does doing your job mean that you are
"doing nothing," at least in terms of this one little girl? Or is it
the best way to save many other children?

For some insight about how journalists address such matters,
consider this story, recounted by war correspondent Peter Arnett.
In South Vietnam in 1963, some Buddhist monks were committing
suicide by public self-immolation to protest their government's
policies. Arnett witnessed and photographed one of these suicides, and when pictures of the burning monk were published
around the world, reporters on the scene were criticized by some
for not trying to save the monk's life.

Arnett responded that he might have been able to kick the
monk's gasoline can away, but "as a human being I wanted to; as
a reporter I couldn't. . . . If I had attempted to prevent [him] doing
this I would have propelled myself directly into Vietnamese politics; my role as a reporter would have been destroyed along with
my credibility."[20]

Of course, said some of Arnett's critics, taking and publishing
the photos of the suicide also constituted intervention in
Vietnamese politics. Rebutting that, Arnett said he was merely
being a messenger, carrying information, which was his job.[21]

The most intriguing and disturbing element of Arnett's comments is the dichotomy he establishes between "human being"
and "reporter." The human being wanted to intervene; the
reporter felt he couldn't. Are these two different species? Does

journalism require the reporter to abandon his or her humanness? Is this profession by necessity intrinsically amoral?

Answering these questions is essential in defining the role of compassion in the news business. News consumers and news professionals alike must ponder how to reconcile the demands of journalism and those of basic humanity. These issues are at the heart of understanding this profession's ethics.

For Discussion

1. When covering the aftermath of a hurricane that destroyed hundreds of homes, would you try to interview people who are wandering dazed in the wreckage of their houses? Would you air video of people sobbing as they look at their devastated homes?

2. Can compassion get in the way of reporting fully and accurately?

3. As a television photographer, should you shoot video of the relatives of victims of a tragedy on the theory that a producer or editor will decide later whether to use the footage? Or, in these circumstances, is the act of photographing itself unethically intrusive?

4. What is the general public perception of journalists—people who care about individuals and society as a whole or people who care only about gathering news regardless of others' feelings?

5. If you were a newspaper editor in charge of covering the aftermath of a tragedy such as the 1995 Oklahoma City bombing, what are some guidelines you would ask your reporters to follow?

6. Do crime victims deserve special treatment from journalists?

CHAPTER EIGHT

High-Tech Ethics

"Global village" may seem a classic oxymoron. The vastness of the globe and the intimacy of the village are so different that the pairing appears illogical.

But the phrase, made famous by Marshall McLuhan, makes perfect semantic sense in the era of high-tech communications. News from the other side of the globe can reach us as quickly as gossip from across the village street.

Between the writing and the publication of this chapter, communication technology undoubtedly will have moved past the cutting-edge tools of 1996, such as the satellite telephone and the small home satellite receiving dish. Regardless of the specific devices available at the moment, the array of sophisticated gadgets has transformed the news business.

This evolution has been anything but slow. Within the past three decades, change has roared through the news business. While broadcasting live during a bombing attack on Baghdad in the early days of the 1991 Gulf War, CNN's Peter Arnett reflected that early in his career he had filed Associated Press dispatches by Morse key. He asked his anchorperson in Atlanta and his worldwide audience, "Would you believe, from Morse key to speaking live to the world in thirty years?"[1]

Along similar lines, James Yuenger, a *Chicago Tribune* foreign correspondent, recalled that during his posting to Moscow in

1970, "I wouldn't get a telephone call from the U.S. but once a year. The phones were lousy. The only way to communicate was with a telex at 66 words a minute. Now [1994], with a computer, it's 1,000 words a minute."[2] And today, even Yuenger's computer is obsolete.

Most computers depend on telephone lines, which are vastly improved but still not infallible. Satellites are better. The reporter at the scene of a war or earthquake who has a satellite telephone can establish the wireless link to the satellite and send his or her story from computer to satellite to home office. This is the same satellite technology that allows Cable News Network (CNN) to broadcast to more than 140 countries and territories.[3] Satellites also are not foolproof, but they are becoming more numerous and more reliable. The scope of news coverage reflects that.

Millions of people around the world can now watch events as they happen. No more delays and anticipation; the world comes into your living room—LIVE!

That speed, however, brings with it considerable ethical peril. When broadcast media cover any event live—be it international or local—much editorial control is abandoned. For example, if a television station does a live report from the scene of an airplane crash that has happened just a short time before, the photographer may inadvertently show bodies or other images normally considered too graphic for broadcast. The editing process has been sacrificed in exchange for immediacy. Former NBC News president Lawrence Grossman has noted that live television "eliminates what journalist Theodore H. White called 'the protective filter of time.'" Grossman added, "Reporters get much of their information at the same time the audience does."[4]

Sometimes the rapid delivery of dramatic news—particularly when accompanied by striking pictures—can lead to equally rapid reaction. That is not always beneficial. The tortoise's pace may be wiser than the hare's.

On Sunday, August 13, 1961, East Germany closed the border between East and West Berlin by erecting the first version of what was to become the Berlin Wall. A CBS News crew in Berlin rushed film of the event to the United States. In those days, that meant the film traveled as airplane cargo. The story aired on Tuesday, August 15, seventy-two hours after the East Germans' action.[5]

With public communication moving slowly, President John Kennedy responded deliberately, avoiding provocative rhetoric and signalling the Soviet Union that he planned to do nothing rash. The American public learned about this new Berlin crisis over several days, first from newspaper and then from television reports. The news, filtered by time, generated no instant demand for Kennedy to do something dramatic in response. The president knew that his options were limited. To have sent American troops to knock down the East Germans' barriers would have meant risking war with the Soviet Union. He didn't want that, and he didn't want politicians or news media pushing him in that direction.

Real-Time News

Imagine if today's technology had existed then and if the sealing of the Berlin border had been televised live. Those raw pictures might have touched raw emotions in the United States, creating political pressure on Kennedy to respond rapidly and forcefully.

Journalists may argue that political reaction to their stories is not their concern. Their job is to present the news accurately and to let events take their course. That is true and not so true. Certainly, delivering the news is their principal task, but it is disingenuous to disclaim all responsibility for the reactions those reports stimulate.

Another example—involving less speculation than the hypothetical version of the Berlin story—is coverage of the 1992 Los Angeles riots. When a jury found police officers not guilty in the beating of Rodney King, the verdict was relayed instantly via local television and radio stations. Given the newsworthiness of this story and the intense public interest in the verdict, that was the only logical course for local news organizations.

But then, when angry public reaction flared, live coverage of isolated disorder was seen by a large audience in Los Angeles. The spasms of outrage soon became a full-fledged riot that police were unable to control. Looking back several months later, some journalists said the live reports were like a virus that raised the temperature of the entire community and helped spur the violence that leapfrogged through South Central Los Angeles.

The ethical issue here is the importance of journalists' recognizing that news has effect. A live television report does not simply vanish into the ether; particularly when it is about an event such as the Rodney King verdict, it stirs emotions and stimulates action. As a practical matter, however, the desire to get news to the public as quickly as possible, plus the competitive pressure of knowing that someone else will do it if you don't, will make intensive live coverage of a big story seem the logical, instinctive thing to do.

But actions produce reactions. If this Newtonian law of motion is applied to journalism, it might be stated as, "A big story is going to produce a big reaction; inflammatory coverage is going to generate inflamed response." This bridge between physics and ethics may be wobbly, but the premise of linkage is worth pondering. News organizations should consider adopting guidelines that recognize the impact that their coverage—especially their live or rapid-delivery coverage—might have.

CASE: The Gulf War and the CNN Effect

The Vietnam War was called the "living room war" because for the first time a war was brought via television into American homes every night. None of that coverage, however, was live. The technology of the 1960s and early 1970s required that film, then videotape, be shipped and relayed before it could be broadcast.

In 1991 another war reached living rooms also through television but without any delay. Viewers could listen to the American bombing of Baghdad and watch the Iraqi Scud missile attacks on Israel and Saudi Arabia as they happened. For television news organizations the new standard of excellence was real-time coverage—the war as it happened, when it happened.

The reports were certainly gripping; audiences watched, transfixed, for hours on end. But are the standards of drama and ethical journalism the same?

Lawrence Grossman, who was president of NBC News from 1984 to 1988, wrote that the dramatic tended to prevail:

> Rumors, gossip, speculation, hearsay and unchecked claims were televised live, without verification, without sources, without editing, while we watched newsmen scrambling for gas masks and reacting to missile alerts. . . . In their impatience to get on the air live rather than wait to find out what was going on, television reporters wondered aloud on-screen what they were seeing and what was happening. No longer did they perform as reporters trying to filter out true information from false. Instead, they were merely sideline observers, as ill-informed as the rest of us. Was it the sound of "thunder" or a "lethal rocket attack" outside? Was it the odor of "nerve gas" or "conventional explosives" that was seeping into the TV studio in Tel Aviv? (It turned out to be bus exhaust.)[6]

The leader in Gulf War coverage was CNN. With its commitment to constant, intensive reporting, it was well suited to meet the public's interest in uninterrupted coverage. Rear Admiral Brent Baker, the U.S. Navy's chief of information, noted that CNN held the attention of the government as well as of the public. "It is clear," he said, "that CNN sets the competitive speed or pace of all major news coverage. Go to any military command center or any newspaper in America—they will both have CNN on 24 hours, as the first electronic cue to what's happening."[7]

Baker also saw tangible evidence of CNN's effect on the public:

> During the war in the Gulf, all the services had 1-800 numbers manned 24 hours for next-of-kin calls if they were concerned about their loved ones. On our Navy–Marine Corps numbers we received over 450,000 calls during Desert Shield/Desert Storm, most of them clearly reacting to a CNN report about an action or incident. In our 24-hour phone center, we watched CNN, and if the report was about a Navy ship hitting a mine, the Navy lines would light up. If a Marine unit was reported under fire, the Marine lines would light up. What this told me as I stood in our

phone center is how far we have gone in touching people's lives in this age of instant communications.[8]

That impact on the audience—particularly those viewers with a high personal stake in the events being covered—underscores the need for accuracy. But this basic responsibility for journalism—getting it right—sometimes was a victim of the emphasis on speed and gripping video above all else.

This sloppiness meant more to some than to others. Although Secretary of Defense Dick Cheney was among those who acknowledged on the eve of the war that he was relying on CNN for information, General H. Norman Schwarzkopf was less impressed. He told an interviewer after the war that he had "turned the TV off in headquarters very early on because the reporting was so inaccurate I did not want my people to get confused."[9]

Within the news business, the contrarian view has a few champions. Former CBS anchorman Walter Cronkite told a congressional committee in 1991, "I don't see what this rush to print or rush to transmit is all about."[10] Veteran television journalist Bernard Kalb wrote: "The *instancy* of today's journalism confronts us with a question: Has all the speed made for better reporting?"[11]

And former NBC News president Grossman advocates "even in this era of real-time technology, the need to value accuracy over speed." He added:

> CNN's instantaneous, continuing live coverage must be shaped by more journalistic discipline and stronger editorial control, even if what gets on the air is delayed until the reporters and their editors are sure the story is right. The networks' chief role should be to provide thoughtful, expert reporting after the fact, rather than mere live narration over an endless stream of satellite pictures.[12]

These points are reiterations of a traditional journalism maxim: "Get it first, but first get it right."

Journalists might claim to be not at fault for government officials' rising emphasis on matching television's speed and compression with the promptness and terseness of their own responses. The argument goes: "We just cover them; they still have the power. They can respond at whatever pace they choose."

That is not realistic. Government representatives know they will pay an intolerably high political price if they do not meet news demands and the public expectations that parallel those demands. Saying, "We don't have an answer yet" will probably elicit accusations of stonewalling. Anyone trying that approach is unlikely to receive praise for being temperate about important matters.

These issues will become more critical as instant global coverage expands. CNN does not have the field to itself. Among its competitors are Worldwide Television News (owned principally by ABC/Capital Cities), the British Broadcasting Corporation's World Service Television, and Reuters Television (including the former Visnews). Others are certain to join the competition. Shifts in the communications industry require consideration of important questions: "If huge, new companies are allowed to control both the conduits and the content that moves over them, what are the dangers? If the system develops as pay-per-view, what are the implications for news programming?"[13]

As technology advances and related issues loom larger, a question that some will consider archaic is not out of place: Even if the public has a "right to know" whatever high-speed journalism can deliver, does it have the *need* to know so much so quickly?

In this context a corollary question is, "What is newsworthy?" Media critic Tom Rosenstiel warns against "confusing newness with importance. Breaking news is not always hard news; being 'live' does not mean being serious."[14]

High-Tech Manipulation

Journalists must be cautious about their media being coopted and used for selfish advantage by those who are ostensibly the subjects of coverage. This can occur in a number of contexts; terrorism is among the most excruciating of these.

CASE: Terrorism

Frank Perez, deputy director of the State Department's Office for Combatting Terrorism during the Reagan administration, said,

"The press is very important to the terrorist in terms of getting their message out, engendering sympathy and support for their cause, articulating their demands, and putting pressure on both governments and populations."[15] Journalists, knowing how they fit into terrorists' plans, face a dilemma: how to bring newsworthy information to the public without aiding terrorism and without further complicating a difficult situation. Live coverage makes this balancing act more difficult.

Consider this case (a hypothetical based on fact): An American commercial passenger jet is hijacked over Europe and flown to Algiers. There the hijackers and their allies on the ground make a series of demands, threatening to kill the plane's passengers unless the U.S. government agrees to the terrorists' terms. As negotiations slowly proceed, television networks carry the terrorists' daily news conferences live and, with the terrorists' permission, interview some of the hostages.

The terrorists are not coy about their manipulation of the media. During a news conference, one of their spokespersons looks directly at the cameras and tells the American audience thousands of miles away, "Urge your president to meet our demands so your fellow countrymen can be set free." Add to this the terrorist leaders' willingness to be interviewed by American network anchorpersons, whose celebrity takes them beyond the level of interviewer to that of de facto negotiator.

Other live coverage includes reporters passing along the latest rumors, such as speculation about an American military rescue mission that may be in the works. Also broadcast live is a terrorist-arranged interview with the airplane's pilot, who warns against such a rescue attempt.

Is this intensive coverage of the terrorist spectacular providing good journalism, or is it merely being a pawn for international outlaws and an irresponsible impediment to the U.S. government's ability to conduct its foreign policy? Or can the coverage, if it shows the hostages being decently cared for, benefit the government by reducing some of the political pressure to act with dramatic quickness?

Answers to these questions depend to some extent on the circumstances of the particular incident. Live coverage of hostages telling their families not to worry will obviously have far different impact than will live coverage of a hostage being executed. Because reporting about terrorist incidents apparently exists with little thoughtful planning, the good or bad ramifications of coverage may turn out to depend on the terrorists' disposition.

Journalist Terry Anderson, who was kidnapped in Lebanon in 1985 and held hostage for almost seven years, writes: "In my experience, publicity has been at once a primary goal and a weapon of those who use terror against innocent people to advance political causes or simply cause chaos. . . . Without the world's attention, these acts of viciousness are pointless."[16]

Veteran print journalist Michael J. O'Neill has some crisp criticism of television coverage of terrorist activity. He says, "It is impossible to argue that the public has to have the news instantly, in the middle of terrorist negotiations, when the real motive for rushing on the air is competition."[17] He adds, "Modern terrorism is a shotgun wedding that marries violent spectaculars to spectacular technology."[18]

The argument that coverage is out of control suggests a need to tighten the reins on technology. But how should that be done? At one end of the spectrum is full-blown, continuous live reporting; at the other is a news blackout. This noncoverage may eliminate some problems, but it will create new—and perhaps more severe—difficulties. O'Neill notes that "cutting off coverage would only feed rumors, increase fears, and incite terrorists to ever-greater atrocities."[19]

As a practical matter, these issues require journalists to find some middle ground. No news organization is going to abandon coverage of a major terrorist event. The public does need to know what is going on. Also, in the real world of news business economics, no news organization is going to become so ethically finicky that it allows itself to be resoundingly scooped by competitors.

Former hostage Terry Anderson offers this advice: "In each case [journalists] must weigh the theoretical or philosophical value of what they do with the fact that individual human lives are at stake. What they report can have a direct impact on the victims, as terrorists pay enormous attention to the news reports about the things they do."[20]

This middle ground may be discovered by taking a more minimalist approach to covering terrorism: less speculation, more background; fewer live reports, more careful evaluation of information before it is broadcast. In the end, the public will still be getting plenty of information, and the terrorists will not be as likely to find an unwitting pawn in the news media.

Political Gamesmanship

The power inherent in evolving television technology is well appreciated by politicians searching for ways to enhance their own clout. Ways to use live coverage to their advantage are seen in all news forums, from the live local broadcast of a city council member's speech to the grand scheming of world leaders. When traditional diplomatic channels are clogged or simply seem unsuited for the politician's task at hand, television offers an alternative pulpit.

Media critic Tom Rosenstiel offers two striking examples:

- "In 1986, as the reign of Philippines President Ferdinand Marcos was coming to an unseemly end, a Marcos aide called CNN's Tokyo bureau, asking if the network would broadcast a speech Marcos wanted to deliver to the United States. 'He sensed he was losing the White House,' CNN's executive vice president Ed Turner . . . explained later. 'And he wanted to talk to a handful of lawmakers on Capitol Hill to shore up his support."
- "When U.S. troops invaded Panama in 1989 the Soviet foreign ministry did not send a formal protest through diplomatic channels. It called CNN so that a Soviet official could broadcast a statement condemning the invasion."

In these and similar instances, says Rosenstiel, the effect of coverage was "to accelerate the pace with which international events would turn, and to give voice to political leaders who otherwise lacked political standing." CNN, he adds, "was not so much supplanting the diplomatic pouch as adding another dimension."[21]

During the days leading up to the 1991 Gulf War, give-and-take between news subjects and those who covered them intensified. For instance, CNN would broadcast a story from Atlanta about the Iraqi parliament. Saddam Hussein's government would watch it and take offense at some aspect of the story. A Hussein aide would call the CNN producer in Baghdad to complain. The CNN producer would call Atlanta to relay the complaint.[22] All this might take place within a few minutes. It's a long way from reading a newspaper story, thinking about it, and then writing a letter to the editor.

A narrow line sometimes exists between gathering news and being used. The temptations of power with which global television is laden make the ethical journalist's job particularly difficult. Efforts to manipulate the press are as old as the institution itself, but high-speed delivery of information raises the stakes.

If journalists surrender to the passion for speed and fail to adhere to basic standards of accuracy (verified facts, corroborated sources, etc.), ethics will be trampled in the chaotic rush to use journalism as merely a way to transmit propaganda.

This is not an esoteric issue; the stakes at any given time may be enormous. Robert Wiener, CNN's executive producer in Baghdad at the beginning of the Gulf War, related CNN chairman Ted Turner's comments about his network's role: "We have to be there [Baghdad]! We're a global network! Also, if there's a chance for peace . . . it might come through us. Hell, both sides aren't talking to each other, but they're talking to CNN. We have a major responsibility."[23]

Impact on Policy

In one way or another, news coverage can drive policy. This was true in 1898, when sensational reporting in William Randolph Hearst's *New York Journal* played a big role in pushing the United States into the Spanish-American War. After the U.S. warship

Maine was sunk mysteriously in the Havana, Cuba, harbor, *Journal* readers were presented with headlines such as "THE WHOLE COUNTRY THRILLS WITH THE WAR FEVER," "HAVANA POPULACE INSULTS THE MEMORY OF THE MAINE VICTIMS," and "NOW TO AVENGE THE MAINE." While Hearst ignited public opinion, President William McKinley and the Spanish government were trying to avoid war. But Hearst and his jingoistic allies prevailed.

Today, new technology enhances that influence. One recent example was the 1994 coverage of the bloody damage done by a single mortar round that landed in Sarajevo's crowded Markale market. Television news crews were close at hand, and their pictures of dismembered innocents galvanized public opinion. Public opinion then galvanized politicians. Polls showed the public becoming more hawkish, and the Clinton administration appeared more ready to bomb the Bosnian Serbs.

This television-enhanced democracy should be celebrated cautiously. Dangers exist if policymaking is to depend on the breadth of the camera's vision and the sharpness of its focus. Television news, with its penchant for the dramatic and its impatience with process, has priorities that are often incompatible with those of responsible governance.

The burden in such instances may rest more heavily on those who govern. But those who report the news—those who deliver the words and pictures that help shape public opinion and influence government action—also have profound responsibilities.

The global village does exist, but it is of fragile construction, always ready to splinter. This raises the ethical stakes for the journalists who cover this village's news.

Altering Reality

CASE: Real and Unreal Photographs

The choice of the cover story for the week of June 19, 1994, was never in question: O. J. Simpson, football hero and media star, had been arrested and charged with murdering his ex-wife and one of her friends. It was pop culture doused in blood—an irresistible tale for the weekly news magazines as well as for virtually every other news organization in America.

The material for the cover was readily available, courtesy of the Los Angeles Police Department: Simpson's mug shot, with the falling hero looking sad and stunned as he stared into the camera, his case number at the bottom of the frame.

Newsweek ran the color picture with no alteration; its credit line read, "Photo by Los Angeles Police Department." At first glance, *Time*'s cover appeared to be the same picture . . . but not quite. The image seemed darker, more menacing. The credit line read, "Photo-illustration for *Time* by Matt Mahurin." Mahurin is an artist, not a photographer. The *Time* cover, although looking like a photograph, was something else.

Added to the Simpson furor was now the charge that *Time*'s cover was racially insensitive and unfair, that by making Simpson ominously darker, it made him look guiltier.

As *Time* managing editor James R. Gaines later explained, the magazine had three options for its cover that week: the LAPD photo, a painting of Simpson, and the photo-illustration. If the painting had been used, no controversy would have arisen. The public would have known that this was an artist's impression of Simpson, not the reality that a photograph is presumed to depict precisely. But the image on *Time*'s cover was confusing. One journalist asked, "*Time*'s editors obviously know what a 'photo-illustration' is, but do the rest of us?"[24]

That question gets to the key ethical issue: Does the public have a right to expect a photograph (or what it believes to be a photograph) to be a mirror image of a real person, place, or event?

Time managing editor Gaines addressed the controversy in a "To Our Readers" column two weeks after the Simpson cover. He said, in part:

> To a certain extent, our critics are absolutely right: altering news
> pictures is a risky practice, since only documentary authority
> makes photography of any value in the practice of journalism. On
> the other hand, photojournalism has never been able to claim the

transparent neutrality attributed to it. Photographers choose angles and editors choose pictures to make points, after all (should President Clinton be smiling this week, or frowning?). And every major news outlet routinely crops and retouches photos to eliminate minor, extraneous elements, so long as the essential meaning of the picture is left intact. . . . If there was anything wrong with the cover, in my view, it was that it was not immediately apparent that this was a photo-illustration rather than an unaltered photograph.[25]

Gaines's response addresses the major issue at hand: making the public aware that this cover was not a true photograph. But he also raises another, broader question: Are alterations of photos acceptable as long as the essential meaning of the picture is left intact, or is any tampering with the mirror image improper?

This is important because computer technology has transformed the cut-and-paste obviousness of composite photographs into a digital data science that makes alterations virtually undetectable. This certainly makes layout editors' lives easier. Photos can be altered to look better and to fit whatever page format is being used. For example, in 1982 *National Geographic* editors wanted to use a particular photograph from Egypt on their cover. But the horizontal composition of the photo did not fit the vertical format of the cover. So, through electronic retouching, one of the Great Pyramids of Giza was moved slightly so the picture would fit the format.

This was not an effort to deceive, nor was it a major alteration of the photo. But this case still draws notice because the notion of moving one of the Great Pyramids seems somehow sacrilegious.

In another instance, during the 1984 Olympics in Los Angeles, the *Orange County* (CA) *Register* "changed the color of the sky in every one of its outdoor Olympics photos to a smog-free shade of blue."[26] The Los Angeles sky without smog? This may have been an instance of altering a photo as an exercise in wishful thinking.

Any abuse of technology will affect the credibility of all photography because the public will be uncertain which pictures reflect "real reality" and which are computerized concoctions. Jack Corn, director of photography for the *Chicago Tribune*, noted: "People used to be able to look at photographs as depictions of reality. Now that's being lost."[27]

As this technology improves, ethical questions will loom larger. News organizations will have to be more careful about the sources of their photos because tampering will be undetectable. Journalist J. D. Lasica asks, "Can newspapers rely on the truthfulness of any photo whose authenticity cannot be verified?"[28]

Some journalists defend alteration of photos as long as it is disclosed to the public with the disclaimer "composite" or "retouched" or some other explanation. Of course, it is the photo itself that gets the audience's attention; many people are likely to ignore the fine print.

In February 1994, as ice skaters Nancy Kerrigan and Tonya Harding arrived in Lillehammer, Norway, for the Olympics, *New York Newsday* ran a front-page photograph of Kerrigan and Harding apparently skating just a few feet apart. A subheadline on the page said, "Tonya, Nancy to Meet at Practice," implying that they had not yet met on the ice, and a caption in smaller print said the two "appear to skate together in this *New York Newsday* composite illustration."

The disclaimer is explicit, but the photo dominates the page and the attention of anyone looking at it on a newsstand or elsewhere. With the Kerrigan-Harding conflict the dominant sensation of the moment, this portrait of apparent reconciliation was sure to sell papers.

Media critic Ellen Hume calls disclosure that the image was invented merely a "fig leaf" to cover the departure from accuracy.[29] Her point is a good one. Disclosure does not absolve the creator of the fiction. A disclaimer is only as good as the public's awareness and understanding of it, and both are often limited.

Beyond the disclaimer, photojournalists and editors might ask two questions about these matters:

- If the photo has to be altered to be acceptable to news consumers, does it really need to run?

- Can another photo be found that will illustrate the story adequately without having to be altered?[30]

At the very least, these questions should be addressed before even considering photo alteration.

These issues extend beyond the print media into television. Computer technology is likely to make videotape obsolete, replacing it with images recorded on discs and computer chips. The engineering particulars are less important than the end result: the prospect of "creativity" crossing ethical boundaries and undermining the journalistic integrity of all visual images.

Already, electronic game playing can mislead television audiences. On the January 26, 1994, edition of ABC's "World News Tonight," anchorman Peter Jennings introduced a report from correspondent Cokie Roberts "at Capitol Hill." Roberts was seen standing in front of the Capitol, wearing an overcoat. But she actually was in ABC's Washington Bureau, with a picture of the Capitol electronically placed in back of her. She put on the overcoat to complete the illusion that she was on the scene at the Capitol.

ABC News formally reprimanded correspondent Roberts and producer Rick Kaplan for this. ABC News vice president Richard Wald told his staff in a memo that the ruse was "serious because it misled our audience." (It also misled Jennings, who did not know that Roberts was not at the Capitol.)[31]

In all these cases, ethical standards are shoved aside in the rush to embrace the snazziest new technology. The rationale seems to be, "We have these new gadgets, so we're obligated to use them." Also, the assertion of "no damage done" is persistently invoked to excuse this tampering with truth.

Such facile reasoning can wreck the ethical foundation of the news business. The technology is not in itself intrinsically unethical. Rather, it is the use of the technology in ways that may mislead that is ethically flawed.

Television and Reality

Television lends itself to "enhancements of reality" that go beyond the electronic reconstruction of visual images. Producing a television news story that has extra appeal to the eye and ear sometimes involves gimmicks that make things happen on the screen differently than they actually did. The effect of this is often to heighten the drama or to intensify the emotion of the story.

One of these techniques is slow motion. This fills a variety of needs for the news producer. Suppose your story is about someone who has been arrested for a major crime. The only footage you have of this person is the five seconds of his being hustled out of a police car and into the city jail, but ten seconds of video is needed to cover the narration of this part of the story. The solution: When the videotape is edited, stretch your five seconds into ten by using slow motion.

Proponents of this technique argue that it is neither deceptive nor misleading and that the use of slow motion is obvious to viewers (in contrast to the computerized alteration of pictures discussed earlier). The counterargument rests on the mirror-of-reality principle: The transfer of the prisoner did not happen at that pace, and the slow-motion segment is not real. The distortion may not mislead the viewer, but it still is untruthful.

A variation on this is "point-of-view" video, which means the camera can take on the point of view of the person whose story is being re-created. ABC, for example, allows this as long as no people are shown. In a news story, the reporter can say that a person walked up these steps and opened this door, with the camera re-creating what he or she may have seen, but the story cannot show a person doing it or a hand opening the door or feet walking up the steps.[32]

Another technique—sometimes used to accompany slow motion—is the addition of extraneous music to a story. This, too, is usually obvious to the audience. Nevertheless, it can have a powerful, almost subliminal impact on the emotions of those watching the story. (Consider, on a grander scale, the effect on movie audiences of a film's soundtrack.) Once again, it is not real, in the sense that the event being watched on the television screen did not have this musical accompaniment when it happened.

A television news story stimulates viewer reaction in a number of ways: by visual image, by the narration (on camera or off) of the reporter or anchorperson, by interviews with persons involved in the story, and by the "natural sound" that accompanies whatever is being seen.

For example, a story from the scene of a plane crash will include video of the crash site and rescue efforts, the reporter's narration about the event, background/natural sound (such as rescuers' shouts and ambulance sirens), and perhaps the voice of someone interviewed by the reporter.

All this comes together to constitute the reality of the event. If it is a well-written, well-produced story, it will convey the emotional power of the crash's aftermath. That power might be boosted if the pictures are accompanied by emotion-tugging music. Doing this might help the story more firmly grasp viewers' attention, but is this a good enough reason to distort reality?

Production of television news stories incorporates a steadily growing amount of high-tech wizardry. Most of this enhances journalism by making complex topics more understandable, and it can be done without distortion of the facts. But caution is advisable. Pursuit of ever-better technology should not be allowed to overwhelm the journalist's allegiance to the truth.

Evolving News Formats

As one century ends and another begins, the ascendance of electronic media continues. For newspapers, that means facing up to the declining percentage of Americans who read newspapers and changing the product to keep up with what the public wants.

In the past, newspapers were interested in new technology for incremental changes, such as how to keep ink from rubbing off on their readers' hands. Now they're exploring how newspapers can survive and perhaps thrive without ink—and maybe without paper.[33]

Major newspaper companies are intensively researching online versions of their products. The principal selling point for the electronic newspaper is its ability to engage the personal interests of its reader. The menu of such news reports will offer more than does today's newspaper. For example, in addition to a story about a treaty signing, the reader will have access on request to the full text of the treaty itself, the background documents used in negotiating the pact, and detailed biographies of the negotiators and signers. Or, on the sports page, every conceivable statistic about last night's baseball games can be called up. All this will be within electronic reach of anyone who wants it and easily ignored by those who want just streamlined information.

Ethical issues accompany newspapers' technological transformation. One benefit will be the ability to segregate material that might offend readers. The *Washington Post*'s Joann Byrd says of the new format: "Readers have to give their consent, and they'll be braced for what they might see. In the menu with the accident story, or the homicide story, or the famine story, the electronic newspaper could offer the option, 'graphic' (or 'sensitive' or 'distressing') photo."[34]

A broader question involves news judgment more generally. Online newspapers will have vastly greater "page space," but that does not necessarily mean that an uncontrolled flood of information should be provided. New York University professor Jay Rosen points out that "interpreting the news and separating out the extraneous is pivotal to the profession. Therefore, dumping a load of facts into a bottomless database would do little to aid public discourse, inform the community or attract a new generation of readers."[35] Editorial discrimination and ethical judgments will remain important.

The pace of change is extremely rapid. Kate McKenna writes:

> Much of the new activity within the print industry is fired by the same fuel propelling computer, telephone, cable and entertainment companies: fear. Technology is breaking down the barriers between these once-distinct industries, allowing unforeseen competitors into the new markets. This same technology could render any one of these industries obsolete.[36]

The television business, like newspapers, recognizes the need to change to keep up with consumer expectations. One big change already well in place is consumer-controlled time shifting. Viewers have become accustomed to recording programs to watch at a more convenient time. When they belatedly watch, they may also fast-forward through the commercials, to advertisers' great dismay.

But far greater change is coming. Here is how Ted Koppel describes it:

> Imagine a three-button remote control: An on-off switch, a button that lets you scroll through the menu until you come to the word "news"; hit enter. Now scroll through the available options until you come to "Nightline." Hit the enter button, at your convenience. You could also, if you wish, scroll through the available "Nightline" programs by date or subject matter—more than 3,500 of them. And as we all become more "interactively" literate, there will be a whole new world of options available. How about the entire interview you did with Ross Perot in 1971, Ted? Not just the fragment that you replayed 23 years later on "Nightline." Play it for me. And I want to see all of your outtakes on that series of programs you did with President Clinton in Europe.[37]

As with the electronic newspaper, a television newscast will place considerable editorial decision making in the hands of news consumers. If you want just international news, you can skip all that domestic politics stuff. And if you want the latest about health care in China, you will be able to pick the two-minute or twelve-minute version of the story. It's your choice. Gradually, says Koppel, "the paternalistic world of television news as presented by a small group of reporters, producers and editors can be replaced by a brave new world of news you can choose."[38]

Television news organizations will still have the responsibility of deciding what to cover and what to include in the menu presented to viewers. Competitive pressures will drive some of those decisions, but so should basic ethical standards in terms of deciding what is newsworthy. This will be particularly important for the viewers who are *not* well informed, who will look at a huge menu of stories without the background knowledge to know which are most important. Viewers with narrow interests may not seek to expand them and will miss out on stories that are not merely interesting but are essential to their well-being.

For instance, if a measles epidemic has broken out in a community, parents need to know that. With a traditional format, a local news organization could lead with that story and be fairly certain that most of its audience would pay attention. But the viewer scanning the story menu might miss "Measles outbreak" or think that it is a medical science feature.

News organizations can provide cues, such as labeling some items "top stories." Such efforts will be part of journalists' responsibilities in the "brave new television world" Koppel describes.

A fundamental reason why news organizations provide information is to build the public's body of knowledge so that the democratic society can be governed by a thoughtful, aware populace. As the revolution in information technology proceeds and as the social fabric of the global village becomes more tightly knit, journalists' ethical duties will increasingly center on this relationship between information and knowledge.

For Discussion

1. Is instant journalism better journalism?

2. What dangers may arise when news organizations rush to get information to the public after an event such as the 1995 Oklahoma City bombing?

3. What guidelines should TV journalists adopt when covering volatile situations such as the early stages of the 1992 Los Angeles riots?

4. Is anything ethically wrong with making minor changes of reality in a news product, such as slightly altering composition of a photograph?

5. What impact does slow motion or added music have on TV news viewers?

6. Is the public likely to be better informed or simply over-whelmed by the growing electronic flood of news?

CHAPTER NINE
_____

The Changing Newsroom

The news business is constantly evolving. Technological advances make the gathering and dissemination of news faster and more comprehensive. Emerging issues challenge the resourcefulness of those who must explain them to the public. Expanding interests of news consumers mean new expectations about the quantity and quality of news available to them.

The state of journalism is itself a public issue. How the news is gathered, who reports it, and how news organizations maintain ties to news consumers are important factors in the news media's ability to act in the public interest. Fairness in coverage is unlikely to exist unless there is fairness within news organizations. Important issues might not be covered if journalists are not aware of their audience's interests and needs.

All these matters get much attention from those who run news organizations, but perhaps the news business's dominant internal issue of the moment is the quest for diversity—the effort to make coverage and those who provide the coverage more representative of the communities they serve.

The Case for Diversity

Buzzwords abound: "diversity," "inclusiveness," "moral leadership," "comprehensiveness," and others. Although the term of choice may vary, the issue remains constant—making certain that coverage represents a broad array of viewpoints and is sensitive to the rights and dignity of all who make and consume the news.

This has not always been a prime concern in the news business. Slurs and sloppiness have been commonplace, even in stories about national heroes. Consider this passage from a 1939 *Life* magazine profile of Joe DiMaggio: "Italians, bad at war, are well-suited for milder competition. . . . Although he learned Italian first, Joe, now 24, speaks English without an accent, and is otherwise well adapted to most U.S. mores. Instead of olive oil or smelly bear grease, he keeps his hair slick with water. He never reeks of garlic and prefers chicken chow mein to spaghetti."[1]

That was a long time ago; such comments couldn't happen now, right? Here is a part of an on-air conversation between a Los Angeles television anchorman and a reporter during coverage of looting in the 1992 Los Angeles riots: "Tell me, Linda, do these people look like illegal aliens?" "Yes, they do, Paul."[2] Nice and chatty and bigoted.

Or consider this headline on a 1995 ad for the ABC News program "Day One": "Give us your tired, your poor, your huddled masses yearning to stick up a liquor store."[3]

Some people might see no problem with the attitudes reflected in these anti-immigrant messages. But others certainly will be angered and hurt by them.

Although overt bias still turns up, it is the least of today's problems because its visibility makes it vulnerable to prompt countermeasures (assuming that anyone cares to take them). More insidious are subtle biases such as news organizations' tendency to rely on sources drawn from a relatively small pool of Anglo men. Some news organizations are aggressively seeking to change this. At the *Washington Post,* a 1994 memorandum from top editors said, in part: "We must strive always to get a rich variety of voices into the paper. . . . We must all look for new specialists—especially women, younger people, people of color, unconventional thinkers and people who aren't routinely quoted by us and other media outlets."[4]

About this, *Post* columnist Richard Harwood wrote: "There is nothing particularly revolutionary here. It is primarily a restatement of the belief that 'truth' is relative and subjective—that there may be black truths, white truths, male truths, female truths and so on. And, if all your sources are white males, you are getting a very limited version of truth."[5]

This imbalance can be quantified. A 1993 study by the Women, Men, and Media Project (based at the University of Southern California and New York University) found that "men were referred to or solicited for comment 85 percent of the time in front-page news stories. . . . Of those interviewed during the network nightly news [ABC, CBS, and NBC], 75 percent were males. One evening during the study period, not one woman was interviewed for any of the stories reported. Twenty-one males were."[6]

In addition to presenting a view of the world distorted by its narrowness, this limited pool of sources helps perpetuate the stereotype of white males being the keepers of all wisdom. Consider the impact, for instance, on children who grow up watching television news and seeing that all "experts" are white men. Unless that myth is debunked at home or school it becomes accepted as reality. The harmful effect on young women, in particular, should not be underrated.

Other prejudices also are reinforced when news organizations are inadequately sensitive to diversity issues. Here are some of the problems:

- *Not considering relevance and irrelevance of race in news stories.* In this news item—"Police arrested John Smith, a black man, age 25"—Smith's race is irrelevant, adding nothing to the story except a reinforcement of the pejorative blacks-are-criminals stereotype. On the other hand, in a story saying "Colin Powell is the first black general to be chairman of the Joint Chiefs," race *is* relevant (as long as the reference is not repeated constantly) because of the historic nature of his role.
- *Failing to recognize the range of minority groups.* Some stories about minority group members discuss issues in terms of

white and black, neglecting Hispanics, Asian-Americans, Native Americans, and others. Critics have noted that this practice means that members of these groups are left out "of the civic discussions that the news media make possible and that often drive public policy."[7] Also, some people object to the word "minority." In a *USA Today* column, Barbara Reynolds wrote: "Minority—a debasing term—is a label I refuse to wear. The root word means small, insignificant. . . . You salute and promote majors but pity, divide and give the leftovers to minors."[8]

- *Ignoring the representative in favor of the sensational.* Extreme viewpoints should be covered, but context should be defined. If the views are not widespread, that should be made clear. For instance, in stories about Nation of Islam leader Louis Farrakhan and black-Jewish relations, much of the coverage omitted data about what African-Americans as a group think about Jews. Concerning such matters, *Washington Post* writer Juan Williams said: "The media typically wants to hear the person who's the most extreme and outrageous and offensive and that person emerges as the true and authentic black voice. . . . You rarely hear the reasoned and thoughtful response from the other 99 percent."[9]

- *Perpetuating negative stereotypes.* The impact of news coverage is determined only rarely by one story or a few stories. The substance and tone of coverage over a lengthy period are more influential. Describing television news coverage of African-Americans, Northwestern University professor Robert Entman wrote: "Television news is uniquely poised to reduce racial stereotyping. But to do so, TV journalists must realize that their words and images, however accurate on a story-by-story basis, accumulate over time to exacerbate racial tensions. A deliberate choice to introduce more complexity and variety in images of African Americans could, on balance, make TV news less likely to arouse white antagonism rooted in misunderstanding and stereotype — while offering a more comprehensively accurate depiction of African-American life."[10] Along the same lines, Sidmel Estes-Sumpter, president of the National Association of Black Journalists, said, "The portrayal of people of color in the news industry has a direct effect on how society feels about those people of color."[11]

These are just a few of the issues related to diversity. At the heart of the matter—especially for local news media—is the relationship between news content and news audience. A news organization unconcerned about diversity is unlikely to be able to provide coverage of the breadth and depth that its community wants and needs.

For example, in the aftermath of the 1992 Los Angeles riots that followed the acquittal of police officers accused of beating Rodney King, some local news organizations were accused of being out of touch with the minority communities. When the California State Assembly held hearings about the causes of the riots, some witnesses said that although television and print reporters documented the violence as it happened, they "failed to put the upheaval in the context of the social and economic problems of the city's disadvantaged" residents.[12]

Establishing context for public consideration of issues—especially crises—is an important task for the news media. Editors and news directors are likely to be surprised with increasing frequency by events in their communities frequency unless they make thoughtful, consistent efforts to expand the range of sources of information coming to them as well as to expand the flow of information being delivered to the public. A news organization cannot adequately serve its community—be it small town or the nation as a whole—if it does not know its constituencies and understand their interests.

Diversity Issues in the Newsroom

Simple logic dictates that diversity in coverage is largely a function of diversity among those who produce that coverage.

Multicultural perspectives are essential in any news organization that wants to cover adequately a multicultural community or nation.

The range of categories to be represented is great: race, gender, sexual orientation, ideology, economic class. *Washington Post* columnist Richard Harwood has noted that this last criterion—socioeconomic status—is paid too little attention. He writes:

"Journalism, in this view, has become in the past half-century a gentrified occupation, dominated overwhelmingly by middle-class and upper-middle-class college graduates who in very important ways neither look like nor think like the mythical 'America' in our heads. They used to be predominantly white males. Today the cast of characters in our newsrooms is more 'diversified' in the sense that it contains more blacks, Asians, Hispanics and women than in earlier times. But the class structure has changed very little."[13]

The kind of narrowness Harwood addresses is certainly a significant issue, but by no means have other problems of representativeness been resolved. For instance, although many major news organizations tout their efforts to build more-diverse news staffs, newspapers remain 90 percent white.[14] The Women, Men, and Media Project reported that in 1993 men reported 86 percent of the stories on ABC, CBS, and NBC.[15] A 1994 survey of members of the National Association of Black Journalists found widespread dissatisfaction with opportunities in the news business and with the treatment of African-American news professionals by their white colleagues. Two-thirds of those surveyed said their newsroom managers did not care about retaining and promoting black journalists. Illustrating the different perspectives on this issue, 94 percent of managers disagreed, saying they were seriously committed to this. Also, 89 percent of the black journalist respondents said the lack of mentors and role models for black journalists was a serious problem. Seventy-seven percent of the managers agreed with this.[16]

Gannett White House correspondent Deborah Mathis, who is an African-American, notes that she sometimes receives mail addressed to "the affirmative action columnist." She says: "If you're black, the assumption is you're part of some quota plan. It can never be because you earned it—and probably overearned it. It's this stealthy little thing that says you don't quite measure up."[17] Minority reporters also object to the "ghettoization" in some newsrooms that limits minority reporters to covering "minority stories."[18]

The litany of protest stemming from anger, frustration, and sadness is endless. The new emphasis among minority journalists is to bring substantive change to news coverage and hiring policies. A major part of this effort was the Unity '94 conference organized by the Asian American Journalists Association, the National Association of Black Journalists, the National Association of Hispanic Journalists, and the Native American Journalists Association. A report produced by Unity '94 included these recommendations for news organizations:

- Institute measurable hiring goals.
- Conduct annual surveys of diversity efforts.
- Audit news content to make sure coverage is diverse and not racist, sexist, or homophobic.
- Identify and nurture potential minority employees, beginning with participants in high school and college journalism programs and with particular emphasis on local residents who can be brought into entry-level jobs.
- Develop closer ties with ethnic media and with minority journalists' organizations.[19]

These measures will produce no instant transformation of the news business. They probably will, however, provide considerable impetus for change, opening doors and keeping them open.

Plenty of pessimism exists among minority journalists and others who believe that reforms in coverage and hiring are essential. One journalist covering Unity '94 wrote: "Throughout the conference, the conclusion seemed inescapable: Newspaper executives by and large see diversity as a way of making money, while minority journalists see it as a means to transform both the newspaper product itself and the people who work at newspapers."[20]

Some enlightenment was evident at Unity '94. For example, *New York Times* publisher Arthur Sulzberger, Jr., told one session that diversity is "about changing the way we view each other and the way we view the news."[21] But these issues are far from new, and encouraging words tend to be outweighed by the news business's long history of foot-dragging. In 1968 the National Advisory Commission on Civil Disorders (known as the Kerner Commission after its chairman, Illinois Governor Otto Kerner) included a study of news coverage in its analysis of the riots that wracked the country in 1967.

The commission's report included these observations:

> The news media have failed to analyze and report adequately on racial problems in the United States and, as a related matter, to meet the Negro's legitimate expectations in journalism. . . . The media report and write from the standpoint of a white man's world. The ills of the ghetto, the difficulties of life there, the Negro's burning sense of grievance, are seldom conveyed. . . . [The press] repeatedly, if unconsciously, reflects the biases, the paternalism, the indifference of white America.[22]

The report also concluded that "the journalistic profession has been shockingly backward in seeking out, hiring, training, and promoting Negroes."[23] Figures cited by the report have improved, but not as appreciably as might have been expected considering that three decades have passed since the report was written.

Consider this passage: "Along with the country as a whole, the press has too long basked in a white world, looking out of it, if at all, with white men's eyes and a white perspective. That is no longer good enough."[24] That, too, comes from the Kerner Commission report, but the message is only slightly less true in the 1990s than it was in the 1960s.

Although race has been the dominant focus of reform efforts in journalism, other groups have become increasingly vocal in their demands for change. As with racial minorities, women have made only slight progress in journalism; their ranks remain far smaller in the news business than in the overall population.

The 1993 study of twenty newspapers by the Women, Men and Media Project found that women wrote only 34 percent of front-page stories and 26 percent of opinion pieces.[25] In 1990 a study of television network evening newscasts found that only 12 percent of the stories were reported by female correspondents.[26] A 1988 survey of network television news found that men received salaries from 15 percent to 81 percent higher than those paid to women for comparable work.[27]

The Women, Men and Media study also found that "women's comments and expert opinions are being sought out minimally—by male and female reporters—particularly on key societal issues" and that disproportionate attention was given to sexist trivia, such as Hillary Rodham Clinton's wardrobe and hairstyle.[28]

Reporting on a study of the networks' evening newscasts from 1983 through 1989, Southern Illinois University professor Joe Foote observed that most women correspondents "were locked into a static underclass, going neither up nor down. . . . Most women correspondents do not have the quality, permanent assignments that guarantee regular visibility."[29]

This last point is particularly important because only when women receive such assignments will television news organizations move beyond tokenism. Women in television news also find that physical appearance is a far more important criterion for them than for men and that as they move into and past middle age, they are far more likely than men to have their careers cut short or at least put into a perpetual holding pattern with little chance of advancement. Television journalist Linda Ellerbee wrote in 1985 that "not so long ago I was told to lose weight if I wished ever to anchor again at NBC News. I wonder if anyone's ever said that to Charles Kuralt."[30]

Along the same lines, Ellerbee noted:

> Because there are so few women in management, it is men who do most of the hiring, which may account for the disproportionate number of pretty, pearl-wearing vacant-headed paper dolls—the kind of women you swear blow-dry their teeth—that you see reporting the news on television. If too many women in my business

seem to concentrate more on their looks than on their brains, perhaps it's because men do the hiring and, as someone pointed out, men see better than they think.[31]

In the years since Ellerbee wrote that, things have improved, but the problems she mentioned have certainly not been wholly solved. *New York Times* executive Seymour Topping addressed this at a 1993 symposium presented by the Freedom Forum Media Studies Center:

> Women in [newspaper] newsrooms are challenging old sins and any backsliding that may appear in news reports or how staff is managed. Nevertheless, subtle discrimination persists. The same is true of the other news media, whether we are speaking of how rape cases are covered, sexual references and allusions, or whether subjects and issues of prime concern to women are adequately addressed. The problem will not be fully solved until we have more women in executive positions. On reporter and junior editor levels, we have fair representation of women in most shops; in fact, the gender mix now in journalism schools indicates that women will be in the majority in newsrooms in the next decade. However, there is a lag in promotion of women to top editorial jobs. Media, to be fair and adequate, require diversity at the executive level. That is the only way to achieve a degree of sensitivity in the management of media that will eliminate discrimination.[32]

In this same symposium, Linda Ellerbee summed up the position of many advocates of the rights of women in the news business: "What I'm looking for in the '90s is my highest hope—more women without apology."[33]

Participation without apology is also a goal for gay journalists. After long keeping their sexual orientation closeted, homosexuals in the news business have gradually become more open. This has been spurred by the growing number of news organizations that cover homosexual issues and that do not discriminate against homosexual staff members.

When hosting a reception for members of the National Lesbian and Gay Journalists Association in 1993, *New York Times* publisher Arthur Sulzberger, Jr., said: "When I was a reporter at the *New York*

Times, a lot of my friends and colleagues were gay and terrified. Imagine the psychic pressure of having a secret and keeping it hidden and worrying about being fired and your career being ruined if you were discovered." He added, "Now we are covering the totality of gay life, that gays are more than just victims of AIDS."[34]

In 1992 Deb Price of the *Detroit News* began writing the first column about gay issues to appear regularly in a major daily newspaper. She said "a newspaper doesn't have to be pro-gay to have a gay columnist; it only has to be pro-news."[35]

This coverage involves some special ethical issues. Among these is deciding when it is appropriate to identify someone as a homosexual. Bob Murphy, a senior vice president at ABC News, told the National Lesbian and Gay Journalists Association 1993 convention that as a gay man he knew that "coming out" was painful and that "outing"—revealing that someone is a homosexual—should not be done unless it is dictated by overriding news value. He said, "I find it abhorrent that we as gay journalists would advocate the widespread invasion of private lives."[36]

Des Moines Register editor Geneva Overholser agreed about the need to exercise care in identifying someone as being gay unless sexual orientation was relevant to the story. She added, however, "We need to be careful about keeping things out of the paper," and said that AIDS was not taken seriously sooner because newspapers had long refused to identify it as the cause of death in obituaries.[37]

Some industry codes address these matters only obliquely, such as the Society of Professional Journalists provision: "The news media must guard against invading a person's right to privacy."[38] The code of the Public Radio News Directors Incorporated is more specific about this: "Strive to eliminate personal, station, or community bias and balance matters of race, creed, religion, ethnic origin, gender, and sexual preference."[39]

The diversity issue in the news business comes down to this: The news audience is composed of varied groups with varied interests. That breadth needs to be recognized in coverage, which requires news staffs of comparable breadth. Just as "one size fits all" rarely satisfies clothing customers, so, too, does "one news approach covers all" rarely satisfy the diverse news audience. The enormous power of the news media should be wielded not by one subgroup of the population—Anglo males—but rather by professionals whose race, gender, and sexual orientation reflect the diversity of the public they serve.

Civic Journalism

Some news organizations, as part of their efforts to strengthen ties to their communities, have embraced "civic journalism"—an approach to news that emphasizes problem solving and participation of the public in deciding what issues are newsworthy. This involves some combination of polling, focus groups, community meetings, and other efforts to tell the public: "Let us know what you are interested in, and we will cover it. Tell us about the most serious problems facing this community and how we can help you solve them." Such surrogacy and partnership are designed at least partly to break down some of the distrust that obstructs relations between news media and public.

Civic journalism—also known as "public journalism"—has its passionate advocates and its equally passionate critics. Its defenders say that strengthening press-community links helps offset perceptions that the news media have become too cynical and too cozy with the privileged and powerful forces that they are supposed to be covering aggressively. Jay Rosen, a New York University professor who is one of the leading exponents of civic journalism, has cited survey research that has found that 71 percent of Americans believe that the media get in the way of the public solving its problems. Rosen said of this, "While journalists treasure their role as watchdog and critic, increasingly they are seen as insiders themselves, part of a discredited political class."[40]

Civic journalism might change the impression that journalists are inveterate naysayers, wallowers in conflict, and voices of doom that harp on the negative and ignore the positive. This doesn't mean that journalists should abandon assertive reporting and replace it with mush. Rather, it involves a reordering of priorities.

Frank Denton, editor of the *Wisconsin State Journal* in Madison and a supporter of public journalism, said: "Our journalism is not here to fry people—although we fry people all the time. Our main goal is in helping the public find the solutions to problems." This process includes inviting civic leaders to meet with journalists to identify problems and ponder solutions. This takes place while the news gathering is going on, rather than after stories have been published, making the outsiders partners of sorts with the journalists. Denton said of this, "Instead of making them feel like targets—and almost victims—of our journalism we are trying to make them, ultimately, instruments of solutions."[41]

One of Mr. Denton's competitors takes a dim view of the *State Journal's* approach. Dave Zweifel, editor of Madison's *Capital Times,* said: "My idea of public journalism is finding out what's going on and raising hell about it. But I don't think I should go down to the mayor's office and hold his hand."[42]

Another critic is *Washington Post* editor Leonard Downie, who worries about the links forged between journalists and the people they cover. He said, "Too much of what's called public journalism appears to be what our promotion department does, only with a different kind of name and a fancy, evangelistic fervor."[43] Downie also argues that a journalist's job should consist of nothing more than telling readers what is happening. He said: "We've got a terrible fiscal problem in the District [of Columbia] and we cover the hell out of it. But we don't want our coverage to tell people how they should deal with it. That's up to the voters and the Congress and the city council and the mayor."[44]

Along similar lines, *Newsday* editor Howard Schneider said, "I don't think you have to lead the parade in order to report on the parade."[45]

One field in which civic journalism is being used is political coverage. Voters are asked to define the issues they think most important (through polls, focus groups, or other solicitations of opinion), and the journalists then act as their direct surrogates, asking the candidates to address those issues. Newspapers such as the *Wichita Eagle* and the *Charlotte Observer* and television stations such as Dallas's WFAA adopted this approach in part because journalists, readers, and viewers all were fed up with campaigns being trivialized by flashy media events at the expense of substance. Journalists recognized their de facto complicity with politicians that resulted because they were covering the media events and not doing an adequate job when reporting about issues.

Prior to election day, voters rarely can exercise their clout unless the news media act on their behalf; the chances of an individual voter being able to pose a question to a candidate are far slimmer than are those of a reporter acting as the voter's agent. Also, when news organizations try to decide on their own what issues the public needs to know about, they may overlook some that are really closest to voters' hearts. *Charlotte Observer* editor Rich Oppel said: "We sought to engage readers in developing the agenda for the campaign and to help readers assert that agenda throughout the campaign. We tried not to pursue our own agenda via eight editorial writers sitting around a table."[46]

One danger inherent in civic journalism is that selecting issues by referendum may mean reinforcing the status quo while news organizations surrender their leadership in identifying topics deserving journalistic scrutiny. John Bare, a scholar who has studied civic journalism, cites historical evidence of the need for independent news judgment:

> Editors often have been alone in believing an issue is important, and their persistently unpopular stands have helped change society for the better. Two decades ago, outspoken newspaper editors in the South who denounced Jim Crow and endorsed civil rights were hated in their communities. Speaking out against racism was a noble but dangerous tactic, yet the progressive writings of these editors eventually helped bring about change. If those editors had established their news agenda by survey research, they certainly would have found that citizens wanted something else.[47]

Civic journalism raises a number of ethical questions:

- Are news organizations being properly inclusive, or are they improperly abdicating leadership when they involve the public in agenda setting?

- Does a conflict of interest exist when journalists create a story through this process and then report about it?
- Should journalists orchestrate solutions to problems or merely report about the problems and then let voters and appropriate public officials develop solutions?
- Should news organizations be so concerned about the public's opinion of them that they institute civic journalism as an exercise in self-promotion to restore public faith in the good citizenship of journalists?

For the most part, the intentions of the practitioners of civic journalism are noble. Does that, however, legitimize the blurring of lines between reporting about and participating in the news?

Diversity and civic journalism will be important issues as the news media enter the twenty-first century. This is modern journalism, but it also is very traditional. The goal is simple: to provide better and broader coverage.

For Discussion

1. What are the main reasons why diversity in the newsroom is important?

2. Should reporters be assigned to stories based on their ethnicity? For example, should only black reporters cover Jesse Jackson?

3. What are some examples of news coverage reinforcing negative stereotypes of minority group members?

4. Do you think your local news organizations do a good job of covering all groups within your community?

5. Do you detect economic bias in news coverage: emphasis on stories that appeal primarily to an upper-income audience? If so, what might be some causes of this tilt?

6. Does civic journalism require journalists to abandon their agenda-setting role?

Chapter Ten

Toward a More Ethical Journalism

$\mathbf{M}$ore than a century ago, in an essay about the British press, Ralph Waldo Emerson wrote, "No journal is ruined by wise courage."[1]

Wisdom without courage or courage without wisdom can ruin a profession committed to fairness and public service. A balance of the two is essential not just to effective journalism, but also to ethical journalism.

The extensive duties and powers of the American news business constitute a mandate for ethical behavior. Pervasive and influential, journalism exists as a complex mix of rights and responsibilities. First Amendment freedom must be nurtured and protected against infringement, but for the most part—particularly when compared to the prerogatives of journalists in other nations—the constitutional foundation is solid. Much less well defined, however, is the latticework of obligations that the press has to those whom it serves.

Reading, watching, and listening to the news are of varied importance to each person. One may treat a network television newscast as gospel, another may consider it mere propaganda. Most people's attitudes fall somewhere in between. But whatever the attitude toward the product, the consumption of news in one form or another is an integral part of American life. Even the professed news-hater may sit for hours avidly watching coverage of the O. J. Simpson trial. And someone who regards the local newscast as sensationalized trivia may read a half-dozen news magazines each week and devotedly watch C-SPAN's reports about politics.

Journalism's virtues—or lack thereof—depend to considerable extent on the eye of the beholder. That can make "ethical journalism" difficult to define. What one person considers to be good, aggressive reporting may seem to someone else to be unprincipled intrusiveness. Setting out to establish comprehensive rules that would precisely govern journalists' work is neither practical nor desirable; they almost certainly would be either too vague or too inhibiting to be useful.

But that doesn't mean that journalists should rely on situational ethics—a "hum a few bars and I'll fake it" approach to moral judgments. As is discussed in Chapter 1, the rights and responsibilities of journalists should be accompanied by a carefully reasoned loyalty to some theory or theories of ethics that can guide the day-to-day practice of the profession. The trick is to come up with a solid foundation on which flexible case-by-case applications can be built. As journalism moves into the new century, its ethical groundings need reinforcement, using a mix of classical theory and up-to-date practical application that takes into consideration new technologies, new constituencies, and the evolving relationship between news organizations and news consumers.

Even the most thoughtfully constructed ethical structure is certain to be tested by the constant storms of the news business. Although decked out in noble trappings, journalism remains a profit-driven industry. The concentration of news media ownership in the hands of a relatively small number of large corporations is likely to accelerate, particularly with looser federal regulation of the telecommunications industry. Before too long, chain ownership of television stations may approach the level of newspaper chain control.

That is not necessarily bad; a case can be made that more efficient management and higher profits will lead to a better news product. But clashes between financial and journalistic judgments will continue, particularly when the distance grows between news organization policymakers and news consumers. Some things will not change; the advertiser unhappy about a news story will always be ready to complain and threaten to pull ads. A larger concern, however, may be found in the conflicts of interest that are inherent in conglomerate ownership of news organizations.

For example, General Electric owns NBC. NBC's "Today" show omits from a news story about faulty aircraft engines the fact that a defective part was made by General Electric.[2] Even if such omissions are not caused by direct corporate pressure, journalists certainly know who signs their paychecks, and that may cause them to be more selective about what they report, treading carefully to avoid stomping on certain toes. This makes it more difficult to follow H. L. Mencken's prescription for journalists: "Comfort the afflicted and afflict the comfortable."

The prospect of financial gain also heightens the allure of tabloid journalism. Presumably a big audience will always exist for the sensational, intrusive, and gory. That may be so, and plenty of print and electronic vehicles deliver "flash and trash." It may be tempting to be ethically prissy about this and to denounce all in the news business who fall short of the highest standards of veracity and taste. But for the most part publications such as the *National Enquirer* and programs such as "A Current Affair" do little harm to those who enjoy them or even to the journalism purists who decry them. Those who find them annoying should remember that the "right to annoy" is an implicit corollary of the First Amendment.

Rather than sniff righteously about the purported transgressions of avowedly sensationalist papers and programs, the mainstream media should pay more attention to their own drift toward tabloidism. The commercial success of the tabloids may be a compelling inducement to adopt the same style and standards, but a merging of tabloid and mainstream journalism may leave the public with an indigestible stew. The reader of the *National Enquirer* should be able to know that other stories and other versions of the same story are available in the *Philadelphia Inquirer* and that coverage of even an inherently sensational story such as the O. J. Simpson trial will be different in the two papers. The papers' names may be similar, but their approaches to journalism have little in common. If the distinction becomes blurred, readers' options will dwindle. When, for instance, some mainstream news organizations followed the tabloids' lead in covering the Gennifer Flowers controversy during the 1992 presidential campaign, standards were sacrificed to expediency.

Within the next few years, the biggest threat of encroaching tabloidism will probably be in television, where the popularity of TV versions of the sensationalist papers has led some news executives to try to out-tabloid the tabloids. Local television news, in particular, has long been susceptible to the appeal of offering glitzy, simplistic coverage. The rationale seems to be that the largest audiences are to be captured by gearing news reports to an intellectual level slightly above that of a hamster. Given the quality of some newscasts, that may be an unfair knock on hamsters, but the point remains that true quality in journalism—as in other professions—can be elusive.

Evolving technology plays a role in this, as in so many other aspects of the news business. The expanding availability of live television pictures and the intrinsic drama they so often contain mean that news consumers are likely to be given ever stiffer doses of unedited reality. The abandonment of judgment in favor of speed is an ethically dangerous trade-off. Part of journalists' responsibility is to establish context so that readers or listeners or viewers can understand what they are reading or hearing or seeing. The capability to fast-forward that process may be progress in a technical sense, but not necessarily in an intellectual or ethical sense.

As is discussed in Chapter 4, among ethical standards that are most vulnerable to being overrun by tabloidism, respect for privacy ranks high. Journalists' perceived lack of respect for privacy also is near the top of complaint lists of people who don't like the news media. Some reporters use "the public's right to know" as a rationale for treating everyone's private life as public property. Whether the topic at hand is Bill Clinton's marriage or the ordeal of a crime victim, many news consumers do not want to know *everything*. Journalists and the public are out of synch about this.

As long as the disparity in values continues, more damage will be done to people's trust in those who gather news.

Along similar lines, techniques of news gathering also change, not always for the better. Again, technology sometimes drives this evolution. For instance, video cameras now are available that are so tiny that their undercover use is easy and—for some journalists—irresistible. Tabloid-style tactics of checkbook journalism, reenactments, ambush interviews, and other such measures tiptoe along the edge of dishonesty. Does the public need, want, or even like these ploys? Survey research indicates considerable impatience with deception as a journalistic tactic. Once again, news organizations should consider the virtues of restraint. The public's own ethical standards may not be as pliable as some journalists apparently assume them to be.

The news media have plenty to do without seeking to expand the definition of sleaze. The public will continue to count on journalists to perform traditional functions such as keeping a sharp eye on politicians. This is yet another journalistic field that is steadily changing. As is discussed in Chapter 6, news organizations grapple with a range of issues: reporting substance instead of being suckered by vacuous "media events"; ranking germaneness above titillation when covering candidates' "character"; deciding how much to rely on increasingly sophisticated polling in shaping coverage priorities; serving as referee to give the public some guidance when politicians make contradictory claims. The list goes on, seemingly forever.

The anger vented on talk radio and the dissatisfaction that helped produce nineteen million votes for an independent presidential candidate in 1992 are evidence of an uneasy electorate. It is not the job of the news media to say, "Everything is fine," but journalists do have a responsibility to make certain that people have thorough, accurate information on which to base their political decisions.

This is a daunting but not impossible task. More information is available than ever before about issues, campaigns, and how government works. In addition to the traditional array of print and electronic sources, newer players such as C-SPAN, computer networks, talk programs, and other emerging media offer a flood of news, data, and opinions. Part of the journalist's job is to help the public sort through all this—to clear the path between the availability of information and the acquisition of knowledge.

While improving the substance of the news product, journalists also might show more concern about the style with which they gather and present the news. Aggressive reporting and civility are not mutually exclusive; humane journalism is not an oxymoron; compassion is not an outmoded virtue.

Compassionate journalism can produce tangible as well as moral benefits. It may make subjects of coverage feel more comfortable about dealing with reporters and make them be willing to provide deeper, more insightful information. Of course, a reporter is not a caseworker; unpleasant truth is often an essential part of news stories. Balancing compassion and toughness is not easy, but it is a task that journalists should think about.

The nature of news gathering often makes this issue crucial to maintaining personal as well as professional moral integrity. You're a photojournalist covering the war in the former Yugoslavia, and one day in Sarajevo you are watching a seven-year-old boy playing just a few feet in front you. Suddenly, he is shot by a sniper. People instantly rush to his aid. First, you take a picture; after all, your job is to report the reality of the war. Then you join those trying to help the boy. Mortally wounded, he is taken to a hospital. You remain on the Sarajevo street, your clothing covered with his blood.

This may sound dramatic, but it is, sadly, a plausible scenario. As a human being, you're deeply shaken. That's the natural response. But as a journalist, what will you do? Having witnessed this shooting, can you remain objective, or will you—and your coverage—become biased, not about just this incident but also in your continuing reporting about the war? If so, if you do tilt your reporting, is that ethically wrong, or are you within moral bounds to put a partisan edge on your reporting to try to stir up a lethargic public? Journalists should be prepared to grapple with such issues. Answers will not come easily, but the questions still need to be addressed.

These issues are part of the larger issue of viewing news makers as human beings. Certainly, the journalist would feel compassion for the wounded child, but would that feeling lead you to refrain from interviewing the child's mother? Such restraint might seem compassionate; you want to leave her alone while she grieves. But in the aftermath of the shooting she might well have some compelling things to say about the war—things that your audience should hear. What would you do?

Such traditional dilemmas coexist in the news business with questions arising from the industry's constantly changing technologies. Throughout this book, questions about how stories are reported are based on matters of technique as well as content. In Chapter 8, much attention is paid to "real-time news." Live coverage of events satisfies the public's desire (real or perceived?) to get information as quickly as possible. News organizations such as CNN have built reputations on the ability to be fast and first.

The concept itself is marvelous—to be able to watch events throughout the world as they happen. But journalism involves more than mere delivery of information. Part of the job is to make discriminating judgments about newsworthiness and accuracy before passing "news" on to the public. This decision making can shrink or evaporate when speed is given precedence above all else. As technical capabilities expand even more, this issue of priorities will deserve continuing consideration from news executives.

Technology is not the only force behind change in the news business. Questions about what gets covered and who does the covering are receiving much attention from news organizations that take seriously the need to improve ties between themselves and the communities they serve.

For most of its history, the American news business has been dominated by Anglo men as journalists, subjects of coverage, and sources. Belatedly, it has occurred to those who run this industry that such reliance ensures a too-narrow view of the world. For the foreseeable future, news executives are likely to put new emphasis on diversity within their organizations and in defining the breadth of their coverage. Because of the news media's power, hiring and coverage decisions should include consideration of the importance of representativeness in gender, ethnicity, sexual orientation, ideology, and other characteristics.

Related to this are the fundamentals of "civic journalism," which in its best form emphasizes aggressive surrogacy—determining what the public wants and needs to know and then getting that information. In addition, it recognizes journalism's role in helping the public find solutions to the problems reported as news. When addressing hiring policies, community involvement, and other matters discussed in Chapter 9, news organizations should beware of detours into tokenism and self-promotion.

The greater the pervasiveness and influence of the news media, the greater the need to behave ethically. This may appear to be a simple formula, but in practice it is infinitely complex. Sometimes it may mean setting aside financial gain or changing long-established procedures in pursuit of vaguely noble goals that are more philosophical than pragmatic.

Ethical behavior has its price. But it also has its rewards: increased public trust in journalism, greater effectiveness in monitoring the sources of power in society, and more self-respect as an honorable profession.

Doing journalism is rarely easy. As Walter Lippmann wrote in 1931, that should come as no surprise: "For the ability to present news objectively and to interpret it realistically is not a native instinct in the human species; it is a product of culture which comes only with knowledge of the past and acute awareness of how deceptive is our normal observation and how wishful is our thinking."[3]

These challenges to the men and women who report and interpret the news may be daunting, but they also are energizing. The job is a difficult one, but it can be done. And it can be done ethically.

Appendix

Many news organizations have devised their own codes of ethics to state general principles and to govern employees' behavior. The following are excerpts from the guidelines adopted by the *Dallas Morning News.*

Dallas Morning News

*News Department Guidelines**

- Fairness: All sides of an issue should be included in any report. Every effort will be made to obtain a prompt, complete rebuttal where any accusations are made either against an individual or a company. Similar play will be given for initial accusations and their final resolutions. (For example, a trial is launched on the front page—then its verdict is also reported in a similar position on the front page.) Rebuttals are included in the main or deck portion of a headline as well as in the early paragraphs of a story, certainly before it jumps from the cover page of a section.
- Corrections and Clarifications: These will be published promptly after their accuracy is determined. Memos from appropriate staffers will explain how the error occurred. Every staffer is an ombudsman in this sense, and we pursue each complaint vigorously. Every complaining party must get a response, whether or not we publish a correction or clarification. The purpose is not punitive, but rather to ensure we do not repeat errors. Do not be defensive; simply explain what is correct or needs to be clarified.
- Freebies, Integrity, Products for Review: Freebies—do not accept them. Any gift should be returned to the sender or given to charity. Insignificant items ($10 and under) may be retained or disposed of as you wish. Do not abuse your position with the paper to obtain a better deal on goods and services. Products (books, recordings, videotapes) other

*"News Department Guidelines" reprinted by permission of the *Dallas Morning News.*

than those retained for review are sent to the appropriate public library.

- Plagiarism: Don't do it. This is a firing offense and includes lifting material from *Dallas Morning News* stories as well as other sources. This is lifting identical material and does not preclude using specific facts from research.
- Racism, Sexism: Racial identifications are used only when necessary to the story. Racial stereotypes and sexism have no place in this newspaper. Ignorance leads to insensitivity and is certainly no excuse.
- Public Relations: Respond promptly to all phone calls and letters. A reader's contact with you may be his or her only contact with this newspaper, so courtesy is essential. Newspapers must combat the perception of being aloof, arrogant and divorced from the community. . . .
- Obscenities: With few exceptions, we don't print them. Either the executive editor or managing editor must approve in advance any obscenity in this newspaper. Source and context will be considered. Obscenities offend many readers and we do not need to shock people. The English language is sufficiently varied for an educated writer.
- Sources: They should be fully identified and anonymous only when absolutely essential. Avoid off-the-record comments and reports. Do not commit this newspaper to publish any story on any particular date or on any particular page or section. . . . Unnamed sources must be aware that they could be identified in lawsuits. . . .
- Political Activity: Avoid any political activity, including contributions which would be on public record and could be used in endorsements without your knowledge. Do not run for office, speak or campaign for any candidate or in behalf of any issue except for professional journalism groups. This is not intended to discourage your voting.
- Obituaries: Be sensitive. Discuss with your editor any suicides or AIDS-related deaths. Be certain that any contacts related to a death are handled with care and sensitivity.

- Photographs, Graphics: Visuals have a tremendous impact on our readers. Follow good taste and good sense. As in many areas of taste, these should be discussed on their individual merits with appropriate photo editors.
- Expenses/Entertainment: We accept no free travel from businesses, governments, political parties or others. . . .
- Crime Victims, Arrests: Rape victims are not named. Crime victims may be protected by imprecise locations of homes such as blocks rather than specific house addresses. An arrested individual usually is not named until charges are filed. . . .
- Misrepresentation: No staffer will represent himself or herself as being anything other than a *Dallas Morning News* reporter, editor, photographer, artist, columnist or whatever with the paper. If for security or other reasons you must avoid identification, you must advise your editor in advance as soon as possible. The managing editor and executive editor must be notified.
- Police Relations: We neither have nor desire any police authority. We cooperate fully with all police. If you feel any public authority is interfering with your duties as a journalist, notify your editor immediately. Proper press identification is available to appropriate staffers and should not be abused.
- Our Name: Do not use the name of the *Dallas Morning News*, the paper's stationery or your business cards in any personal application. (For example, you do not identify yourself as a *News* staffer when complaining about poor service at a store.) The paper's name must not be used directly or by implication in your personal activities.
- Finally, no guidelines or codes can or should anticipate every situation. Individual cases require daily individual discussion. . . . We don't hesitate to take on tough, sensitive subjects. We have the experience and reputation to back up our work. Always be guided by fairness, accuracy and good common sense.

Radio-Television News Directors Association

Code of Ethics*

The responsibility of radio and television journalists is to gather and report information of importance and interest to the public accurately, honestly and impartially.

The members of the Radio-Television News Directors Association accept these standards and will:

1. Strive to present the source or nature of broadcast news material in a way that is balanced, accurate and fair.

   A. They will evaluate information solely on its merits as news, rejecting sensationalism or misleading emphasis in any form.
   B. They will guard against using audio or video material in a way that deceives the audience.
   C. They will not mislead the public by presenting as spontaneous news any material which is staged or rehearsed.
   D. They will identify people by race, creed, nationality or prior status only when it is relevant.
   E. They will clearly label opinion and commentary.
   F. They will promptly acknowledge and correct errors.
2. Strive to conduct themselves in a manner that protects them from conflicts of interest, real or perceived. They will decline gifts or favors which would influence or appear to influence their judgments.
3. Respect the dignity, privacy and well-being of people with whom they deal.
4. Recognize the need to protect confidential sources. They will promise confidentiality only with the intention of keeping that promise.

*RTNDA Code of Ethics, copyright by Radio-Television News Directors Association. Reproduced here with permission of RTNDA.

5. Respect everyone's right to a fair trial.
6. Broadcast the private transmissions of other broadcasters only with permission.
7. Actively encourage observance of this Code by all journalists, whether members of the Radio-Television News Directors Association or not.

Unanimously Adopted by the RTNDA Board of Directors
August 31, 1987

National Press Photographers Association

Code of Ethics*

The National Press Photographers Association, a professional society dedicated to the advancement of photojournalism, acknowledges concern and respect for the public's natural-law right to freedom in searching for the truth and the right to be informed truthfully and completely about public events and the world in which we live.

We believe that no report can be complete if it is not possible to enhance and clarify the meaning of words. We believe that pictures, whether used to depict news events as they actually happen, illustrate news that has happened or to help explain anything of public interest, are an indispensable means of keeping people accurately informed; that they help all people, young and old, to better understand any subject in the public domain.

Believing the foregoing we recognize and acknowledge that photojournalists should at all times maintain the highest standards of ethical conduct in serving the public interest. To that end the National Press Photographers Association sets forth the following Code of Ethics which is subscribed to by all of its members.

*Code of Ethics reprinted by permission of National Press Photographers Association.

1. The practice of photojournalism, both as a science and art, is worthy of the very best thought and effort of those who enter into it as a profession.
2. Photojournalism affords an opportunity to serve the public that is equaled by few other vocations and all members of the profession should strive by example and influence to maintain high standards of ethical conduct free of mercenary considerations of any kind.
3. It is the individual responsibility of every photojournalist at all times to strive for pictures that report truthfully, honestly and objectively.
4. Business promotion in its many forms is essential, but untrue statements of any nature are not worthy of a professional photojournalist and we severely condemn any such practice.
5. It is our duty to encourage and assist all members of our profession, individually and collectively, so that the quality of photojournalism may constantly be raised to higher standards.
6. It is the duty of every photojournalist to work to preserve all freedom-of-the-press rights recognized by law and to work to protect and expand freedom-of-access to all sources of news and visual information.
7. Our standards of business dealings, ambitions and relations shall have in them a note of sympathy for our common humanity and shall always require us to take into consideration our highest duties as members of society. In every situation in our business life, in every responsibility that comes before us, our chief thought shall be to fulfill that responsibility and discharge that duty so that when each of us is finished we shall have endeavored to leave the level of human ideals and achievement higher than we found it.
8. No Code of Ethics can prejudge every situation, thus common sense and good judgment are required in applying ethical principles.

The Society of Professional Journalists, Sigma Delta Chi

Code of Ethics*

The Society of Professional Journalists, Sigma Delta Chi, believes the duty of journalists is to serve the truth.

We BELIEVE the agencies of mass communication are carriers of public discussion and information, acting on their Constitutional mandate and freedom to learn and report the facts.

We BELIEVE in public enlightenment as the forerunner of justice, and in our Constitutional role to seek the truth as part of the public's right to know the truth.

We BELIEVE those responsibilities carry obligations that require journalists to perform with intelligence, objectivity, accuracy, and fairness.

To these ends, we declare acceptance of the standards of practice set forth:

I. Responsibility
The public's right to know of events of public importance and interest is the overriding mission of the mass media. The purpose of distributing news and enlightened opinion is to serve the general welfare. Journalists who use their professional status as representatives of the public for selfish or other unworthy motives violate a high trust.

II. Freedom of the Press
Freedom of the press is to be guarded as an alienable right of people in a free society. It carries with it the freedom and the responsibility to discuss, question, and challenge actions and utterances of our government and of our public and private institutions. Journalists uphold the right to speak unpopular opinions and the privilege to agree with the majority.

*Code of Ethics reprinted by permission of the Society of Professional Journalists.

III. Ethics

Journalists must be free of obligation to any interest other than the public's right to know.

1. Gifts, favors, free travel, special treatment or privileges can compromise the integrity of journalists and their employers. Nothing of value should be accepted.
2. Secondary employment, political involvement, holding public office, and service in community organizations should be avoided if it compromises the integrity of journalists and their employers. Journalists and their employers should conduct their personal lives in a manner that protects them from conflict of interest, real or apparent. Their responsibilities to the public are paramount. That is the nature of their profession.
3. So-called news communications from private sources should not be published or broadcast without substantiation of their claims to news values.
4. Journalists will seek news that serves the public interest, despite the obstacles. They will make constant efforts to assure that the public's business is conducted in public and that public records are open to public inspection.
5. Journalists acknowledge the newsman's ethic of protecting confidential sources of information.
6. Plagiarism is dishonest and unacceptable.

IV. Accuracy and Objectivity

Good faith with the public is the foundation of all worthy journalism.

1. Truth is our ultimate goal.
2. Objectivity in reporting the news is another goal that serves as the mark of an experienced professional. It is a standard of performance toward which we strive. We honor those who achieve it.
3. There is no excuse for inaccuracies or lack of thoroughness.
4. Newspaper headlines should be fully warranted by the contents of the articles they accompany. Photographs and

telecasts should give an accurate picture of an event and not highlight an incident out of context.

5. Sound practices makes clear distinction between news reports and expressions of opinion. News reports should be free of opinion or bias and represent all sides of an issue.

6. Partisanship in editorial comment that knowingly departs from the truth violates the spirit of American journalism.

7. Journalists recognize their responsibility for offering informed analysis, comment, and editorial opinion on public events and issues. They accept the obligation to present such material by individuals whose competence, experience, and judgment qualify them for it.

8. Special articles or presentations devoted to advocacy or the writer's own conclusions and interpretations should be labeled as such.

V. Fair Play
Journalists at all times will show respect for the dignity, privacy rights, and well-being of people encountered in the course of gathering and presenting the news.

1. The news media should not communicate unofficial charges affecting reputation or moral character without giving the accused a chance to reply.

2. The news media must guard against invading a person's right to privacy.

3. The media should not pander to morbid curiosity about details of vice and crime.

4. It is the duty of news media to make prompt and complete correction of their errors.

5. Journalists should be accountable to the public for their reports and the public should be encouraged to voice its grievances against the media. Open dialogue with our readers, viewers, and listeners should be fostered.

VI. Pledge
Adherence to this code is intended to preserve and strengthen the bond of mutual trust and respect between American journalists and the American people.

The Society shall—by programs of education and other means—encourage individual journalists to adhere to these tenets, and shall encourage journalistic publications and broadcasters to recognize their responsibility to frame codes of ethics in concert with their employees to serve as guidelines in furthering these goals.

Code of Ethics adopted in 1926; revised 1973, 1984, 1987

American Society of Newspaper Editors

A Statement of Principles*

Preamble

The First Amendment, protecting freedom of expression from abridgment by any law, guarantees to the people through their press a constitutional right, and thereby places on newspaper people a particular responsibility.

Thus journalism demands of its practitioners not only industry and knowledge but also the pursuit of a standard of integrity proportionate to the journalist's singular obligation.

To this end the American Society of Newspaper Editors sets forth this Statement of Principles as a standard encouraging the highest ethical and professional performance.

ARTICLE I—Responsibility

The primary purpose of gathering and distributing news and opinion is to serve the general welfare by informing the people and enabling them to make judgments on the issues of the time. Newspapermen and women who abuse the power of their professional role for selfish motives or unworthy purposes are faithless to that public trust.

The American press was made free not just to inform or just to serve as a forum for debate but also to bring an independent scrutiny to bear on the forces of power in the society, including the conduct of official power at all levels of government.

*Code of Ethics reprinted with permission of the American Society of Newspaper Editors.

ARTICLE II—Freedom of the Press
Freedom of the press belongs to the people. It must be defended against encroachment or assault from any quarter, public of private.

Journalists must be constantly alert to see that the public's business is conducted in public. They must be vigilant against all who would exploit the press for selfish purposes.

ARTICLE III—Independence
Journalists must avoid impropriety and the appearance of impropriety as well as any conflict of interest or the appearance of conflict. They should neither accept anything nor pursue any activity that might compromise or seem to compromise their integrity.

ARTICLE IV—Truth and Accuracy
Good faith with the reader is the foundation of good journalism. Every effort must be made to assure that the news content is accurate, free from bias and in context, and that all sides are presented fairly. Editorials, analytical articles and commentary should be held to the same standards of accuracy with respect to facts as news reports.

Significant errors of fact, as well as errors of omission, should be corrected promptly and prominently.

ARTICLE V—Impartiality
To be impartial does not require the press to be unquestioning or to refrain from editorial expression. Sound practice, however, demands a clear distinction for the reader between news reports and opinion. Articles that contain opinion or personal interpretation should be clearly identified.

ARTICLE VI—Fair Play
Journalists should respect the rights of people involved in the news, observe the common standards of decency and stand accountable to the public for the fairness and accuracy of their news reports.

Persons publicly accused should be given the earliest opportunity to respond.

Pledges of confidentiality to news sources must be honored at all costs, and therefore should not be given lightly. Unless there is clear and pressing need to maintain confidences, sources of information should be identified.

These principles are intended to preserve, protect and strengthen the bond of trust and respect between American journalists and the American people, a bond that is essential to sustain the grant of freedom entrusted to both by the nation's founders.

This statement of Principles was adopted by the ASNE board of directors, Oct. 23, 1975; it supplants the 1922 Code of Ethics ("Canons of Journalism").

Notes

Chapter One

1. Philip Seib and Kathy Fitzpatrick, *Public Relations Ethics* (Fort Worth: Harcourt Brace College Publishers, 1995), 29.
2. Herbert Strentz, *News Reporters and News Sources* (2nd ed.) (Ames, Iowa: Iowa State, 1989), 4.
3. Ralph D. Barney, "Responsibilities of a Journalist: An Ethical Construct," *Mass Communications Review* 14(3) (1987), 18–19.
4. Philip Patterson and Lee Wilkins, *Media Ethics* (Dubuque, Iowa: Wm. C. Brown Publishers, 1991), 106.
5. Ibid.
6. See Clifford G. Christians, Mark Fackler, and Kim B. Rotzoll, *Media Ethics* (3rd ed.) (White Plains, N.Y.: Longman, 1991), for additional discussion on ethical philosophies.
7. Carl Hausman, *Crisis of Conscience* (New York: HarperCollins, 1992), 24.
8. See Marlin Shipman, "Putting Ethics to Work: Applying Two Codes of Ethics to the Question of Whether Executions Should Be Televised or Photographed," presented at the Association for Education in Journalism and Mass Communications Southeast Colloquium, March 4, 1994, for an examination of how this ethical issue might be resolved. See also Cynthia Barnett, "Covering Executions," *American Journalism Review* (May 1995), 26–31.
9. Christians et al., *Media Ethics*, 3.
10. See Gene Goodwin and Ron F. Smith, *Groping for Ethics in Journalism* (3rd ed.)

(Ames, Iowa: Iowa State, 1994), 29.

11. Michael Josephson, "Teaching Ethical Decision Making and Principled Reasoning," in *Business Ethics (Annual Editions 1993–1994* (Guilford, Conn.: Dushkin, 1993), 15.

12. John L. Hulteng, *Playing It Straight* (Chester, Conn.: Globe Pequot, 1981), 80.

13. Patterson and Wilkins, *Media Ethics*, 29.

14. Christians et al., *Media Ethics*, 11.

15. See, e.g., Daniel Brudney, "Two Links of Law and Morality," *Ethics* 103(2) (January 1993), 301.

16. See, e.g., Leonard J. Brooks, "Corporate Codes of Ethics," *Journal of Business Ethics* (February/March 1989), 117.

17. Andrew Belsey and Ruth Chadwick, *Ethical Issues in Journalism and the Media* (London: Routledge, 1992), 8.

18. See, e.g., John Galey, "Society of Professional Journalists' Code of Ethics: Influences of Criticism and Professionalism," presented at the Association for Education in Journalism and Mass Communications Southeast Colloquium, March 5, 1994.

19. Ibid., 11.

20. Ibid.

21. See, e.g., Galey, "Society of Professional Journalists," and Appendix.

22. Deni Elliott, "Creating the Conditions for Ethical Journalism," *Mass Communications Review* 14(3) (1987), 6.

23. Jay Black, Bob Steele, and Ralph Barney, *Doing Ethics in Journalism* (Needham Heights, Mass.: Allyn & Bacon, 1995).

24. David Boeyink, "How Effective Are Codes of Ethics? A Look at Three Newsrooms," *Journalism Quarterly* (Winter 1995), 902–903.

25. Richard L. Johannesen, *Ethics in Human Communication* (3rd ed.) (Prospect Heights, Ill.: Waveland, 1990), 169–170.

26. Philip Seib and Kathy Fitzpatrick, *Public Relations Ethics*, 24.

27. Brian Richardson, "Four Standards for Teaching Ethics in Journalism," *Journal of Mass Media Ethics* 9(2) (1994), 110.

28. Ibid.

29. Robert Schmuhl, "Introduction: The Road to Responsibility," *The Responsibilities of Journalism* (Notre Dame, Ind.: University of Notre Dame Press, 1995), 13–14.

30. Clarence Pennington, "Revise and Boil Down Declaration of Ethics," *Nieman Reports* (Summer 1994), 66.

31. Louis A. Day, *Ethics in Media Communications: Cases and Controversies* (Belmont, Calif.: Wadsworth, 1991), 28.

32. *New World Dictionary,* 2nd college ed. (Cleveland: William Collins Publishers, 1979), 1134.

33. Jeffrey Olen, *Ethics in Journalism* (Englewood Cliffs: Prentice-Hall, 1988), 30.

34. Philip Seib and Kathy Fitzpatrick, *Public Relations Ethics,* 121.

35. Norman E. Isaacs, "20 Years Later: 33 Ombudsmen," *Washington Journalism Review* (October 1978), 40.

36. James P. Gannon, "Betrayal: Media 'Scandal' Erodes Public Confidence," *Detroit News,* February 14, 1993, 1A.

37. Martha Fitzsimon and Lawrence T. McGill, "The Citizen as Media Critic," *Media Studies Journal* (Spring 1995), 101.

38. Ibid., 91.

39. Michael J. Robinson and Norman J. Ornstein, "Why Press Credibility Is Going Down," *Washington Journalism Review* (January/February 1990), 34.

40. Lou Hodges, "Cases and Commentaries," *Journal of Mass Media Ethics* 9(4) (Fall 1992), 173–181.

Chapter Two

1. William Glaberson, "Departures at Paper Ignite Debate on Owners' Priorities," *New York Times,* February 15, 1995, C16.

2. Alicia C. Shepard, "Geneva Talks," *American Journalism Review* (September 1995), 31–33.

3. Glaberson, "Departures at Paper Ignite Debate on Owners' Priorities," C1.

4. Ben H. Bagdikian, *The Media Monopoly* (4th ed.) (Boston: Beacon Press, 1992), xxxi.

5. Marc Gunther, "All in the Family," *American Journalism Review* (October 1995), 37–41.

6. Ed Bark, "Deal Puts ABC in Prickly Spot," *Dallas Morning News,* August 6, 1995, 1C/3C.

7. Ibid., 3C.

8. Michael J. O'Neill, "Who Cares About the Truth?" *Nieman Reports* (Spring 1994), 14.

9. Jacqueline Sharkey, "Judgment Calls," *American Journalism Review* (September 1994), 20.

10. Ibid.

11. See Jonathan Kwitny, "The High Cost of High Profits," *Washington Journalism Review* (June 1990), 19–29.

12. "ABC Altered TV Images for Jackson," *Dallas Morning News*, June 26, 1995, 27A.

13. Ibid.

14. Karl Idsvoog, "TV Sitting on Stories to Improve Ratings," *Nieman Reports* (Spring 1994), 38.

15. Ibid.

16. Ibid.

17. Bill Winter, "Another View on New Journalism," *Editor & Publisher*, April 4, 1992, 50.

18. Leonard Silk, "The Ethics and Economics of Journalism," in *The Responsibilities of Journalism* (South Bend, Ind.: University of Notre Dame Press, 1994), 49–50.

19. John McManus, "Serving the Public and Serving the Market," *Journal of Mass Media Ethics* (Winter 1992), 196.

20. Warren K. Agee, Philip H. Ault, and Edwin Emery, *Introduction to Mass Communication* (New York: HarperCollins, 1994), 100.

21. Bagdikian, *The Media Monopoly*, 232.

22. Robert W. Snyder, Jennifer Kelley, and Dirk Smillie, "Critics with Clout— Nine Who Matter," *Media Studies Journal* (Spring 1995), 11–12.

23. Jonathan Cohn, "Perrier in the Newsroom," *The American Prospect* (Spring 1995), 15.

24. Richard Harwood, "Are Journalists Elitist?" *American Journalism Review* (June 1995), 29.

25. Ed Bark, "Channel 5 Suspends Snyder After Rally Remarks," *Dallas Morning News*, August 30, 1994, 1A.

26. Ibid., 9A.

27. Ken Auletta, "Fee Speech," *The New Yorker*, September 12, 1994, 40.

28. Alicia C. Shepard, "Take the Money and Talk," *American Journalism Review* (June 1995), 21.

29. Alicia C. Shepard, "Bradlee," *American Journalism Review* (March 1995), 42.

30. Shepard, "Take the Money and Talk," 21.

31. Ibid., 23.

32. Auletta, "Fee Speech," 47.

33. Silk, "The Ethics and Economics of Journalism," 86.

Chapter Three

1. Philip Seib and Kathy Fitzpatrick, *Public Relations Ethics,* 71.

2. See Jeff Blyskal and Marie Blyskal, *PR: How the Public Relations Industry Writes the News* (New York: William Morrow, 1985), 46.

3. Lynne Masel Walters and Timothy N. Walters, "Environment of Confidence: Newspaper Daily Use of Press Releases," *Public Relations Review* (Spring 1992), 36.

4. See Doug Newsome, Alan Scott and Judy VanSlyke Turk, *This Is PR: The Realities of Public Relations* (5th ed.) (Belmont, Calif.: Wadsworth, 1992), 248.

5. Michael Ryan and David L. Martinson, "Public Relations Practitioners, Journalists View Lying Similarly," *Journalism Quarterly* 71(1) (Spring 1994), 210.

6. Ibid.

7. Dennis W. Jeffers, "Performance Expectations as a Measure of Relative Status of News and PR People," *Journalism Quarterly* (Summer 1977), 306.

8. Mary Anne Ramer, "A PR Practitioner's Memo to Journalists," *Editor & Publisher,* October 10, 1992, 64.

9. See David L. Martinson, "How Should the PR Practitioner Respond When Confronted with Unethical Journalistic Behavior?" *Public Relations Quarterly* (Summer 1995), 19.

10. Ibid., 20–21.

11. Ramer, "A PR Practitioner's Memo," 64.

12. Lee W. Baker, *The Credibility Factor: Putting Ethics to Work in Public Relations* (Homewood, Ill.: Business One Irwin, 1993), 122–127.

13. Ibid., 121.

14. Ibid.

15. Ibid., 123.

16. Ibid., 124.

17. Robert M. Bleiberg, "Turned Off, Tuned Out," *Barron's*, May 20, 1991, 10.

18. Laura Bird, "First Advertorials; Now Advernewscasts," *Wall Street Journal*, September 29, 1994, B14.

19. Dennis L. Wilcox, Philip H. Ault, and Warren K. Agee, *Public Relations Strategies and Tactics* (4th ed.) (New York: HarperCollins, 1995), 630.

20. Ibid., 132.

21. Bird, "First Advertorials," B1.

22. Wilcox et al., *Public Relations Strategies and Tactics*, 133.

23. Bird, "First Advertorials," B14.

24. See, e.g., George E. Belch and Michael A. Belch, *Introduction to Advertising and Promotion* (2nd ed.) (Homewood, Ill.: Business One Irwin, 1993), 825.

25. Alicia Shepard, "Those Sensitive Auto Dealers Strike Again, and Another Newspaper Caves," *American Journalism Review* (September 1994), 14.

26. Ibid.

27. Hulteng, *Playing It Straight*, 78.

28. Shepard, "Those Sensitive Auto Dealers," 15.

29. Lawrence C. Soley and Robert L. Craig, "Advertising Pressures on Newspapers: A Survey," *Journal of Advertising* (December 1992), 1.

30. Ibid.

31. Ann Marie Kerwin, "Behind the Waltzing," *Editor & Publisher*, June 13, 1992, 18.

32. "Ad Pressure on Writers," *Editor & Publisher*, June 13, 1992, 6.

33. Kerwin, "Behind the Waltzing," 6.

34. Mike Haggerty and Wallace Rasmussen, *The Headline vs. The Bottom Line: Mutual Distrust Between Business and the News Media* (Arlington, Va.: The Freedom Forum, 1995), 85.

35. Ibid., 88.

Chapter Four

1. Lexington, "One Nation Under O. J.," *The Economist*, July 16, 1994, 30.

2. Ibid.

3. Jacqueline Sharkey, "Interviews for Sale," *American Journalism Review* (September 1994), 22.

4. Molly Ivins, "The Pea and the Shell," *The Progressive* (March 1994), 46.

5. Mortimer B. Zuckerman, "Behind the Paula Jones Story," *U.S. News & World Report,* May 23, 1994, 82.

6. Ibid.

7. Joe Saltzman, "Tabloid Hysteria," *USA Today* (May 1994), 21.

8. Mitchell Stephens, *A History of News* (New York: Viking, 1988), 204.

9. Oliver Carlson, *The Man Who Made News: James Gordon Bennett* (New York: Duell, Sloan and Pearce, 1942), 168.

10. Ibid., 185.

11. Ibid., 169.

12. Charles Dickens, *Martin Chuzzlewit* (Oxford: Oxford University Press, 1981), 256.

13. Richard Harwood, "Read All About It," *Washington Post,* July 13, 1994, A25.

14. Philip Weiss, "Bad Rap for TV Tabs," *Columbia Journalism Review* (May/June 1989), 38.

15. Joshua Gamson, "Incredible News," *The American Prospect* (Fall 1994), 31.

16. Jack W. Germond and Jules Witcover, *Mad As Hell* (New York: Warner, 1993), 173.

17. Jerry Nachman, "Look at Tonya and Nancy," *New York Times Magazine,* June 26, 1994, 34.

18. Ibid.

19. Sharkey, "Interviews for Sale," 20.

20. Ibid.

21. Mike Tharp and Betsy Streisand, "Tabloid TV's Blood Lust," *U.S. News & World Report,* July 25, 1994, 48.

22. Ibid.

23. Carl Hiassen, "Media and Public Deserve Each Other in O. J. Fiasco," *Dallas Morning News,* June 24, 1994, 21A.

24. Everette E. Dennis, "Simpson Coverage Makes for Bad Television," *Communique* (November 1994), 2.

25. William Glaberson, "Times Criticized for Use of Tabloid Account," *New York Times,* December 23, 1994, A9.

26. Jonathan Alter, "They're on Candid Camera," *Newsweek,* October 31, 1994, 59.

27. Gamson, "Incredible News," 31.

28. Jonathan Cohn, "Diary of the American Nightmare," *The American Prospect* (Fall 1994), 36.

29. Ibid., 37.

30. Thomas E. Patterson, *Out of Order* (New York: Vintage, 1994), 140.

31. Ron LaBrecque, "Stay Tuned for the Execution of Robert Harris," *Washington Journalism Review* (June 1991), 35.

32. Ibid., 37.

33. Richard Lacayo, "Tarting Up the Gray Lady of 43rd Street," *Time*, May 6, 1991, 44.

34. Meg Greenfield, "In Defense of Sensationalism," *Newsweek*, September 26, 1994, 72.

35. "Indecent Exposure," *The New Yorker*, May 23, 1994, 6.

36. Paula LaRocque, "The Excesses of Tabloid Journalism Can Be Contagious," *Quill* (January/February 1994), 58.

37. Nancy E. Bernhard, "The Lecher, the Witch and the Weirdo," *Nieman Reports* (Summer 1993), 16.

38. Ibid., 18.

39. Ibid., 20.

40. Jay Black, Bob Steele, and Ralph Barney, *Doing Ethics in Journalism* (Needham Heights, Mass.: Allyn & Bacon, 1995), 157.

41. Ibid.

42. Harold Evans, "Facing a Grim Reality," *American Photo* (May/June 1991), 48.

43. "Story Dilemma for TV," *Society of Professional Journalists 1987-88 Ethics Report*, 5.

44. Scott J. Higham, "Photos a Dilemma for Press," *Allentown Morning Call*, January 23, 1987, A2.

45. Ibid.

46. Fred Behringer, "Press Debates Photo Use," *Society of Professional Journalists 1987–88 Ethics Report*, 6.

47. Ibid.

48. Edwin Guthman, "Why the Inquirer Ran Those Budd Dwyer Photos," *Philadelphia Inquirer*, February 1, 1987, 7F.

49. Ibid.

50. Fred Behringer, "Dwyer Suicide Called a 'Statement' to Press," *Society of Professional Journalists 1987–88 Ethics Report*, 4.

51. Chevel Johnson, "Televised Suicide Raises Questions About TV Journalism," Associated Press wire, September 16, 1994.

52. Roy Peter Clark, "Natural Born Killers," *New York Times*, October 14, 1994, A17.

53. Jim Upshaw and John Russial, "See No Evil?" *Columbia Journalism Review* (January/February 1994), 9.

54. Ibid.

55. Richard P. Cunningham, "Seeking a Time-Out on Prurience," *Quill* (March 1992), 6.

56. Ibid.

57. Gene Goodwin and Ron F. Smith, *Groping for Ethics in Journalism* (3rd ed.), (Ames, Iowa: Iowa State, 1994), 250.

58. Ibid., 251.

59. Carl Sessions Stepp, "When a Public Figure's Private Life Is News," *Washington Journalism Review* (December 1986), 40.

60. Goodwin and Smith, *Groping for Ethics*, 252.

61. Lou Prato, "It Was Like a Shark Attack," *American Journalism Review* (May 1994), 48.

62. Marguerite Johnston, "David X," *Columbia Journalism Review* (May 1984), 9.

63. Louise Mengelkoch, "When Checkbook Journalism Does God's Work," *Columbia Journalism Review* (November/December 1994), 38.

Chapter Five

1. Nancy Doyle Palmer, "Going After the Truth—In Disguise," *Washington Journalism Review* (November 1987), 20.

2. Goodwin and Smith, *Groping for Ethics*, 136.

3. Ibid., 141.

4. Tom Goldstein, *The News at Any Cost* (New York: Simon & Schuster, 1985), 131.

5. Steve Robinson, "Pulitzers: Was the Mirage a Deception?" *Columbia Journalism Review* (July/August 1979), 16.

6. Marcel Dufresne, "To Sting or Not to Sting?" *Columbia Journalism Review* (May/June 1991), 50.

7. Goldstein, *The News at Any Cost,* 144.

8. Robinson, "Pulitzers," 14.

9. Sissela Bok, *Secrets: On the Ethics of Concealment and Revelation* (New York: Pantheon, 1982), 264.

10. Russ W. Baker, "Truth, Lies, and Videotape," *Columbia Journalism Review* (July/August 1993), 27.

11. Howard Kurtz, "Hidden Network Cameras: A Troubling Trend?" *Washington Post* (November 30, 1992), A4.

12. Baker, "Truth, Lies," 28.

13. Kurtz, "Hidden Network Cameras," A4.

14. Colman McCarthy, "Getting the Truth Untruthfully," *Washington Post,* December 22, 1992, D21.

15. Kurtz, "Hidden Network Cameras," A4.

16. Robert Lissit, "Gotcha!" *American Journalism Review* (March 1995), 20.

17. Baker, "Truth, Lies," 28.

18. Kurtz, "Hidden Network Cameras," A1.

19. Goodwin and Smith, *Groping for Ethics,* 184.

20. Black, Steele, and Barney, *Doing Ethics,* 126.

21. "A Discussion of Newspaper Ethics for Associated Press Managing Editors," presented to APME members September 23, 1993, 48.

22. Goodwin and Smith, *Groping for Ethics,* 193.

23. Ibid., 194.

24. Goldstein, *The News at Any Cost,* 110.

25. Neil Postman and Steve Powers, *How to Watch TV News* (New York: Penguin, 1992), 89.

26. Ibid., 92.

27. Goodwin and Smith, *Groping for Ethics,* 201.

28. *New York Times Co. v. United States,* 403 U.S. 713 (1971).

29. "A Discussion of Newspaper Ethics," 44.

30. Sissela Bok, *Lying: Moral Choice in Public and Private Life* (New York: Pantheon, 1978), 121.

31. William Safire, "Pleasure of My Company," *New York Times,* August 14, 1984, 15.

32. Goodwin and Smith, *Groping for Ethics,* 111.

33. "A Discussion of Newspaper Ethics," 59.

34. Stephen D. Reese, August Grant, and Lucig H. Danielian, "The Structure of News Sources on Television," *Journal of Communication* (Spring 1994), 85.

35. Alicia C. Shepard, "Anonymous Sources," *American Journalism Review* (December 1994), 23.

36. Marvin Kalb, *The Nixon Memo* (Chicago: University of Chicago, 1994), 64.

37. Shepard, "Anonymous Sources," 20.

38. David S. Broder, *Behind the Front Page* (New York: Simon & Schuster, 1987), 319.

39. Shepard, "Anonymous Sources," 24.

40. Ibid., 20.

41. Ibid., 22.

42. Gene Foreman, "Confidential Sources: Testing the Readers' Confidence," *Social Responsibility: Business, Journalism, Law, Medicine,* 10 (1984), 24.

43. Monica Langley and Lee Levine, "Broken Promises," *Columbia Journalism Review* (July/August) 1988, 22.

44. Bill Salisbury, "Burning the Source," *Washington Journalism Review* (September 1991), 22.

45. Larry Bodine, "Broken Promises," *Quill* (March 1991), 32.

46. Lawrence Savell, "Cover Yourself When You 'Mask' Sources," *Editor & Publisher,* October 23, 1993, 3.

47. Black, Steele, and Barney, *Doing Ethics,* 11.

48. Bill O'Reilly, "We Pay for News. We Have To," *New York Times,* February 26, 1994, 17.

49. Sharkey, "Interviews for Sale," 22.

50. Jeffrey Toobin, "Cash for Trash," *New Yorker,* July 11, 1994, 38.

51. Bruce Selcraig, "Buying News," *Columbia Journalism Review* (July/August 1994), 45.

52. Ibid.

53. Mengelkoch, "When Checkbook Journalism," 38.

54. Walter Lippmann, *Public Opinion* (New York: Free Press, 1965), 226.

55. Kevin McManus, "The, Uh, Quotation Quandary," *Columbia Journalism Review* (May/June 1990), 54.

56. Ralph L. Holsinger and Jon Paul Dilts, *Media Law* (3rd ed.) (New York: McGraw-Hill, 1994), 186.

57. McManus, "The, Uh, Quotation Quandary," 56.

Chapter Six

1. Lippmann, *Public Opinion,* 229.

2. Peter Arnett, *Live from the Battlefield* (New York: Simon & Schuster, 1994), 90.

3. James Deakin, *Straight Stuff* (New York: William Morrow, 1984), 88.

4. Simon Serfaty, "Neither Hero Nor Villain," in Simon Serfaty (ed.), *The Media and Foreign Policy* (New York: St. Martin's, 1991), 230.

5. Jon Hall, "Stop! This Is a Warning . . . Suppressing News at Police Request," *Fine Line* (October 1989), 6.

6. Ibid.

7. Robin DeRose, "95 Million Tune In O. J. Televised Chase," *USA Today*, June 22, 1994), D3.

8. Dennis Moore, "Newsmags Score Big with O. J. Stories," *USA Today*, June 29, 1994, D3.

9. "Headline Grabbers," *USA Today* (June 21, 1994), A1.

10. M. L. Stein, "Can O. J. Get a Fair Trial?" *Editor & Publisher* (July 9, 1994), 9.

11. B. Drummond Ayres, Jr., "Court of Public Opinion Is First to Try Simpson," *New York Times*, June 21, 1994, A6.

12. Stein, "Can O. J. Get a Fair Trial?" 33.

13. Kathy Fitzpatrick and Alice Kendrick, "Public Perception of Media Coverage of the O. J. Simpson Story One Week After 'The Chase,'" *Southwestern Journal of Mass Communication* (October 1995), 81.

14. Forrest Sawyer, "ABC's Nightline," January 13, 1995.

15. A. M. Rosenthal, "The Press and Simpson," *New York Times*, June 6, 1994, A11.

16. Bill Thompson, "Trial by Headline Is Not What Justice Is Supposed to Be About," *Tampa Tribune-Times*, June 19, 1994, 3.

17. Jerome Berger, "Hit-and-Run Journalism," *Nieman Reports* (Summer 1994), 67.

18. Steve McClellan and Steve Coe, "TV Chases Another Hot Story," *Broadcasting and Cable*, June 27, 1994, 20.

19. John L. Hulteng, *Playing It Straight* (Chester, Conn.: Globe Pequot, 1981), 5.

20. Peter A. Levin, "You Want Me to Read a What?" *Media Studies Journal* (Fall 1992), 173.

21. Ibid

22. Joann Byrd, "Gaga Over O. J. Simpson," *Washington Post*, October 16, 1994, A22.

23. *Sheppard v. Maxwell*, 384 U.S. 333 (1986).

24. Ralph Frasca, "Estimating the Occurrence of Trials Prejudiced by Press Coverage," *Judicature* (October/November 1988), 162.

25. *Press Enterprise Co. v. Riverside County Superior Court*, 464 U.S. 501 (1984).

26. *Richmond Newspapers, Inc. v. Virginia*, 448 U.S. 555 (1980).

27. Carole Gorney, "Litigation Journalism Is a Scourge," *New York Times*,

February 15, 1994, A21.

28. Archibald Cox, "Freedom of the Press," *University of Illinois Law Review*, 1 (1983), 5.

29. John C. Merrill, "Good Reporting and Ethics," *Journalism Educator*, 42 (1987), 28.

30. "Naming the Victim," *Columbia Journalism Review* (July/August 1991), 54.

31. Al Neuharth, "O. J. Drama Gives Us Media's Best, Worst," *USA Today*, June 24, 1994, 11A.

32. Lyle Denniston, *The Reporter and the Law: Techniques of Covering the Courts* (New York: Hastings House, 1980), xvii.

33. Timothy Crouse, *The Boys on the Bus* (New York: Random House, 1973), 8.

34. Austin Ranney, *Channels of Power* (New York: Basic Books, 1983), 86.

35. Michael Kinsley, "Election Day Fraud on Television," *Time*, November 23, 1992, 84.

36. Gail Sheehy, *Character* (New York: Morrow, 1988), 12.

37. Germond and Witcover, *Mad as Hell*, 474.

38. Philip Seib, *Campaigns and Conscience* (New York: Praeger, 1994), 55.

39. Tom Rosenstiel, *Strange Bedfellows* (New York: Hyperion, 1993), 66.

40. Ibid., 69.

41. Ibid., 70.

42. Ibid., 66.

43. Davis Merritt, *Public Journalism and Public Life* (Hillsdale, N.J.: Lawrence Erlbaum Associates, 1995), 61.

44. Debra Gersh, "News Reports More Important Than Commercials," *Editor & Publisher*, October 31, 1992, 23.

45. Mark Crispin Miller, "Political Ads: Decoding Hidden Messages," *Columbia Journalism Review* (January/February 1992), 36.

46. Seib, *Campaigns and Conscience*, 102.

47. Rosenstiel, *Strange Bedfellows*, 273.

48. James Boylan, "Where Have All the People Gone?" *Columbia Journalism Review* (May/June 1991), 33.

Chapter Seven

1. Jane Schorer, "The Story Behind a Landmark Story of Rape," *Washington*

Journalism Review (June 1991), 21.

2. Ibid., 22.

3. Martin J. Smith, "Media as God," *Quill* (November/December 1993), 22.

4. Ibid.

5. Jim Sachetti, "We Can't Back Off When the Reporting Is Tough," *Pennsylvania Newspaper Publishers' Association Press* (January 1995), 3.

6. Gypsy Hogan, "Covering the Catastrophe," *Editor & Publisher*, June 10, 1995, 16.

7. Ibid.

8. Schorer, "The Story Behind," 21.

9. Charles B. Seib, "Could a Little Caring Have Prevented a Hoax?" *Presstime* (June 1981), 35.

10. Ibid.

11. Ibid.

12. Fawn Germer, "'How Do You Feel?'" *American Journalism Review* (June 1995), 39.

13. Goodwin and Smith, *Groping for Ethics*, 321.

14. Eddie Adams, "The Tet Photo," in A. Santoli (ed.), *To Bear Any Burden* (New York: Ballantine, 1985), 184.

15. Steve Lehman, "Eyewitness to Carnage," *Newsweek*, January 9, 1995, 48.

16. Jim Wooten, "Parachuting into Madness," *Columbia Journalism Review* (November/December 1994), 46.

17. Ibid.

18. Ibid., 47.

19. Scott Williams, "TV Doctor Saves Rwanda Youngster," Associated Press wire, August 16, 1994.

20. Arnett, *Live from the Battlefield*, 119.

21. Ibid.

Chapter Eight

1. Arnett, *Live from the Battlefield*, 405.

2. Alicia Shepard, "An American in Paris (and Moscow and Berlin and Tokyo . . .)," *American Journalism Review* (April 1994), 23.

3. Ibid.

4. Lawrence K. Grossman, "A Television Plan for the Next War," *Nieman Reports*

(Summer 1991), 27.

5. Richard Reeves, *President Kennedy* (New York: Simon & Schuster, 1993), 213.

6. Grossman, "A Television Plan," 27.

7. Brent Baker, "Decisions at the Speed of TV Satellites," *Vital Speeches,* July 15, 1992, 582.

8. Ibid., 581.

9. Grossman, "A Television Plan," 28.

10. Baker, "Decisions at the Speed," 583.

11. Bernard Kalb, "Follow That Tank!" *Media Studies Journal* (Winter 1995), 120.

12. Grossman, "A Television Plan," 30.

13. Katherine Fulton, "A New Agenda for Journalism," *Nieman Reports* (Spring 1994), 16.

14. Tom Rosenstiel, "The Myth of CNN," *The New Republic,* August 22/29, 1994, 33.

15. Sarah Midgley and Virginia Rice (eds.), *Terrorism and the Media in the 1980's* (Washington: The Media Institute, 1984), 19.

16. Terry Anderson, "Terrorism and Censorship: The Media in Chains," *Journal of International Affairs* (Summer 1993), 128.

17. Michael J. O'Neill, *Terrorist Spectaculars* (New York: Priority Press, 1986), 33.

18. Ibid., 35.

19. Ibid., 63.

20. Anderson, "Terrorism and Censorship," 135.

21. Rosenstiel, "The Myth of CNN," 28.

22. Robert Wiener, *Live from Baghdad* (New York: Doubleday, 1992), 194.

23. Ibid., 253.

24. Michael Gartner, "Why Risk Enhancing News?" *USA Today,* June 28, 1994, 13A.

25. James R. Gaines, "To Our Readers," *Time,* July 4, 1994, 4.

26. J. D. Lasica, "Photographs That Lie," *Washington Journalism Review* (June 1989), 22.

27. Ibid., 23.

28. Ibid.

29. William Glaberson, "Newsday Imagines an Event and Sets Off a Debate," *New York Times,* February 17, 1994, A12.

30. Black, Steele, and Barney, *Doing Ethics,* 166.

31. "ABC Admits Phony News Setting," Associated Press Wire, February 15, 1994.

32. Tom Rosenstiel, "Not Necessarily the News," *Esquire* (January 1995), 77.

33. Kate McKenna, "The Future Is Now," *American Journalism Review* (October

1993), 17.

34. Joann Byrd, "News You Can Choose," *Washington Post*, August 28, 1994, A24.

35. McKenna, "The Future Is Now," 22.

36. Ibid., 19.

37. Ted Koppel, "The Worst Is Yet To Come," *Washington Post*, April 3, 1994, G9.

38. Ibid.

Chapter Nine

1. Geoffrey C. Ward and Ken Burns, *Baseball* (New York: Knopf, 1994), 268.

2. Susan Paterno, "Under Fire," *Editor & Publisher*, August 15, 1992, 18.

3. *Dallas Morning News TV Magazine*, January 8, 1995, 23.

4. Richard Harwood, "Sources Who Supply 'The News,'" *Washington Post*, January 7, 1995, A 21.

5. Ibid.

6. Junior Bridge, "The Media Mirror: Reading Between the (News) Lines," *Quill* (January/February 1994), 18.

7. Center for Integration and Improvement of Journalism, *News Watch* (San Francisco: Center for Integration and Improvement of Journalism, 1994), 14.

8. Barbara Reynolds, "White-Male Thinking Still Dominates News Coverage," *USA Today*, July 29, 1994, 13A.

9. Center for Integration and Improvement of Journalism, *News Watch*, 38.

10. Robert M. Entman, "African Americans According to TV News," *Media Studies Journal* (Summer 1994), 37.

11. Debra Gersh, "Unity '94 Report on Newsroom Diversity," *Editor & Publisher*, March 13, 1993, 22.

12. Paterno, "Under Fire," 18.

13. Harwood, "Sources Who Supply," A21.

14. Howard Kurtz, "The Media's Diversity Dating Game," *Washington Post*, July 29, 1994, D1.

15. Bridge, "The Media Mirror," 19.

16. National Association of Black Journalists, "Muted Voices: Frustration and Fear in the Newsroom," August 1994, 4.

17. Howard Kurtz, "The Culture Clash Between the Lines," *Washington Post*,

July 28, 1994, C1.

18. Ibid.

19. Gersh, "Unity '94," 22.

20. Mark Fitzgerald, "Diversity's Delineations," *Editor & Publisher,* August 13, 1994, 14.

21. Ibid., 37.

22. National Advisory Commission on Civil Disorders, *Report* (New York: Bantam, 1968), 366.

23. Ibid., 384.

24. Ibid., 389.

25. Debra Gersh, "Women Still Underrepresented," *Editor & Publisher,* May 15, 1993, 20.

26. Joe S. Foote, "Women Correspondents' Visibility on the Network Evening News," *Mass Communication Review,* 19 (1 and 2) (1992), 37.

27. Ibid., 36.

28. Gersh, "Women Still Underrepresented," 21.

29. Foote, "Women Correspondents' Visibility," 39.

30. Linda Ellerbee, *"And So It Goes"* (New York: Putnam, 1986), 110.

31. Ibid., 102.

32. "In the Media, A Woman's Place," *Media Studies Journal* (Winter/Spring 1993), 57.

33. Ibid., 50.

34. Howard Kurtz, "Gay Journalists 'Asserting Themselves' in the Media," *Washington Post,* September 12, 1993, A4.

35. Tony Case, "Gay Journalists Ponder Obstacles," *Editor & Publisher,* October 2, 1993, 11.

36. Ibid., 12.

37. Ibid.

38. Black, Steele, and Barney, *Doing Ethics,* 8.

39. Ibid., 9.

40. Tony Case, "Public Journalism Denounced," *Editor & Publisher,* November 12, 1994, 14.

41. William Glaberson, "From a Wisconsin Daily, a Progress Report on a New Kind of Problem-Solving Journalism," *New York Times,* February 27, 1995, C6.

42. Ibid.

43. Case, "Public Journalism Denounced," 14.

44. Alicia C. Shepard, "The Gospel of Public Journalism," *American Journalism Review* (September 1994), 33.

45. Richard Harwood, "Civic Journalism 101," *Washington Post*, January 17, 1995, A23.

46. John Barc, "Case Study—Wichita and Charlotte: The Leap of a Passive Press to Activism," *Media Studies Journal* (Fall 1992), 151.

47. Ibid., 157.

Chapter Ten

1. Ralph Waldo Emerson, *English Traits* (Boston: Houghton Mifflin, 1903), 272.

2. Gene Goodwin and Ron F. Smith, *Groping for Ethics in Journalism* (3rd ed.) (Ames, Iowa: Iowa State, 1994), 106.

3. Clinton Rossiter and James Lare (eds.), *The Essential Lippmann* (New York: Random House, 1963), 405.

Bibliography

Books

Agee, Warren K., Phillip H. Ault, and Edwin Emery. *Introduction to Mass Communication.* New York: HarperCollins, 1994.

Arnett, Peter. *Live from the Battlefield.* New York: Simon & Schuster, 1994.

Bagdikian, Ben H. *The Media Monopoly* (4th ed.). Boston: Beacon, 1992.

Baker, Lee W. *The Credibility Factor: Putting Ethics to Work in Public Relations.* Homewood, Ill.: Business One Irwin, 1993.

Belch, George E., and Michael A. Belch. *Introduction to Advertising and Promotion* (2nd ed.). Homewood, Ill.: Business One Irwin, 1993.

Belsey, Andrew, and Ruth Chadwick. *Ethical Issues in Journalism and the Media.* London: Routledge, 1992.

Bernstein, Carl, and Bob Woodward. *All the President's Men.* New York: Warner, 1975.

Black, Jay, Bob Steele, and Ralph Barney. *Doing Ethics in Journalism.* Needham Heights, Mass.: Allyn & Bacon, 1995.

Bok, Sissela. *Lying: Moral Choice in Public and Private Life.* New York: Pantheon, 1978.

———. *Secrets: On the Ethics of Concealment and Revelation.* New York: Pantheon, 1982.

Broder, David S. *Behind the Front Page.* New York: Simon & Schuster, 1987.

Carlson, Oliver. *The Man Who Made News: James Gordon Bennett.* New York: Duell, Sloan and Pearce, 1942.

Center for Integration and Improvement of Journalism. *News Watch.* San Francisco: Center for Integration and Improvement of Journalism, 1994.

Christians, Clifford G., Kim B. Rotzoll, and Mark Fackler. *Media Ethics* (3rd ed.). White Plains, N.Y.: Longman, 1991.

Commission on Freedom of the Press. *A Free and Responsible Press.* Chicago: University of Chicago, 1947.

Crouse, Timothy. *The Boys on the Bus.* New York: Random House, 1973.
Day, Louis A. *Ethics in Media Communications: Cases and Controversies.* Belmont, Calif.: Wadsworth, 1991.
Deakin, James. *Straight Stuff.* New York: William Morrow, 1984.
Denniston, Lyle. *The Reporter and the Law: Techniques of Covering the Courts.* New York: Hastings House, 1980.
Dickens, Charles. *Martin Chuzzlewit.* Oxford: Oxford University Press, 1981.
Donovan, Robert J., and Ray Scherer. *Unsilent Revolution.* New York: Cambridge, 1992.
Ellerbee, Linda. *"And So It Goes."* New York: Putnam, 1986.
Emerson, Ralph Waldo. *English Traits.* Boston: Houghton Mifflin, 1903.
Garment, Suzanne. *Scandal.* New York: Doubleday/Anchor, 1992.
Germond, Jack W., and Jules Witcover. *Mad as Hell.* New York: Warner, 1993.
Goldstein, Tom. *The News at Any Cost.* New York: Simon & Schuster, 1985.
Goodwin, H. Eugene. *Groping for Ethics in Journalism* (2nd ed.). Ames, Iowa: Iowa State, 1987.
Goodwin, Gene, and Ron F. Smith. *Groping for Ethics in Journalism* (3rd ed.). Ames, Iowa: Iowa State, 1994.
Gora, Joel M. *The Rights of Reporters.* New York: First Discus, 1974.
Haggerty, Mike, and Wallace Rasmussen. *The Headline vs. the Bottom Line: Mutual Distrust Between Business and the News Media.* Arlington, Va.: The Freedom Forum, 1995.
Hausman, Carl. *Crisis of Conscience.* New York: HarperCollins, 1992.
Holsinger, Ralph L., and Jon Paul Dilts. *Media Law* (3rd ed.). New York: McGraw-Hill, 1994.
Hulteng, John L. *Playing It Straight.* Chester, Conn.: Globe Pequot, 1981.
Jaksa, James A., and Michael S. Pritchard. *Communication Ethics* (2nd ed.). Belmont, Calif.: Wadsworth, 1994.
Kalb, Marvin. *The Nixon Memo.* Chicago: University of Chicago, 1994.
Knightley, Phillip. *The First Casualty.* New York: Harcourt Brace Jovanovich, 1975.
Kurtz, Howard. *Media Circus.* New York: Times Books, 1993.
Lippmann, Walter. *Public Opinion.* New York: Free Press, 1965.
Matelski, Marilyn J. *TV News Ethics.* Boston: Focal Press, 1991.
Merritt, Davis. *Public Journalism and Public Life.* Hillsdale, N.J.: Lawrence Erlbaum Associates, 1995.
Meyer, Philip. *Ethical Journalism.* New York: Longman, 1987.
Midgley, Sarah, and Virginia Rice (eds.). *Terrorism and the Media in the 1980's.* Washington: The Media Institute, 1984.
National Advisory Commission on Civil Disorders. *Report.* New York: Bantam, 1968.
Newsome, Doug, Alan Scott and Judy Vanslyke Turk. *This Is PR: The Realities of Public Relations* (5th ed.). Belmont, Calif.: Wadsworth, 1992.
Olen, Jeffrey. *Ethics in Journalism.* Englewood Cliffs, N.J.: Prentice-Hall, 1988.
O'Neill, Michael J. *Terrorist Spectaculars.* New York: Priority Press, 1986.
Patterson, Thomas E. *Out of Order.* New York: Vintage, 1994.
Postman, Neil, and Steve Powers. *How to Watch TV News.* New York: Penguin, 1992.
Powell, Jody. *The Other Side of the Story.* New York: William Morrow, 1984.

Ranney, Austin. *Channels of Power*. New York: Basic Books, 1983.

Reeves, Richard. *President Kennedy*. New York: Simon & Schuster, 1993.

Rosenstiel, Tom. *Strange Bedfellows*. New York: Hyperion, 1993.

Rossiter, Clinton, and James Lare (eds.). *The Essential Lippmann*. New York: Random House, 1963.

Seib, Philip. *Campaigns and Conscience*. New York: Praeger, 1994.

Seib, Philip, and Kathy Fitzpatrick. *Public Relations Ethics*. Fort Worth: Harcourt Brace, 1995.

Sheehy, Gail. *Character*. New York: Morrow, 1988.

Smith, Zay N., and Pamela Zekman, *The Mirage*. New York: Random House, 1979.

Stephens, Mitchell. *A History of News*. New York: Viking, 1988.

Stevens, John D. *Shaping the First Amendment: The Development of Free Expression*. Beverly Hills, Calif.: Sage, 1982.

Strentz, Herbert. *News Reporters and News Sources* (2nd ed.). Ames, Iowa: Iowa State, 1989.

Swain, Bruce M. *Reporters' Ethics*. Ames, Iowa: Iowa State, 1978.

Wagman, Robert J. *The First Amendment Book*. New York: Scripps Howard, 1991.

Ward, Geoffrey C., and Ken Burns. *Baseball*. New York: Knopf, 1994.

Warner, Rawleigh, Jr., and Leonard Silk. *Ideas in Collision: The Relationship between Business and the News Media*. New York: Carnegie-Mellon University Press, 1979.

White, Thomas I. *Right and Wrong: A Brief Guide to Understanding Ethics*. Englewood Cliffs, N.J.: Prentice-Hall, 1988.

Wiener, Robert. *Live from Baghdad*. New York: Doubleday, 1992.

Wilcox, Dennis L., Philip H. Ault, and Warren K. Agee. *Public Relations Strategies and Tactics* (4th ed.). New York: HarperCollins, 1995.

Wilcox, Dennis L., and, Lawrence W. Nolte. *Public Relations: Writing and Media Techniques* (2nd ed.). New York: HarperCollins, 1995.

Articles and Other Sources

"ABC Admits Phony News Setting." Associated Press wire, February 15, 1994.

"ABC Altered TV Images for Jackson." *Dallas Morning News*, June 26, 1995, 27A.

"Ad Pressure on Writers." *Editor & Publisher*, June 13, 1992, 6.

Adams, Eddie. "The Tet Photo." In A. Santoli (ed.), *To Bear Any Burden*. New York: Ballantine, 1985.

Alter, Jonathan. "They're on Candid Camera." *Newsweek*, October 31, 1994, 59.

Anderson, Terry. "Terrorism and Censorship: The Media in Chains." *Journal of International Affairs* (Summer 1993), 127.

Argyris, Chris. "The Media and Their Credibility Under Scrutiny." *Nieman Reports* (Winter 1989), 31.

Auletta, Ken. "Fee Speech." *The New Yorker*. September 12, 1994, 40.

———. "Raiding the Global Village." *The New Yorker*, August 2, 1993, 25.

Ayres, B. Drummond, Jr. "Court of Public Opinion Is First to Try Simpson." *New York Times*, June 21, 1994, A 6.

Bailey, Charles W. "Conflicts of Interest: A Matter of Journalistic Ethics." *Report to the National News Council,* 1984.
———. "Newspapers Need Ombudsmen." *Washington Journalism Review* (November 1990), 29.
Baker, Brent. "Decisions at the Speed of TV Satellites." *Vital Speeches,* July 15, 1992, 581.
Baker, Russ W. "Truth, Lies, and Videotape." *Columbia Journalism Review* (July/August 1993), 25.
Bare, John. "Case Study—Wichita and Charlotte: The Leap of a Passive Press to Activism." *Media Studies Journal* (Fall 1992), 149.
Bark, Ed. "Channel 5 Suspends Snyder After Rally Remarks." *Dallas Morning News,* August 30, 1994, 1A.
———. "Deal Puts ABC in Prickly Spot." *Dallas Morning News,* August 6, 1995, 1C.
———. "Media Closer to Indicting Simpson Than Prosecutors Are." *Dallas Morning News,* June 17, 1994, 19A.
Barnett, Cynthia. "Covering Executions." *American Journalism Review* (May 1995), 26.
Barney, Ralph D. "Responsibilities of a Journalist: An Ethical Construct." *Mass Communications Review,* 14(3), 1987, 14.
Barron, James. "Dueling Magazine Covers: A Police Photo vs. a 'Photo-Illustration.'" *New York Times,* June 21, 1994, 19.
Behringer, Fred. "Dwyer Suicide Called 'Statement' to Press." *Society of Professional Journalists 1987–88 Ethics Report,* 4.
———. "Press Debates Photo Use." *Society of Professional Journalists 1987–88 Ethics Report,* 6.
Berger, Jerome. "Hit-and-Run Journalism." *Nieman Reports* (Summer 1994), 67.
Bernhard, Nancy E. "The Lecher, the Witch and the Weirdo." *Nieman Reports* (Summer 1993), 16.
Berniker, Mark. "Path to Interactive TV a Rough One." *Broadcasting & Cable,* August 29, 1994, 23.
Bird, Laura. "First Advertorials, Now Advernewscasts." *Wall Street Journal,* September 29, 1994, B1.
Bivins, Thomas H. "A Worksheet for Ethics Instruction and Exercises in Reason." *Journalism Educator* (Summer 1993), 4.
Bleiberg, Robert M. "Turned Off, Tuned Out." *Barron's,* May 20, 1991, 10.
Bodine, Larry. "Broken Promises." *Quill* (March 1991), 31.
Boeyink, David. "How Effective Are Codes of Ethics? A Look at Three Newsrooms." *Journalism Quarterly* (Winter 1994), 893.
Bovee, Warren G. "The End Can Justify the Means—But Rarely." *Journal of Mass Media Ethics* (1991), 135.
Boylan, James. "Where Have All the People Gone?" *Columbia Journalism Review* (May/June 1991), 33.
Boyle, Patrick. "Standards for Photography's Cutting Edge." *Washington Journalism Review* (November 1992), 12.
Bridge, Junior. "Media Mirror: Distorted Reflections—Distorted Treatment." *Quill* (April 1994), 16.
———. "The Media Mirror: Reading Between the (News) Lines." *Quill* (January/February 1994), 18.

Brooks, Leonard J. "Corporate Codes of Ethics." *Journal of Business Ethics* (February/March 1989), 117.

Brudney, Daniel. "Two Links of Law and Morality." *Ethics* (January 1993), 280.

Byrd, Joann. "Gaga Over O. J. Simpson." *Washington Post,* October 16, 1994, A22.

———. "News You Can Choose." *Washington Post,* August 28, 1994, A24.

———. "The Vulture Syndrome." *Washington Post,* March 20, 1994, A24.

Carey, John L. "Professional Ethics Are a Helpful Tool." *Public Relations Journal* (March 1957), 7.

Carmody, Deirdre. "Time Responds to Criticism Over Simpson Cover." *New York Times,* June 25, 1994, 7.

Carter, Bill. "Networks' Simpson Vigil: A Low-Cost Reply to CNN." *New York Times,* July 11, 1994, D1.

Case, Tony. "Gay Journalists Ponder Obstacles." *Editor & Publisher,* October 2, 1993, 10.

———. "Public Journalism Denounced." *Editor & Publisher,* November 12, 1994, 14.

———. "Recruiting Gay Journalists." *Editor & Publisher,* September 11, 1993, 10.

Clark, Roy Peter. "Natural Born Killers." *New York Times,* October 14, 1994, A17.

Cohn, Jonathan. "Diary of the American Nightmare." *The American Prospect* (Fall 1994), 36.

———. "Perrier in the Newsroom." *The American Prospect* (Spring 1995), 15.

Cox, Archibald. "Freedom of the Press." *University of Illinois Law Review (1)* (1983), 3.

Cunningham, Richard P. "Seeking a Time-out on Prurience." *Quill* (March 1992), 6.

Dalton, Terry A. "Another One Bites the Dust." *Quill* (November/December 1994), 39.

Dennis, Everette E. "Avoid Path of Wretched Excess in Simpson Case." *Communique* (July/August 1994), 2.

———. "News, Ethics, and Split Personality Journalism." *Television Quarterly* (Winter 1994), 29.

———. "Simpson Coverage Makes for Bad Television." *Communique* (November 1994), 2.

DeRose, Robin. "95 Million Tune in O. J. Televised Chase." *USA Today,* June 22, 1994, D3.

"A Discussion of Newspaper Ethics for Associated Press Managing Editors." Presented to APME members September 23, 1993.

Dobkin, Bethami A. "Paper Tigers and Video Postcards." *Western Journal of Communication* (Spring 1992), 143.

"Don't Mean Diddly." *The New Yorker,* July 11, 1994, 4.

Dowling, Ralph E. "Terrorism and the Media: A Rhetorical Genre." *Journal of Communication* (Winter 1986), 12.

Dozier, Steve. "Enough With Technology." *Editor & Publisher,* September 4, 1993, 9.

Dufresne, Marcel. "To Sting or Not to Sting?" *Columbia Journalism Review* (May/June 1991), 49.

Duke, Paul. "The Wayward Media." *The Virginia Quarterly Review* (Summer 1994), 393.

Dwyer, Paula. "CNN Copycats Get Set for a Catfight." *Business Week,* March 6, 1995, 50.

"Editor's Note." *Columbia Journalism Review* (January/February 1994), 8.

Elliott, Deni. "Creating the Conditions for Ethical Journalism." *Mass Communications Review* 14 (3) (1987), 6.

Entman, Robert M. "African Americans According to TV News." *Media Studies Journal* (Summer 1994), 29.

Evans, Harold. "Facing a Grim Reality." *American Photo* (May/June 1991), 48.

Fibich, Linda. "Under Siege." *American Journalism Review* (September 1995), 16.

Fitzgerald, Mark. "Diversity's Delineations." *Editor & Publisher,* August 13, 1994, 14.

Fitzpatrick, Kathy, and Alice Kendrick. "Public Perception of Media Coverage of the O. J. Simpson Story One Week after 'The Chase.'" *Southwestern Journal of Mass Communication* (October 1995), 81.

Fitzsimon, Martha, and Lawrence T. McGill. "The Citizen as Media Critic." *Media Studies Journal* (Spring 1995), 91.

Foote, Joe S. "Women Correspondents' Visibility on the Network Evening News." *Mass Communications Review* 19 (1 and 2) (1992), 36.

Foreman, Gene. "Confidential Sources: Testing the Readers' Confidence." *Social Responsibility: Business, Journalism, Law, Medicine* 10 (1984), 24.

Frasca, Ralph. "Estimating the Occurrence of Trials Prejudiced by Press Coverage." *Judicature* (October/November 1988), 162.

Fulton, Katherine. "A New Agenda for Journalism." *Nieman Reports* (Spring 1994), 15.

Gaines, James R. "To Our Readers." *Time,* July 4, 1994, 4.

Galey, John. "Society of Professional Journalists' Code of Ethics: Influences of Criticism and Professionalism." Presented at the Association for Education in Journalism and Mass Communication Southeast Colloquium, March 5, 1994.

Gamson, Joshua. "Incredible News." *The American Prospect* (Fall 1994), 28.

Gannon, James P. "Betrayal: Media 'Scandal' Erodes Public Confidence." *Detroit News,* February 14, 1993, 1A.

Gartner, Michael. "Why Risk 'Enhancing' News?" *USA Today,* June 28, 1994, 13A.

Germer, Fawn. "'How Do You Feel?'" *American Journalism Review* (June 1995), 36.

Gersh, Debra. "News Reports More Important Than Commercials." *Editor & Publisher,* October 31, 1992, 23.

———. "Unity '94 Report on Newsroom Diversity." *Editor & Publisher,* March 13, 1993, 22.

———. "Women Still Underrepresented." *Editor & Publisher,* May 15, 1993, 20.

Glaberson, William. "ABC Altered Images for Jackson." *Dallas Morning News,* June 28, 1995, 27A.

———. "Departures at Paper Ignite Debate on Owners' Priorities." *New York Times,* February 15, 1995, C1.

———. "From a Wisconsin Daily, a Progress Report on a New Kind of Problem-Solving Journalism." *New York Times,* February 27, 1995, C6.

———. "Newsday Imagines an Event and Sets Off a Debate." *New York Times,* February 17, 1994, A12.

———. "Times Criticized for Use of Tabloid Account." *New York Times,* December 23, 1994, A9.

Glass, Charles. "The Crisis Coup." *Washington Journalism Review* (September 1985), 24.

Gorney, Carole. "Litigation Journalism Is a Scourge." *New York Times*, February 15, 1994, A21.
Gowing, Nik. "Behind the CNN Factor." *Washington Post*, July 31, 1994, C1.
Green, Bill. "Janet's World." *Washington Post*, April 19, 1981, A1.
Greenfield, Meg. "In Defense of Sensationalism." *Newsweek*, September 26, 1994, 72.
Griffith, Thomas. "Credibility at Stake." *Time*, March 11, 1985, 57.
Grosjean v. American Press Co., 297 U.S. 233 (1936).
Grossman, Lawrence K. "A Television Plan for the Next War." *Nieman Reports* (Summer 1991), 27.
Gunther, Marc. "All in the Family." *American Journalism Review* (October 1995), 37.
Guthman, Edwin. "Why The Inquirer Ran Those Budd Dwyer Photos." *Philadelphia Inquirer*, February 1, 1987, 7F.
Hall, Jon. "Stop! This Is a Warning . . . Suppressing News at Police Request." *Fine Line* (October 1989), 6.
Harwood, Richard. "Are Journalists Elitist?" *American Journalism Review* (June 1995), 26.
———. "Civic Journalism 101." *Washington Post*, January 17, 1995, A23.
———. "Read All About It." *Washington Post*, July 13, 1994, A25.
———. "Sources Who Supply 'The News.'" *Washington Post*, January 7, 1995, A21.
"Headline Grabbers," *USA Today*, June 21, 1994, A1.
Herbert, Bob. "Forget Farrakhan." *New York Times*, June 15, 1994, A25.
Hiaasen, Carl. "Media and Public Deserve Each Other in O. J. Fiasco." *Dallas Morning News*, June 24, 1994, 21A.
Higham, Scott J. "Photos a Dilemma for Press." *Allentown Morning Call*, January 23, 1987, A2.
Hodges, Lou. "Cases and Commentaries." *Journal of Mass Media Ethics* 9 (4) (1994), 257.
Hogan, Gypsy. "Covering the Catastrophe." *Editor & Publisher*, June 10, 1995, 15.
Horn, John. "KABC vs. Ombudsman." *Washington Journalism Review* (October 1987), 8.
Idsvoog, Karl. "TV Sitting on Stories to Improve Ratings." *Nieman Reports* (Spring 1994), 38.
"Indecent Exposure." *The New Yorker*, May 23, 1994, 6.
"In the Media, A Woman's Place." *Media Studies Journal* (Winter/Spring 1993), 49.
Isaacs, Norman E. "20 Years Later: 33 Ombudsmen." *Washington Journalism Review* (October 1987), 40.
Ivins, Molly. "The Pea and the Shell." *The Progressive* (March 1994), 46.
Jeffers, Dennis W. "Performance Expectations as a Measure of Relative Status of News and PR People." *Journalism Quarterly* (Summer 1977), 299.
Johnson, Chevel. "Televised Suicide Raises Questions about TV Journalism." Associated Press wire, September 16, 1994.
Johnson, Paul. "The Media and Truth: Is There a Moral Duty?" in *Mass Media* (annual editions 94/95), ed. Joan Gorham. Guilford, Conn.: Dushkin Publishing Group, 162.
Johnston, David. "The Anonymous Source Syndrome." *Columbia Journalism Review* (November/December 1987), 54.

Johnston, Marguerite. "David X." *Columbia Journalism Review* (May 1984), 9.

Josephson, Michael. "Teaching Ethical Decision Making and Principled Reasoning," in *Business Ethics* (annual editions 1993–1994). Guilford, Conn.: Dushkin, 1993, 15.

Kalb, Bernard. "Follow That Tank!" *Media Studies Journal* (Winter 1995), 119.

Kann, Peter R. "The Media: What's Right and Wrong." *Vital Speeches of the Day,* August 1, 1993, 618.

Kenney, Richard J. "Building a Better Ombudsman: An Ethical Foundation and Framework." Paper presented at the annual convention of the Association for Education in Journalism and Mass Communication, August 1994.

Kerwin, Ann Marie. "Behind the Waltzing." *Editor & Publisher,* June 13, 1992, 18.

Kinsley, Michael. "Election Day Fraud on Television." *Time,* November 23, 1992, 84.

Koppel, Ted. "The Worst Is Yet to Come." *Washington Post,* April 3, 1994, G1.

Kovach, Bill. "New Ethical Questions for a New Age." *Nieman Reports* (Spring 1994), 2.

Kurtz, Howard. "The Culture Clash Between the Lines." *Washington Post,* July 28, 1994, C1.

———. "From Bedroom to Newsroom." *Washington Post,* September 17, 1994, D1.

———. "Gay Journalists 'Asserting Themselves' in the Media." *Washington Post,* September 12, 1993, A4.

———. "Hidden Network Cameras: A Troubling Trend?" *Washington Post,* November 30, 1992, A1.

———. "The Media's Diversity Dating Game." *Washington Post,* July 29, 1994, D1.

———. "Minority Journalists Join Forces to Seek Fairness, Power in Media." *Washington Post,* July 24, 1994, A3.

———. "Why the Press Is Always Right." *Columbia Journalism Review* (May/June 1993), 33.

Kwitny, Jonathan. "The High Cost of High Profits." *Washington Journalism Review* (June 1990), 19.

LaBrecque, Ron. "Stay Tuned for the Execution of Robert Harris." *Washington Journalism Review* (June 1991), 34.

Lacayo, Richard. "Tarting Up the Gray Lady of 43rd Street." *Time,* May 6, 1991, 44.

Lambeth, Edmund B., Christians, Clifford, and Cole, Kyle. "Role of the Media Ethics Course in the Education of Journalists." *Journalism Educator* (Autumn 1994), 20.

Langley, Monica, and Lee Levine. "Broken Promises." *Columbia Journalism Review* (July/August 1988), 21.

LaRocque, Paula. "The Excesses of Tabloid Journalism Can Be Contagious." *Quill* (January/February 1994), 58.

Lasica, J. D. "Photographs That Lie." *Washington Journalism Review* (June 1989), 22.

Lawrence, David Jr. "Avoiding the Trash Trail." *Editor & Publisher,* April 18, 1992, 10.

Lehman, Steve. "Eyewitness to Carnage." *Newsweek,* January 9, 1995, 48.

Levin, Peter A. "You Want Me to Read a What?" *Media Studies Journal* (Fall 1992), 173.

Lewis, Michael. "Lights! Camera! News!" *The New Republic,* February 28, 1994, 11.

Lexington. "One Nation under O. J." *The Economist,* July 16, 1994, 30.

Lissit, Robert. "Gotcha!" *American Journalism Review* (March 1995), 17.

"Marketing Brief." *Wall Street Journal,* June 22, 1994, B4.

Martinson, David L. "How Should the PR Practitioner Respond When Confronted with Unethical Journalistic Behavior?" *Public Relations Quarterly* (Summer 1991), 18.

Marzolf, Marion Tuttle. "Honor Without Influence?" *Media Studies Journal* (Spring 1995), 91.

Matloff, Judith. "Eye on Apartheid: The Legacy of Kevin Carter." *Columbia Journalism Review* (November/December 1994), 57.

McCarthy, Colman. "Getting the Truth Untruthfully." *Washington Post,* December 22, 1992, D21.

McClellan, Steve. "The Growing Focus on Global News." *Broadcasting and Cable,* May 31, 1993, 40.

McClellan, Steve, and Coe, Steve. "TV Chases Another Hot Story." *Broadcasting and Cable,* June 27, 1994, 20.

McKenna, Kate. "The Future Is Now." *American Journalism Review* (October 1993), 17.

McManus, John. "Serving the Public and Serving the Market." *Journal of Mass Media Ethics* (Winter 1992), 196.

McManus, Kevin. "The, Uh, Quotation Quandary." *Columbia Journalism Review* (May/June 1990), 54.

Melcher, Richard A. "Everybody Wants to Get in on CNN's Act." *Business Week,* March 18, 1991, 48.

Mengelkoch, Louise. "When Checkbook Journalism Does God's Work." *Columbia Journalism Review* (November/December 1994), 35.

Merrill, John C. "Good Reporting and Ethics." *Journalism Educator* 42 (1987), 27.

Miller, Mark Crispin. "Political Ads: Decoding Hidden Messages." *Columbia Journalism Review* (January/February 1992), 36.

Moore, Dennis. "Newsmags Score Big with O. J. Stories." *USA Today,* June 29, 1994, D3.

Nachman, Jerry. "Look at Tonya and Nancy." *New York Times Magazine,* June 26, 1994, 34.

"Naming the Victim." *Columbia Journalism Review* (July/August 1991), 54.

National Association of Black Journalists. "Muted Voices: Frustration and Fear in the Newsroom." (August 1994).

Near v. Minnesota, 283 U.S. 697 (1931).

Neuharth, Al. "O. J. Drama Gives Us Media's Best, Worst." *USA Today,* June 24, 1994, 11A.

New York Times Co. v. United States, 403 U.S. 713 (1971).

O'Connor, John J. "Far Away from Home, But Not Far from CNN." *New York Times,* September 17, 1994, 22.

O'Neill, Michael J. "Who Cares About the Truth?" *Nieman Reports* (Spring 1994), 11.

O'Reilly, Bill. "We Pay for News. We Have to." *New York Times,* February 26, 1994, 17.

Palmer, Nancy Doyle. "Going After the Truth—In Disguise." *Washington Journalism Review* (November 1987), 20.

Paterno, Susan. "Under Fire." *Editor & Publisher,* August 15, 1992, 18.

Pennington, Clarence. "Revise and Boil Down Declaration of Ethics." *Nieman Reports* (Summer 1994), 66.
Prato, Lou. "It Was Like a Shark Attack." *American Journalism Review* (May 1994), 48.
————. "No-Win Coverage of Hostage Crises." *American Journalism Review* (May 1993), 44.
————. "Tabloids Force All to Pay for News." *American Journalism Review* (September 1994), 56.
Press Enterprise Co. v. Riverside County Superior Court, 464 U.S. 501 (1984).
Ramer, Mary Anne. "A PR Practitioner's Memo to Journalists." *Editor & Publisher*, October 10, 1992, 64.
Reaves, Shiela. "Digital Retouching: Is There a Place for It in Newspaper Photography?" *Journal of Mass Media Ethics* (Spring/Summer 1987), 40.
Reese, Stephen D., August Grant, and Lucig H. Danielian. "The Structure of News Sources on Television." *Journal of Communication* (Spring 1994), 84.
Reynolds, Barbara. "White-Male Thinking Still Dominates News Coverage." *USA Today*, July 29, 1994, 13A.
Richardson, Brian. "Four Standards for Teaching Ethics in Journalism." *Mass Media Ethics* 9 (2) (1994), 109.
Richmond Newspapers, Inc. v. Virginia, 448 U.S. 555 (1980).
Robinson, Michael J., and Norman J. Ornstein. "Why Press Credibility Is Going Down." *Washington Journalism Review* (January/February 1990), 34.
Robinson, Steve. "Pulitzers: Was the Mirage a Deception?" *Columbia Journalism Review* (July/August 1979), 14.
Rosenthal, A. M. "The Press and Simpson." *New York Times*, June 6, 1994, A11.
Rosenstiel, Tom. "The Myth of CNN." *The New Republic*, August 22/29, 1994, 27.
————. "Not Necessarily the News." *Esquire* (January 1995), 77.
Ryan, Michael, and Martinson, David L. "Public Relations Practitioners, Journalists View Lying Similarly." *Journalism Quarterly* (Spring 1994), 199.
Sachetti, Jim. "We Can't Back Off When the Reporting Is Tough." *Pennsylvania Newspaper Publishers' Association Press* (January 1995), 3.
Safire, William. "Pleasure of My Company." *New York Times*, August 14, 1984, 15.
Salisbury, Bill. "Burning the Source." *Washington Journalism Review* (September 1991), 18.
Saltzman, Joe. "Tabloid Hysteria." *USA Today*, May 1994, 21.
"Save the Front Page." *The Economist*, September 3, 1994, 27.
Savell, Lawrence. "Cover Yourself When You 'Mask' Sources." *Editor & Publisher*, October 23, 1993, 3.
Sawyer, Forrest. "ABC's Nightline," January 13, 1995.
Schmuhl, Robert. "Introduction: The Road to Responsibility," in *The Responsibilities of Journalism*. Notre Dame, Ind.: University of Notre Dame, 1984.
Schorer, Jane. "The Story Behind a Landmark Story of Rape." *Washington Journalism Review* (June 1991), 20.
Seib, Charles B. "Could a Little Caring Have Prevented a Hoax?" *Presstime* (June 1981), 35.
Seib, Philip. "Coverage Shapes Bosnia Policy." *Dallas Morning News*, February 14, 1994, 17A.
Selcraig, Bruce. "Buying News." *Columbia Journalism Review* (July/August 1994), 45.

Serfaty, Simon. "Neither Hero nor Villain," in Serfaty, Simon, ed. *The Media and Foreign Policy.* New York: St. Martin's, 1991, 229.

Sharkey, Jacqueline. "Interviews for Sale." *American Journalism Review* (September 1994), 22.

————. "Judgment Calls." *American Journalism Review* (September 1994), 19.

Shepard, Alicia C. "An American in Paris (and Moscow and Berlin and Tokyo . . .)." *American Journalism Review* (April 1994), 22.

————. "Anonymous Sources." *American Journalism Review* (December 1994), 18.

————. "Bradlee." *American Journalism Review* (March 1995), 41.

————. "Geneva Talks." *American Journalism Review* (September 1995), 31.

————. "The Gospel of Public Journalism." *American Journalism Review* (September 1994), 28.

————. "Talk Is Expensive." *American Journalism Review* (May 1994), 20.

————. "Those Sensitive Auto Dealers Strike Again, and Another Newspaper Caves." *American Journalism Review* (September 1994), 14.

Sheppard v. Maxwell, 384 U.S. 333 (1966).

Shipman, Marlin. "Putting Ethics to Work: Applying Two Codes of Ethics to the Question of Whether Executions Should Be Televised or Photographed." Presented at the Association for Education in Journalism and Mass Communication Southeast Colloquium, March 4, 1994.

Silk, Leonard. "The Ethics and Economics of Journalism," in *The Responsibilities of Journalism.* Notre Dame, Ind.: University of Notre Dame, 1994.

Sitton, Claude. "News in Our Time: A Problem of Perception." *Editor & Publisher,* April 21, 1990, 152.

Slattery, Karen L. "Sensationalism Versus News of the Moral Life: Making the Distinction." *Journal of Mass Media Ethics (1994)* 9 (1) 5.

Smith, Martin J. "Media as God." *Quill* (November/December 1993), 22.

Snyder, Robert W., Jennifer Kelley, and Dirk Smillie. "Critics with Clout—Nine Who Matter." *Media Studies Journal* (Spring 1995), 1.

Soley, Lawrence C., and Robert L. Craig. "Advertising Pressures on Newspapers: A Survey." *Journal of Advertising* (December 1992), 1.

Sommers, Louise. "Confidential Sources: Protection and Prevention." *Editor & Publisher,* March 16, 1991, 32.

Stark, Andrew. "What's the Matter with Business Ethics?" *Harvard Business Review* (May/June 1993), 38.

Stein, M. L. "Can O. J. Get a Fair Trial?" *Editor & Publisher,* July 9, 1994, 9.

————. "The Future of Electronic News." *Editor & Publisher,* May 2, 1992, 70.

Stepp, Carl Sessions. "When a Public Figure's Private Life Is News." *Washington Journalism Review* (December 1986), 39.

"Story Dilemma for TV." *Society of Professional Journalists 1987–88 Ethics Report,* 5.

Swift, Joel H. "Model Rule 3.6: An Unconstitutional Regulation of Defense Attorney Trial Publicity." *Boston University Law Review* 64 (1984): 1003.

Tharp, Mike, and Betsy Streisand. "Tabloid TV's Blood Lust." *U.S. News & World Report,* July 25, 1994, 47.

Thompson, Bill. "Trial by Headline Is Not What Justice Is Supposed to Be About." *Tampa Tribune-Times,* June 19, 1994, 3.

Times Mirror Center for the People and the Press. "The Press and Campaign '92: A Self-Assessment." *Columbia Journalism Review* (March/April 1993), insert.
Toobin, Jeffrey. "Cash for Trash." *New Yorker,* July 11, 1994, 34.
Upshaw, Jim, and John Russial. "See No Evil?" *Columbia Journalism Review* (January/February 1994), 9.
Van Riper, Frank. "A Cautionary Tale." *Nieman Reports* (Spring 1994), 19.
Walters, Lynne Masel, and Timothy N. Walters. "Environment of Confidence: Newspaper Daily Use of Press Releases." *Public Relations Review* (Spring 1992), 31.
Weiss, Philip. "Bad Rap for TV Tabs." *Columbia Journalism Review* (May/June 1989), 38.
Weiss, Philip, and Laurence Zuckerman. "The Shadow of a Medium." *Columbia Journalism Review* (March/April 1987), 33.
Williams, Scott. "Mike Wallace Gets Wrist Slapped by CBS." Associated Press wire, November 17, 1994.
———. "TV Doctor Saves Rwanda Youngster." Associated Press Wire, August 16, 1994
Winship, Thomas. "The New Curmudgeon: Warnings on Going Downmarket." *Editor & Publisher,* April 4, 1992, 11.
Winter, Bill. "Another View on the 'New Journalism.'" *Editor & Publisher,* April 4, 1992, 7.
Wooten, Jim. "Parachuting into Madness." *Columbia Journalism Review* (November/December 1994), 46.
Zoglin, Richard. "How a Handful of News Executives Make Decisions Felt Round the World." *Time,* January 6, 1992, 30.
Zuckerman, Mortimer B. "Behind the Paula Jones Story." *U.S. News & World Report,* May 23, 1994, 82.

INDEX

"Potter Box," 7–8, 22
Potter, Ralph, 7
Presley, Lisa Marie, 28
Price, Deb, 195
"Prime Time Live" (ABC), 64, 92
Pritchard, Peter, 82
privacy, 80–85
public figures, 81
public journalism. *See* civic jour-
   nalism
Public Opinion, 111
public relations, 39–51
Public Relations Society of
   America, 42–45
Pulitzer, Joseph, 60
Ramer, Mary Ann, 45
Rasmussen, Wallace, 54
Rather, Dan, 26
ratings, 27
Rawls, John, 6
Reagan, Ronald, 102, 137
reenactments and staged events,
   96–97
The Responsibilities of Journalism,
   16
Reston, James, 91
Reuters Television, 169
Reynolds, Barbara, 188
Richardson, Brian, 15
Roberts, Cokie, 34, 36, 178
Roberts, Steve, 36
Robertson, Pat, 139
Rose, Stuart, 74
Rosellini, Lynn, 33
Rosen, Ira, 92
Rosen, Jay, 181, 196
Rosenstiel, Tom, 142, 169, 172
Rosenthal, A. M., 125
Ross, Madelyn, 73
Rwanda, 158
Sachetti, Jim, 149
Safire, William, 102

San Jose Mercury News, 52
Sawyer, Diane, 28, 36, 64
Schmertz, Herbert, 41
Schmuhl, Robert, 16
Schneider, Howard, 197
Schorer, Jane, 146–147, 153
Schwarzkopf, Norman, 168
Seattle Times, 106
Seib, Charles B., 155
Serfaty, Simon, 119
Sharkey, Jacqueline, 27
Sheehy, Gail, 138
Shepard, Alicia, 105
Siegel, Joel, 26
Sigma Delta Chi, 12
Silk, Leonard, 30
Simpson, O. J., 26–27, 57–58, 63,
   109–110, 124–128, 175
Sims, Norman, 114
"60 Minutes" (CBS), 46–47, 92,
   110
slow motion, 179
Smith, William Kennedy, 67,
   126–127, 130–131
Snyder, Mike, 33
socializing with sources, 101–103
Society of American Business
   Editors and Writers, 53
Society of Professional Journalists,
   12–13, 31
Soquist, Joseph, 90
sound, 179–180
sources, 101–109
Spanish-American War, 60,
   173–174
speaking fees, 34–37
Springfield News (Springfield, OR),
   79
Stahl, Leslie, 62
The Star, 61, 110
Stephanopoulos, George, 62
Strentz, Herbert, 3